REVOLUTION IN CHINA

REVOLUTION

IN

CHINA

by

CHARLES PATRICK FITZGERALD

FREDERICK A. PRAEGER

NEW YORK

Published in the United States of America in 1952
by Frederick A. Praeger, Inc, Publishers,
105 West 40th Street, New York 18, N.Y.

BOOKS THAT MATTER

TO

SIR DOUGLAS B. COPLAND

K.B.E., C.M.G., D.SC., LITT.D., LL.D.

Vice-Chancellor of the
Australian National University

Australian Minister to China
1946–1948

·PREFACE

THIS BOOK is not intended to be, in any sense, a history of the Chinese Revolution. Such a history cannot yet be written in definitive form, since many of the documents and some of the real facts still remain unknown. Nevertheless the Chinese Revolution presses hard upon the policies of our age; we may not be able to know the whole, true story, but we need to take account of the fact, and to try to assess its significance. This book is therefore an attempt to make such an assessment, an essay in interpretation rather than an outline of history.

It may be that some few new facts are contributed by personal experience, or first-hand evidence. Some of these may help the historian of the future. For certain statements no authority is given in the text, and some incidents not perhaps hitherto recorded are described without citing any source. This unscholarly practice is deliberate; because the source of such statements and the description of the incidents, when not the personal experience of the author, are derived from other first-hand witnesses, both Chinese and foreign, many of whom might suffer embarrassment if identified.

In any interpretation of a revolutionary movement much depends on the standpoint of the observer; the Christian, the Socialist, the Conservative will all lay different emphasis even when all are agreed on facts. The standpoint from which this book is written is that of the historian. An endeavour has been made to relate the present convulsion to causes lying in the past and the long continuing historical factors which have shaped China's destiny. The results of such a study may be disconcerting to those of the Left or Right who hold certain truths to be self-evident.

Since this is a study of revolution in China I have considered movements of Western origin, such as Christianity or Communism, only as they appear in the Chinese context, treating them as integral factors in the Chinese revolutionary situation, but leaving readers who wish to consider the rise and growth of these ideas in their native lands to experts more competent in that field. In this way I believe that the impact of western ideologies on the Chinese mind is shown more sharply and the Chinese reaction more justly appraised.

Revolution in China is primarily the concern of the Chinese people, who suffer, or benefit, from its result. The interest of the West is at second-hand, and mainly concerned with the attitude which revolutionary China will take to Western interests. If the subject is approached only with those interests in mind, from the Western point of view, seeing the Chinese Revolution from the outside, the picture formed is distorted and misleading. To a Chinese sympathetic to the more recent phases of the Revolution the interests of the West appear irrelevant and pernicious; there is perhaps a place for an interpretation of these great events by a Western observer who is sufficiently acquainted with the Chinese point of view to do it some justice, and has yet not lost touch or sympathy with the ideals of Europe.

The book is not thus written from the angle of the Left or the Right of western political opinions; it attempts to be an objective study of the phenomena, and in so far as it expresses a political outlook, it is that of historical experience and philosophic anarchism; that all governments are bad, and some are worse.

For criticisms and suggestions I am indebted to Professor Walter Crocker, of the Australian National University, and to Professor Raymond Firth, both of whom read the book in manuscript.

Canberra, December 1951   C. P. F.

CONTENTS

'. . . but then, there is this consideration: that if the abuse be enormous, nature will rise up, and claiming her original rights, overturn a corrupted political system.'

—DR JOHNSON

CHAPTER ONE

THE ORIGINS OF THE CHINESE REVOLUTION

JUST INSIDE THE Ch'ien Men, the great south gate of the Northern City in Peking, there is a smaller gate, forming the most southerly entrance to the Imperial City which surrounds the still more secluded Forbidden City, the palace of the Emperors. This gate is called the Dynastic Gate, because it carried the name of the ruling dynasty. Thus, when it was built, it was 'Ta Ming Men', the 'Great Ming Gate', then 'Ta Ch'ing Men', 'Great Ch'ing (Manchu) Gate', and now 'Chung Hua Men', 'China Gate', since under the Republic, both the epithet 'great' and the distinctive dynastic title for a regime have been dropped.

It is related, in the gossip of the Peking people, that when the Republic was established in February 1912, workmen were sent with the new name tablet to take down the 'Ta Ch'ing Men' tablet and put up the 'Chung Hua Men'. The workman set up his ladder, took down the old tablet, fixed the new one and then said to the foreman down below, 'what shall I do with the old tablet?' The foreman, a humble official, thought for a moment. The Republic was very new, the idea strange, its duration perhaps uncertain. It would be awkward, should the Emperor regain power, if he, the foreman, should be held responsible for the loss or destruction of the old tablet. Better take no such risk. 'Put it up in the loft, there, under the roof,' he replied.

The workman took the tablet up to the loft, and then called out in surprise, 'but there is one here already'. 'Bring it down and let us have a look,' said the foreman. The tablet found lying in the loft was brought down: the onlookers gathered around, the dust of ages was wiped off, and there was read the inscription 'Ta Ming Men'—'The Great Ming Gate'. Three hundred years before, another workman had had the same wisdom, and devised the same safeguard. No one seems to know whether both these fallen tablets still lie in the loft of the Chung Hua Men.

The Peking people like this kind of story: it appeals to their malicious contempt for all authority, the sophisticated, aloof indifference of the inhabitants of the capital—who see all regimes come and go, and see all their human frailties. Yet the foreman might, this time, have been more careless with impunity. This revolution was no mere change of dynasty, no simple change of name for the long-continuing Empire. This time not only the name but the structure itself must fall, for to wrench away the Throne is to pull out the king-pin of the Chinese civilization. The cloud of dust which obscured the collapse of that ancient fabric has only now begun to settle.

On October 10, 1911, the accidental explosion of a bomb in the home of some Chinese republican conspirators in Hankow precipitated the train of events which brought about the fall of the Manchu Dynasty, the rise and decay of the Republic, the Nationalist dictatorship, and finally the triumph of the Chinese Communist Party. So small a cause, so great a consequence; yet had not the landslide been ready to fall the movement of one small pebble would have been without significance. The Chinese Revolution was made possible by the long growth of elements of instability in Chinese society. The increasing maladjustment of institutions, the ever more apparent inadequacy of the ruling orthodox doctrines, the manifest decline in the prestige and power of the Empire both at home and abroad, all these factors had brought about a situation in which only a small agent was needed to bring the aged structure down in ruin.

Once that fall had begun it could not be stopped until the main constituent parts of the old society had been levelled with the ground and a firm basis found for the construction of a new order. The Revolution began, as it were, in slow motion, but its apparently erratic and spasmodic development was caused by the successive decay and fall of the bastions of the old society, the Throne, Confucian orthodoxy, the Civil

2

Service, the land tenure system, the family system. Each phase of the Revolution saw the crumbling and collapse of some ancient institution, and in its fall the others were in turn shaken and successively overthrown. The Revolution which began with the simple elimination of an effete dynasty has progressively destroyed the fundamental concepts of the ancient civilization, and has substituted others, which seem, at least at first sight, to be wholly alien and diametrically opposed.

In 1911 the Manchu Dynasty ruled over an Empire which in all essentials was the Empire first unified by Ch'in Shih Huang Ti in 221 B.C. and perfected by the great Han Dynasty in the second century B.C. The Empire had been refounded, after foreign invasion and division, by the T'ang Dynasty in the seventh century A.D., refined and embellished by the Sung in the tenth century, usurped by the Mongols, restored by the Ming, and at last taken over, almost without change, by the Manchus; but during these centuries hardly any new institution or idea had modified the political system set up by the Han Emperors two hundred years before the birth of Christ. The T'ang had perfected the Civil Service system; Sung philosophy had brought the reigning Confucian orthodoxy into line with later thought; in the Ming and Manchu periods the development of the novel had produced the last literary form—even though this was considered heterodox and improper.

Nothing, it was often said, both by foreigners and Chinese, had changed; the Chinese civilization was and had been static for centuries. This view was not in fact correct, but the slow tempo of change in China, and the conservation of very ancient forms both in institutions and in material products, contributed to the belief that this was a stable and unchanging order of society. It is true that the European observers and Chinese scholars, although they agreed in the belief that China did not change, held opposite views on the value of this supposed immutability. To the Confucian scholar change could be only decay; the perfect system had been evolved in the remote past by the sage emperors of antiquity and the best that the modern could hope for was to make some passable imitation of that

3

Golden Age. The Confucian therefore opposed all innovation as a further departure from the original and perfect pattern. The orthodoxy which gave him his rank, his outlook and his background constrained him to instinctive rejection of progress or change.

The European critic, usually in the early period a missionary, was often struck with admiration for the harmony and poise of Chinese civilization; his one complaint was that this was a pagan, not a Christian culture. In time, however, he came to realize that the seeming immutability and interdependence of all aspects of Chinese civilization was the real obstacle to the great reform which he lived to promote. The Gospel could not be dissociated from the culture and spirit of the West, yet these things were inimical to the Chinese civilization, and as such firmly rejected by the upholders of Confucian orthodoxy.

Gradually the missionary came to see that only by wide and sweeping changes could China be made accessible to his teaching; such changes would involve either the disappearance or the profound alteration of the culture; as the missionaries and their countrymen in lay life worked towards this end they encountered the ever sharper hostility of the defenders of ancient China. The foreign outlook triumphed, not through large conversions to Christianity, but by the spread of the secular ideas of the West. The Empire fell, Confucius was dethroned, political and ideological anarchy followed the collapse, but the Christian religion did not succeed in synthesizing this chaos and becoming the active principle of the new Chinese civilization.

In the late eighteenth and early nineteenth centuries the West was profoundly ignorant of the real character of Oriental society; neither its true strength nor its failings were detected; obsessed with the prevailing belief in the moral superiority of Christianity and the intellectual supremacy of Greek thought, the Oriental civilizations were dismissed as barbarous because they were manifestly polytheistic and ignorant of the conception of democracy. It was generally accepted that the mission of Europe was to lighten this darkness both by spreading Christianity and introducing the system of democratic government which was then gaining ascendancy in Western Europe and its overseas offshoots. It was hoped that once these changes had been made the Oriental cultures would progress in the European manner, keeping, perhaps, some picturesque native features. It was also confidently assumed that these changes would be speedily brought about, if not by persuasion, then by force.

History has not fulfilled these expectations, and some of the assumptions of the West are no longer widely held even in their lands of origin. The belief, even the hope, that large-scale conversions to some Christian church would transform the society of China or Japan, has long since faded. The expectation and the assurance that democracy as understood in the West was a necessary condition of all human progress and an inseparable characteristic of any modern State died harder, and indeed still lingers. The patent fact of new, powerful and technically all-too efficient authoritarian societies is unwelcome, and felt in some way to be a denial of truth, a travesty of the course of history.

If the real history of the great Oriental civilizations were better known and the true causes of their growth and stability appreciated these modern phenomena would be more easily understood. The conditions and the causes which brought democracy to the West are alike absent in the Far East; fundamental facts of geography, climate and economic circumstance determined the form which society took in China, and will continue to exercise their profound influence on all future change. These basic environmental circumstances differ very widely from those of Europe, in which continent, alone of all the five, the conception of individual liberty arose and flourished.

The great land mass of China is separated from the rest of Asia either by wide deserts or very high and difficult mountain country. It is in itself a fertile region, with a great variety of climate and soil, fit to nourish and sustain a great culture almost wholly isolated from any other. Eastward of China stretches the vast Pacific. A few small islands, the larger Japanese and

Philippine groups, are all that early man could hope to reach by voyaging on that sea. The sea was the end of the world, leading nowhere and linking nothing. The Mediterranean, the central sea of the ancient western world, the bond and highway of the nations, has no counterpart in the Far East.

For very many centuries China was therefore a world apart, even when coasting voyages brought a slight link with southern Asia, and caravans could pass the Central Asiatic deserts; even then the contacts were few and their effects delayed. The Chinese people evolved the main features of their civilization alone, adapted themselves to their peculiar environment, and it was not until the adaptation had long been made, and its pattern set, that foreign influences seeped in to adorn and varify the uniform character of the Chinese culture. The basic elements of the great neolithic culture of the Western world are also found in China; but the next step, the advance to literacy, the organization of State and government, the development of abstract ideas and the conception of religion, all this was done in China, by Chinese alone, without contact with peoples of similar attainments.

For these reasons any observation of Chinese civilization shows at once two outstanding characteristics; the simple, fundamental arts, crafts, concepts and tools are similar to or identical with those of the rest of mankind; the elaborate work of art, the skilled craft, the advanced idea and the specialized instrument are always stamped with that indefinable but instantly recognizable quality which is Chinese, and which can be at once distinguished from the work of any other culture.

The Chinese peasant uses the hoe, the Yang Shao pottery of neolithic China is closely related to that of Turkestan and Eastern Russia; the Chinese clan system is familiar from other parts of the world. But the Chinese write with a brush, not a pen, their ideographs are wholly unlike other scripts; the cultivation of silk worms was a Chinese invention, and for centuries a monopoly; bronze came late to China but Chinese bronzes are in decoration and form purely Chinese, owing nothing to foreign influence. The Chinese conceptions which

6

underlie the theory of government are unique; unlike any others, and evolved in China. The roots are deep and nourished in a soil alien to the West; the flower is therefore also strange, and hard to recognize.

When the Chinese people first become a distinct and recognizable group they are found in and around the Yellow River Valley. North of that region were barbarians, probably of nomadic culture. South of the Yellow River, in the Yang Tze Valley and what is now South China, there were peoples ethnically close to the Chinese, but culturally well below them. Chinese civilization gradually incorporated these peoples and raised them to its own level. To the north a different environment resisted for all time the spread of Chinese civilization, which with the cultivation of crops ended not far from the line of the Great Wall. The Chinese civilization thus arose in an area not, at first sight, particularly blessed by nature or easy to develop. The Yang Tze Valley and those of the South China rivers are fertile, mild in climate and far less subject to destructive floods or droughts than the Yellow River region. In those southern valleys the early inhabitants could find wild rice, and easily cultivate a variety of crops. Perhaps for this reason they were not inspired to do much more than that, like the primitive peoples of the remoter parts of South-East Asia today.

The Yellow River is a formidable and destructive stream. Flowing for hundreds of miles through the *loess* lands of North-West China it becomes silt laden and earns its name of 'Yellow'. In Western Honan it turns east, and soon enters the great plain of North-East China, where no hills confine the river, still four hundred miles from the sea. The current eases, the silt begins to settle, as the river moves east the silt deposit increases rapidly and can in a few years fill the bed. The river shifts its course and spreads like a vast marsh over the flat plains.

It was into this region, so unpromising in its primitive appearance, a wide plain covered with marshes, flooded periodically by the capricious river, but yet rich in the silt deposited by former floods, that the early Chinese first began to organize

7

their communities into kingdoms and to evolve the early beginnings of their civilization.

Before cultivation could be carried on with any hope of security the spreading summer floods of the great river had to be confined by dykes. The marshes must be drained by canals; the dykes maintained, not for a few miles, but for scores, even for hundreds. Central control was essential. No local leader, head of clan or petty noble could find the men to build the great dykes, nor exercise authority over sufficient territory to carry out the work. The king of a large kingdom could alone command the support and control sufficient territory. Kingdoms therefore arose which were even in the earliest stage of considerable dimensions, some not much inferior to those of modern Europe.

At a very early period the states of the Chinese in the Yellow River Valley were grouped together in a loose federation, under the supreme leadership of a monarch who, strictly, was alone entitled to the rank which has been conventionally translated into English as 'king'. The king was both a ruler and a priest. He was the sole priest of the highest deities, and the authority of his inferior nobility was measured by the right to perform certain sacrifices to certain deities. Only the lord of a territory might perform those to the gods of the soil and the crops, only the supreme king those to the deity of heaven. The lesser nobility might sacrifice to their ancestors: the people, it would seem, were probably not allowed this right, and merely worshipped the spirits of the woods, rocks, springs and mountains, as indeed they still do. Thus far back in the beginnings arose the twin concepts of hierarchy and orthodox doctrine. The king was a priest, the director of irrigation and flood conservancy, the general, and the expounder of sacred matters; arbiter of heaven and earth.

Divine monarchy thus became at an early period the set pattern of Chinese government, nor was this form ever questioned until modern times. Chinese political philosophy concerned itself not with the form, but with the content of government. Monarchy was never in dispute: how to train

8

the monarch to perform his proper duty, what system of rule he should follow, who should be the instruments of his government were the problems which for centuries were hotly debated by the Chinese philosophers. These thinkers, men whose speculations upon the nature and purpose of the universe closely paralleled those of their contemporaries the Greeks, never engaged, like the Greeks, in disputation upon forms of government. No ancient Chinese terms meaning 'democracy' or 'aristocracy' ever existed. But the Chinese sages did very actively contend for opposed systems of autocratic rule.

The Legists urged the full rigour of military despotism. 'Agriculture and war' were the purposes for which society existed; nothing that did not contribute to efficiency in agriculture and war should be tolerated by the king. The rule of this autocrat was to be upheld by a cruel and merciless code of criminal laws, to which all were to be equally subjected. Two thousand and more years before Hitler lived, the Legist statesman, the Lord of Shang, formulated the political philosophy of Fascism and put it into practice in the state of Ch'in.

Elsewhere, other doctrines were preached, and partly heeded. Confucius and his school taught that the sovereign must rule by benevolence and sincerity, using only the minimum of force. Every soldier he maintained was proof of a lack of these virtues. The perfect prince would have no need to issue orders, the perfect warrior would be victorious without fighting—because his virtue would so shine that he would be obeyed by spontaneous recognition of his merit. For man was born good and only corrupted by the evil of the world and society.

The Taoist sages despised the world, denied that government was anything but tyranny, advocated a completely passive approach to human relationships, and said that the very existence of institutions proved the decline of virtue, since when all men were sages no laws were needed. 'Govern a great state as you would cook a small fish'; i.e. hardly at all, advised one of the Taoist teachers. Mo Tze, a sublime figure, was the first pacifist statesman known to history. He taught the folly of war, deprecated the ceremony which the Confucians revered, and preached the unity of the human race. From all these diverse teachings the Chinese political system received something, but not one of them was concerned with the existence of monarchy or sought to justify or deny its value.

The Legists left to later China the theory of criminal law, harsh, severe and cruel, fit for the people but not for the scholars, except where treason to the throne was involved. By reason of the severity of this law, which was the sole concern of the State, no other law, civil, commercial or religious, flourished. Law meant what was done to vile criminals. No action not criminal was subject to law, nor concerned the State. All other disputes and causes were settled by custom wielded by the guilds, clans, associations and other bodies in which a citizen was enrolled.

The Confucians, the ultimately dominant party, gave the theory of moral government, the belief in a moral order to which the monarch must conform, and the corollary of unfailing loyalty by the subject to a just prince. From the Taoists came the Chinese conviction that government was a necessary evil, to be reduced to the minimum, and strictly confined to essential spheres of action. The Mohists, perhaps, left the military profession under that abiding stigma which it has endured in China for so many centuries. 'Good iron is not made into nails, nor good men into soldiers.'

This emphasis on content, on conduct and on doctrine, rather than on form, rank and law, marks the essential difference in spirit between Western and Chinese civilization. It is also the source of much error about Chinese history. Since the form of government was not in question it continued, very little changed for millennia. The spirit might alter, slow changes transform the character of absolute rule, but in history as formally recorded by the Chinese this was not made plain. Dynasty succeeds to dynasty; they rise, flourish and decline, and to the reader it might well seem that Amurath to Amurath succeeds with no change or advance. Yet closer study reveals that this was not at all the case. China before the Ch'in Dynasty was not an empire but a very loose federation of feudal states;

power was held by hereditary aristocrats, who alone could excerise authority.

After the Ch'in and Han Revolution in 221-206 B.C., the first and still, perhaps, the greatest in Chinese history, a centralized empire was formed governed by officers chosen by the emperor and dismissed at his pleasure. Men of base origin rose to the highest posts. The emperor who founded the Han was himself a peasant. The social system was transformed and wide changes in the economy took place. After the Han, in the period of weakness and partial foreign conquest, the forms of the old empire were preserved but its power and control was gone. Dynasties rose and fell in two generations, a series of what were in fact military dictatorships are disguised as dynasties.

The Sui and the T'ang (A.D. 589-618) restored the Empire. Really they founded a new one which in many respects differed from its predecessor. The Civil Service, now recruited by public examination, replaced the haphazard choice of the earlier period. Under the Sung the Chinese Empire for a while lived under the rule of two rival parties who in turn received the patronage of the throne, and when out of power were not slain but merely transferred to distant provinces.

The Mongols introduced a foreign bureaucracy of international adventurers—such as Marco Polo—and largely denied to their Chinese subjects the lucrative posts of authority. The Ming restored—or claimed to restore—the system of the T'ang but without its intellectual curiosity and freedom from prejudice. The Manchus, owning themselves as foreigners, and anxious to conciliate the Chinese, adopted everything that the Ming left, enshrined it with a veneration impervious to reform, and crystallized the Chinese Empire.

If even in the supposedly unchanging form of the absolute Empire there was in fact progress, regress, change and decline, so in the general civilization of China there were also great but slow alterations. Unlike Greek civilization Chinese culture did not flower at once in every field. Literature for many centuries lacked some of its greatest forms. Arts developed slowly over many periods. The drama is late in China, the art of painting very early, but not perfected until the tenth century. Poetry did not achieve its finest expression until the T'ang, architecture until the Ming. European observers first coming to China under the Manchus mistook much of what was really recent for high antiquity, since all alike was essentially so alien to their own culture, and by Chinese convention all alike was covered with the approval of Confucian orthodox doctrine.

The dynastic histories relate facts; they do not often theorize upon them, and they follow certain rigid conventions. Thus some of the most important and dynamic movements in Chinese history are disguised to make them conform with the established theory. The early foreign scholars of Chinese were easily deceived by these guides into the belief that all Chinese history had conformed to a pattern. That pattern was laid down by Confucian doctrine. The dynasty which ruled by the Mandate of Heaven was legitimate; rebellion against it, any movement of opposition, was wrong, both treasonable and wicked: unless such a rebellion succeeded. Then 'the Mandate of Heaven' had changed, and forthwith the successful rebel became the legitimate emperor.

This theory was put forward by Mencius in a famous saying —that he had heard that a criminal had been executed, but not that a minister had assassinated his prince. The 'criminal' was the last king of the Shang Dynasty, the executioner, the first king of the succeeding Chou Dynasty, who had in fact held a post under the Shang. Thus an evil monarch, if slain or dethroned, is no longer a king, and can be treated as criminal. This is the theory of the Mandate of Heaven by which every Chinese emperor reigned as the steward of the supreme deity, and could have his patent revoked if he did not carry out his duty.

The theory of the Mandate of Heaven has been called the Chinese Constitution, the Right of Rebellion, but it is important to see who exercised this right, who it was that rebelled successfully, and who failed to 'achieve the Mandate of Heaven'.

Rebellions in China, from the foundation of the centralized Empire, fall into two classes; the great peasant risings, often associated with religious movements, and the insurrections of powerful generals. There have been many great peasant risings. There were two in the first Empire, the Han, another at the end of the T'ang Dynasty; the founder of the Ming was the leader of such a movement; another dethroned his descendants, and in the last century the T'ai P'ing rebellion conformed closely to the type. The Boxer movement at the beginning of the present century was essentially similar. Now with one exception all these great risings, which swept across the Empire, failed to overthrow the feeble and degenerate dynasties which they opposed. All were in the end defeated. They shook the Throne, but could not overturn it.

In each case the weakened dynasty a few years later succumbed to some military adventurer who had risen either in the ranks of rebellion or in the armies raised to suppress the rebels. This was the case with the Red Eyebrows and Yellow Turbans of the Han period, the rebellion of Huang Tsao in the T'ang; of Li Tze-ch'eng at the end of the Ming; and of the T'ai P'ing Heavenly King in the sixties of the last century. Only one exception occurs, the great rebellion which drove the Mongols from the throne of China and founded the Ming Dynasty.

The exception must therefore be examined to see why Ming Hung Wu succeeded when all the others failed. It was certainly not through superior education. Chu Yuan-chang, the man who reigned as Hung Wu of the Ming, was born in the poorest dregs of society. He was left a famine orphan at an early age, became a beggar, a Buddhist monk, a bandit, and then a leader of rebels. For many years he fought his way slowly to the forefront of the great movement of nationalist opposition which in the end drove out the Mongols. His success was in part due to military ability, to skilful alliances with other rebels, and above all to the fact that, leading a movement of peasants risen against the perennial injustices of landlord and official exactions, he welcomed to his standard the scholars who resented their exclusion from the government by the Mongol foreigners.

Ming Hung Wu, in fact, led more than a peasant rising, it was also a national rising, one of the very few in Chinese history before modern times. His success was due to the alliance of scholars and peasants, the two classes upon which all Chinese government must rest. The first by virtue of their education are essential to the workings of government. The second must give their consent to be governed; if they withhold it no regime can stand, if the scholars—the educated— withdraw, no system can work.

No other peasant rising commanded this dual support. The scholars drew back from the incantations and religious rites of the Red Eyebrows and Yellow Turbans. Huang Tsao failed to win their support, Li Tze-ch'eng was a bandit of renown, but no statesman; the T'ai P'ing Heavenly King by adopting a form of Christianity alienated the Confucian scholar class. Thus the scholars would always rally around the Throne, however bad, however weak, if the throne was willing to use them. When the peasants were beaten some general could be allowed to usurp the throne, since he would surely take over the Civil Service as a going concern, and the scholars would for their part ratify his act by declaring that the Mandate of Heaven had passed. The Mongols made the fatal mistake of both fleecing the peasants and excluding the scholars from employment and hopes of preferment. They thus raised up against them the irresistible combined force of both these classes, and were destroyed.

The Mandate of Heaven theory works out in practice as a justification for rebellions which succeed with the blessing of the literate class. Rebellions contrary to the interest of this class did not succeed. If the history of the successful founders of dynasties is examined the same rule holds true. Few of these men were peasants. Ming Hung Wu and the founder of the Han Dynasty are the exceptions. Most were generals, some few were governors or civil ministers. The great dynasties did not succeed each other immediately, but arose after an interval of

14

some years during which power had been disputed between rival military leaders. In all cases the founders of enduring regimes were careful to conciliate the educated class and to relieve the worst distresses of the people. Those despots who seized power without the backing of the scholars did not retain it, those foreign invaders, such as the Mongols, who failed to use the scholars or relieve the peasants proved unable to endure.

The real character of Chinese rebellions is thus twofold; on the one hand there are peasant risings, which do not succeed in founding new regimes, on the other, military usurpations which obtain the backing of the Civil Service and treat the peasants with moderation. The Confucian scholar was certain that whatsoever king might reign he would be the Vicar of Bray, for he was essential to government, he was not merely the vicar of the Chinese Bray he was also the squire and the magistrate too. A Chinese change of dynasty was not a revolution; it was a change of government, sometimes carried out by force, more often by the constraint of superior power without bloodshed. Rebellions rarely overthrew dynasties, and when they did the scholars hastened to enlist under the banner of the victorious rebel and assure him of the Mandate of Heaven—provided he in turn was willing to use them and carry on the system of government they understood and served.

In the belief that this pattern of dynastic succession, which had endured so long, and so seldom suffered disturbance from the outside, would last for ever, the Confucian scholar official was content to serve even a decaying dynasty, knowing that in due course it, but not he, would be replaced. Even if nomadic invaders, such as the Manchus, should seize the throne, they would rely on the Chinese official, and he would control their alien regime as much as he had the native one. The Mongols, who failed to play this game, paid for it with a very short term of power. The Manchus were very careful not to repeat the mistake.

When the Manchus had already held the throne of China for over one hundred years, and were now no longer in the full flush of their power, too satisfied, too rich, a little degenerate, less susceptible to new ideas than before, there occurred two momentous changes in the Chinese position in the world, and one far-reaching development in the internal situation. Under K'ang Hsi and his grandson Ch'ien Lung the Manchus achieved the final and definite conquest of the Mongol tribes of the north, who had for centuries raided China and at times conquered the Empire.

At the same time the advance of the Tsars across Siberia destroyed for the first time in history that great reservoir of nomadic peoples from which Europe and Asia had so long suffered. No Attila, no Tamerlane, no Genghiz Khan could evermore emerge from the steppes, 'threatening the world in high astounding terms and scourging kingdoms with his conquering sword'. The nomad power was for ever broken; neither China, India nor Europe would have to suffer the great invasions of the past. The Great Wall had become an historical monument.

The vast significance of this change, on which, for their part in it, the Manchu emperors could justly congratulate themselves, was not understood either in China or in other countries. Gibbon could indeed, a century later, point out that barbarian invasions would no longer threaten Europe as they had threatened Rome, but the fact that China was now brought by way of Siberia into direct touch with a nation of European culture, Russia, was for long disregarded by Chinese as by Westerners. For the Chinese the end of the nomad menace appeared an unmixed blessing. The one frontier which had been in danger was now for ever quiet. The mountains to the west and south would, as before, keep off the weak and savage tribes beyond. The sea had never mattered. No enemies came from the sea; a few Japanese raids, but no real possibility of invasion or conquest. The Manchus and their Chinese subjects could well believe that peace was now certain and sure. It was hard to wrench the mind away from that northern frontier, so long the danger spot, and pay attention to the acts of a few Western ships from the unknown lands of Europe.

The first European (Portuguese) navigators to reach China had already arrived in the last years of the Ming Dynasty, and during the seventeenth and eighteenth centuries, the first two centuries of the Manchu Dynasty, they came in increasing numbers; the quality of their ships manifestly greatly improved, their military power was shown in the Philippines, in India and in the islands; yet none of these changes made any impression on the Manchus and their Chinese Confucian-trained officials. The conquest of India should have aroused the alarm of China; the size and strength of the Indiamen and ships of the line, with their guns and immense spread of sail, should have pointed a sharp contrast to the antique junks which were still the only ships the Chinese built or sailed. No such impression reached the Court. The Emperor reigned in Peking; the foreigners came only to Canton, two thousand miles away: the Court was pleased to receive gifts of clocks, watches and other ingenious products of Western manufacture. The Chinese, however, did not inquire why the 'barbarians' could make these things better than they could.

It is often argued that this strange indifference to a growing power and increasing danger was due to the effete indolence of the Manchu Court, sunk in degenerate luxury. But this picture is hardly compatible with the fact that under such emperors as Ch'ien Lung, who reigned for sixty years in the last half of the eighteenth century, when the English were already conquering India and the great ships coming to Canton, the Chinese armies, commanded by this active ruler, were completing a great historical task which had proved beyond the powers of the mightiest emperors of the past—the final pacification and conquest of Mongolia.

Ch'ien Lung was no degenerate, and Chinese land power in his reign was probably greater than at any previous time. The Empire was then more populous and had had internal peace for a longer period than ever before; the reign of Ch'ien Lung was by all previous standards glorious and prosperous. Yet within a century of his death the dynasty was at its last gasp; within fifty years his successors saw the 'ocean devils'—the

English in this case—invade the Empire, sack Canton, and impose the first of the Unequal Treaties.

So swift a decline, so unexpected a reversal of fortune must have some deep-seated cause. If the seaborne invaders had merely surprised an Empire unaccustomed to danger from that quarter, and thus gained some early transitory success before the Chinese could organize their defences, the history of the Far East would have been very different. But, on the contrary, the limited attacks of the European powers, their restricted objective of opening the ports to trade, their few missionaries and their still undeveloped but expanding mechanical science proved more than enough to overturn the whole Chinese society, Empire, economy and doctrine alike. Within a hundred years of the Opium War, China was in the last stages of revolution, and the rise of Communism was already the main issue.

The cause of this great upheaval therefore lay principally in China herself; the agency was Western imperialism, but the reaction was far more extensive than the force applied gave any reason to expect. The Westerners banged heavily upon the barred door of the Chinese world; to the amazement of all, within and without, the great structure, riddled by white ants, thereupon suddenly collapsed, leaving the surprised Europeans still holding the door handle.

The Chinese civilization rested, and had for centuries rested securely, on three pillars of support. First the universal Empire, which embraced the civilized world as known to the Chinese and beyond whose frontiers were only barbarians, and beyond them, faint and hardly known, remote peoples whose activities had no political significance and little cultural influence. The Empire had no official foreign relations; admitted no other State to equality, recognized no other monarch as sovereign. The Empire must be universal because it must be the only source of power, of orthodox doctrine and of civilization. Any rival or equal would be a competitor, 'two suns in one sky' and thus a source of war and disaster.

This idea had been evolved in China, in isolation; and for

China in isolation it was true and valid. There is no real possibility of dividing China peacefully into two or more States. The attempt, repeated throughout history in times of confusion, has always led to war and the conquest of the weaker side. No adequate frontier between north and south can be found in the slow merging of millet lands and rice fields, without mountain barrier or desert to divide them. Deep-seated for two thousand years and rooted in their historical experience the belief that the Empire must be universal and co-extensive with civilization coloured all Chinese thinking and inhibited the establishment of normal relations with the Western powers.

The second base of the Chinese civilization was 'the fundamental occupation'—agriculture. Beyond the limits of possible farm land the Chinese neither sought to settle nor aspired to conquer. Throughout the long contest with the nomads of the Mongolian steppe the Chinese debated the dilemma of these northern regions 'where not even a hair will grow'. Unless they were conquered and occupied the nomad menace would soon revive. If they were conquered, how could Chinese settle in a place where the soil yielded no crops? The possibility of Chinese settlers taking to the pastoral life was never regarded as a serious solution.

Chinese agriculture was, in the pre-industrial age, efficient. An immense labour conducted over centuries had transformed flood plains into farm lands, had terraced the hills and graded the valleys so that every field could be irrigated for rice cultivation. Huge works of embankment restrained the rivers. All this activity, directed by the central Empire and its officers, had made possible a large population. As the population grew in the northern plains emigrants moved south into the valleys of South China, or occupied the mountain country of the west. Even at an early time, the first centuries of the Christian era, the Chinese population was considerable.

As agriculture was the fundamental occupation, and taxation was collected in kind, the Empire very soon began to keep accurate records of the population and thus of the yield of the land. These figures, first collected during the Han period, and continued throughout the later dynasties, show that the Chinese population had already attained 46 millions in the third century A.D. By the year A.D. 754, the most prosperous period of the T'ang Dynasty, a very detailed census records the figure of 52,880,488. In 1578 a census of the Ming Dynasty gives a total of 63,601,046. Two hundred years later the annual census of 1778 gives the figure of 242,965,618 for the expressly stated total population, men, women and children.

In the Manchu period there was thus for the first time a heavy increase of population for which no new land was available. The Manchus restricted Chinese migration into the lands beyond the Wall, the original kingdom of the Manchu Dynasty, since they rightly feared that if permitted the Chinese flood would soon overwhelm the native population. The events of the last fifty years have shown that this was a correct view. Equally, since the Manchus were northern aliens and the native Ming Dynasty had found its last support in the far south, the Manchus were unwilling to see their Chinese subjects emigrate beyond the seas, fearing that such colonies would become the resort of the disaffected, and might, with foreign aid, stir up revolt at home. In this also they were correct; it was precisely in the overseas Chinese communities that the strength of the anti-Manchu movement grew and prospered, and it was such an emigrant, Dr Sun Yat-sen, who gave the movement leadership and a modern political objective—the establishment of a republic.

The Manchus were not able to prevent the growth of overseas Chinese settlement, although until the nineteenth century, when they were forced to concede the right of emigration to suit foreign interests, they did greatly restrict it. Nor was the restraint upon emigration the main cause of the very rapid growth of population during the seventeenth and eighteenth centuries. New crops had certainly some influence. The introduction of the sweet potato, of maize and to a lesser extent of the potato had made possible the cultivation of lands unsuitable for rice or wheat.

The fact that the Manchu Empire expanded mainly by conquering nomad tribes whose habitat offered no scope for Chinese settlement was still more important. Under previous dynasties the newly-established regime found the best way to settle the soldiers and ease the pressure on the land was to send the army off to conquer and occupy new lands. The T'ang Dynasty had thus settled the south; the Ming had occupied the south-west. The Manchus excluded the Chinese from Manchuria and because their own army was required for garrison duty in the newly-conquered Empire made no conquests in the south, and in consequence little or no scope was provided for the expanding population.

Pressure of population rose steadily throughout the dynasty, and with the coming of seaborne trade the old economy was still further dislocated. The Chinese peasant had relied, apart from his fields, on the products of craftsmanship. In winter, at slack seasons, and at all times for the surplus hands, various handicrafts had provided a livelihood. With the import of manufactured goods from the West this rural industry was successively attacked, rendered unproductive, and at last in all the provinces accessible to the ports virtually extinguished.

The failure to develop a concurrent expansion of modern industry in China prevented the normal cycle of an industrial revolution from following its course. That failure was in part due to the tariff restrictions which the Western States imposed on China, preventing any protection for her nascent capitalism, but much more to the climate of opinion which formed the minds of the Chinese ruling class. The economic crisis which was swiftly approaching found the Chinese educated class wholly unprepared to meet the situation.

The third pillar of the old civilization, and the greatest of the three, was the orthodox doctrine of Confucian ethical and political teaching. Chinese civilization was for so many centuries the only higher culture known to the Chinese, Chinese thought the only field in which the powers of the intellect could be exercised, that the doctrines which enshrined this thought and which expressed this culture were *ipso facto* the only conceivable expression of civilization.

China had been both the Greece and the Rome of the Far Eastern world. She gave the thought, the arts, the laws and the system of government. Nothing essential to her civilization came from abroad, and when, many centuries after the mould had been formed, Indian Buddhism reached China, the pattern was too set to be remodelled. Buddhism, alone of all the foreign influences reaching China, made a deep impression, but Chinese culture transformed Buddhism more deeply still. India might have become the Holy Land for China, and Buddhism might have become the revealed religion reorientating the whole civilization as Christianity reformed that of the West. It did not happen.

Buddhism is not an organizing force, but a religion for the contemplative and the recluse. The Buddhist monastery is a retreat, set in the farther hills, not the centre of communal worship. Buddhism is a religion teaching the way of salvation for individuals through knowledge, not for a whole people through grace. Buddhism had no real desire to remould a culture, but merely to instruct the minds of those who were fit to receive knowledge. Moreover, even with this absence of evangelical fervour, this failure to condemn, not merely to ignore, the rival gods and the competitive ethical system, Buddhism had a harder task.

When Christianity captured the West the rival systems of polytheism and Greek philosophy were divided among themselves, without any unifying doctrine and coherent system. In China, Confucian order had long been imposed on the contest of the ancient philosophic schools. Taoism might still flourish as an esoteric sect given to the study of magic and astrology. Mohism, the Legists and many smaller sects were wholly extinct. The Confucian doctrine not only ruled the minds of men but also the Empire. To enter the Civil Service it was necessary to pass an examination concerned only to test proficiency in the Confucian philosophy and knowledge of its classical books. This system, not yet perfected when Buddhism first came to China, was one of the main contributions of the great Tʻang Dynasty, which refounded and secured the Central Imperial State.

This fact, that at the very time when Buddhism was in full flood and at the height of its missionary zeal the divided Empire was once more united and stronger than ever, has had a profound influence on Chinese history. At a similar turning-point in the history of the West, it was not the Empire but the Papacy which obtained all and more than the ancient power, it was not the secular State but the theocratic empire of the popes which arose on the ruins of the early Empire to salvage civilization and reshape the world. The rise of the Tʻang Dynasty, the refounding of the Empire, stronger, more perfectly organized, and more extensive than the fallen Empire of the Han, left no room for the rise of theocracy. The emperor was supreme: pope and king. The doctrine which served the Empire, which trained its officers, and which taught the duty of minister to prince, of prince to emperor, and of emperor to heaven, this was inevitably the orthodox doctrine of the Imperial State. The emperors of the Tʻang and the people of China might, and did, devoutly follow the Buddhist teaching, but the State remained Confucian, secular and all powerful. Buddhism willingly left the world to its pomp and sought enlightenment in the hills. Confucianism secured the control of the Empire, contained Buddhism, and asserted its abiding identity with the theory and practice of the Empire.

Thus it had continued through all the changes of dynasty, which were in fact nothing but changes of government in the enduring Empire which the Tʻang had built. With time and the deeply considered philosophy of the Sung thinkers to reinforce it, Confucianism had become so orthodox, so necessary and so accepted, that it was inconceivable to the Chinese that any civilization could exist without this orthodox doctrine to afford it the necessary ethical and spiritual foundation. Yet in the nineteenth century the Chinese became aware that this assumption was wrong. There were other worlds, technically superior, morally perhaps at least equal, and all animated by another philosophy.

At the time when the material power of the Empire was proved inadequate and antiquated, when its claim to universal sovereignty of the civilized world was manifestly disproved, and when the age-old economic balance of population and food supply was evidently being upset, then suddenly came the still more terrible realization that orthodoxy itself was neither infallible nor essential to civilization. There were whole worlds which knew not Confucius; great empires, more powerful than China, which derided her ethical and political system. The foreigner could point to defeat in war, to Chinese famine and poverty, and to the technical and scientific knowledge of the West, and say 'how do you justify your claim to civilization, let alone to superiority?'

The historian, writing centuries hence, will know the answer. He will suggest, perhaps, that technical skills are not good criteria of true civilization, that harmony and balance in a human society are better than restless change and the chimerical search for progress to some undefined goal. He may even decide that wide tolerance both of superstition and of unbelief is a higher good than any attempt to instil one creed, however sublime. Grace of living may seem to him better than material comfort, or even than hygiene. He may think that a system which gives men content, or even resignation, is better than one which gives them violent alternations between Utopian hopes and abysmal fear.

It did not appear to the Chinese of the second half of the nineteenth century in this light. All alike saw that the whole fabric of their culture and life was threatened by the innovations which the West either forced upon them at the cannon's mouth, or spread with the allures of commerce and education. Some thought that China must shut her doors more closely and make a supreme effort to expel the germ of change. Others, recognizing the inevitable, hoped to adopt just so much innovation as was necessary to resist the onrush of the rest. A few, a growing number, came to think that Chinese culture stood condemned; that all must be changed, that only by the out-right adoption of every Western trait could the Chinese be saved. This view came to prevail. It was believed by the early revolutionaries that China must be entirely reshaped on the Western pattern, must become a nation State, and cease to pretend she was a universal empire; must also become a democracy, because that was modern, too, and must be in-dustrialized so as to have the strength to contend with the rest of the inhabitants of the political jungle.

These were, and perhaps to many Chinese still are, the aims of the Revolution, the imperative needs which any change must satisfy. Yet it may be asked, and perhaps the answer will explain some of the contradictions of the Chinese Revolution, whether these aims were attainable, or in the Chinese world really desirable. Could the Chinese Revolution, inevitable though it was, have made China a great democracy, and was such an end the proper aim of the Revolution?

The foundations of democracy in Western Europe and in its overseas daughter lands are not, except by later literary convention, built upon the city-state democracies of ancient Greece and Rome. Those democracies had long since perished, and the Roman World Empire that succeeded them had also collapsed before any sign of what can properly be called demo-cracy had arisen in Western Europe, then a savage land. The origins of the institutions, as opposed to the ideas which were subsequently made to fit them, is much later. Freedom, the idea which preceded the application of democracy to Euro-pean government, is not, as now understood, a classical con-cept. Freedom in the ancient world was the opposite of slavery, and democracy was the privilege of the free—a very small minority of the total population. Ancient democracy was more properly aristocracy.

The idea of freedom, applying to every man, not merely to a select category, would seem to have arisen in Western Europe as a consequence of the wars between different countries, and between Christian and Saracen. The English invasions of France, the Spanish war against the Moors, the Italian resistance to the German Holy Roman Emperors, from these national struggles, which to be won required the co-operation of all social classes, the sense of national freedom, freedom from foreign rule, was born and long preceded the idea of social or class freedoms. Yet once you have taught men the idea of resisting some sort of oppression, even though only foreign oppression, it is hard to make them forget the lesson. Oppressions nearer home, religious, social, political, will in turn be challenged and in turn overthrown. From wars of liberation against the Moors or the Germans it was but a step to wars for liberation of thought, or of freedom from feudal overlordship.

The idea of law, of human rights written in uncontestable covenants played a most significant part in the origin of Western democratic thinking. So, too, in another way, did the Christian doctrine of the individual soul, the equal of any other soul. From these complex factors emerged the institutions which had in them the germs of democratic freedom. From the re-discovered literature of the classical past came a theory with which to adorn and justify these new liberties as a revival of the ancient democracy of Athens. And from the city-states, themselves a product of the Mediterranean environment, came that power of money as opposed to land which nourished the early growth of democracy, and later succumbed to the full-grown monster. The Western world came to accept this as a natural and indeed inevitable sequence of events; it was not perceived that it was in fact a series only possible in the peculiar setting of Europe, and wholly without application to other regions.

In China not one of the causes which gave birth to Western democracy operated. The universal Empire at a very early date, a date prior to the rise of the Roman Empire, extinguished for ever the rudimentary national States of the Far East and made each and all a province of the abiding Empire. War became civil war, and morally wrong. The rebel against the Empire was either a failure, in which case he was branded through history as a traitor, or successful, in which case he took over the Empire and became the legitimate ruler. In no case was he a patriot struggling for freedom. No sense of freedom as against tyranny animated the rebels of Chinese history. Their purpose was to capture the Empire, and then reform it, not to escape from it.

There were no foreign potentates against whom the Chinese struggled for liberation. The Tartars were either barbarians as long as they remained in Mongolia, or the legitimate rulers of China if they conquered the Empire in whole or in part. Only once, against the Mongols, can it be said that the Chinese rose as a people, in a national movement to win 'freedom'. The rising was successful and therefore set up once more the pattern of the Chinese Empire State with all the restoring conservative zeal of nationalism.

If no need for regaining national freedom urged the Chinese to resist absolutism, no question of religious faith or persecution ever imposed the obligation to fight for liberty of conscience. Buddhism, which ignores rather than opposes the other religions of China, did not demand from its votaries any denial of the old gods, or renunciation of Confucian ethics. The dominant state doctrine of Confucianism, which regards most supernatural beliefs as superstition, did not see any reason to demand that the people, who were not literate, nor studied the classics, should be asked to abandon their gods, or the Buddha. Confucian pedants and scholars upbraided the Court for favouring Buddhism, and at times urged the marriage of monks and nuns, as being necessary to the maintenance of the reproduction rate, but such milk and water persecutions would have been tolerance itself among the ferocious European Christians and their Moslem foes. Lacking any belief in a jealous God, the Chinese felt no jealousy towards a neighbour for his religion.

The concept of law in Chinese thought differs from its European counterpart. Law, in so far as it existed, meant criminal law; penalties, usually very harsh, inflicted on bandits, murderers, thieves and swindlers. Civil law was customary. The dispute over a contract was settled by the merchant guild; the dispute over land title or water right, by the village clan elders. Everyone was anxious to keep the official out of their business. There were no lawyers. Family jurisdiction ruled the problems of divorce, marriage, legitimacy and inheritance. Thus the government ignored the whole field of civil law, and left this to the subject and his proper and appropriate organization.

As no church ever rose to power and influence so the question of foundations of organized benevolence and relief was also left to the private citizen and his associations. Temples were built and repaired by associations of merchants, of land-owners, or by some rich official. The work of charity, which the church first undertook in Europe before the State, was in China the responsibility of the clan or great family. If a work-man sickened or lost his livelihood, he returned to his village, to claim and receive the support of his kin. If a poor boy showed promise his kin subscribed for his education so that he might become a scholar and official and so benefit the clan. The great official had his huge train of hangers-on, his relatives, clansmen and fellow countrymen who expected and received relief, employment and patronage from the great man. Few such men left huge fortunes to their descendants, for the obligation of clan support soon whittled away the largest accumulations.

There was no class of lawyers, and therefore no interpreters of rights, no claimants for greater liberty, no politicians. A Chinese official was a loyal servant of the Emperor, or else a scheming and intriguing traitor. He could not be a politician, because opposition was treason, and loyalty meant obedience. He could be, and often was a skilled and capable administrator, a wise counsellor, a perfectly devoted Civil Servant carefully guarding his precedents and citing his authorities, but never claiming rights or alleging laws.

Neither Buddhism, Confucianism, nor the ancient poly-theism grouped under the name of Taoism taught with any assured voice on the life to come nor stressed the individuality of the soul, nor the importance of salvation. The concept of sin, as opposed to crime, is not known to the Far East. Therefore damnation was equally ignored. The Buddhist hell does indeed hold out a lively picture of the horrors which offenders against Buddha's rule must suffer for a long period of time. But these are penalties for crimes: for taking life, for slaying animals; and they are expiation, not damnation. All must in time rise, even from the lowest hell, to enlightenment and so to Buddhahood.

The idea of the individual, so essential to democracy, was blurred in China by the obligations and responsibility of the clan. If a man committed treason, all his kin suffered with him. If he rose to honour, all his kin rose too—'clinging to the hairs of the dragon'. Business, like government, tended to be a family matter. Men did not associate with strangers in a venture, but with their kin. Even in modern times every single person employed in the great banks, down to tea boys and coolies, was a relative of the proprietor and from his own village.

The city-State and the merchant prince were alike unknown in China. Commerce, though extensive on the great rivers and along the south coast, was at best secondary to agriculture, and mainly concerned in the exchange of luxuries. The government with its tribute system undertook the bulk transport of grain for the capital, or in time of famine. Merchants were not one of the esteemed social classes, and except in a few very large cities they catered for the needs of the adjacent country only. Early Chinese legislation, in the Han Dynasty, later often revived, was directed to restraining the rise of the merchant class, and curbing their wealth and luxury. The alliance between merchant and official which occurred to some degree tended to the enrichment and corruption of the official class rather than to the rise to political power of merchants.

The fundamental requisites for democracy were thus lacking, and to supply them would have required a revolution even more profound than that which has taken place. If the fragmentation of Europe into nation-States after the fall of Rome is the first cause of European ideas of liberty, the main preoccupation of the Chinese reformers, as of the conservatives, was how to preserve the Empire. If the Empire had been broken up, or reduced to some federal constitution, it would have at once become the prey of the imperialist powers, who eagerly anticipated such a development. The introduction of a legal system surrounded by the hoary veneration which law has acquired in Europe was obviously impossible. Any legal system had to be brand new. As such it was without sanction of custom, without prestige and without effect.

The growth of individualism in a nation which had thought in terms of clan responsibility for two or three thousand years meant a shedding of responsibility to the clan without the assumption of any duty to the community. Sun Yat-sen, thinking in political terms, compared China to a 'heap of sand', meaning that each man or family thought for themselves and had no national consciousness. This was in any case an exaggeration, but it is interesting to see that the great Chinese democrat himself saw individualism not as the necessary basis of democracy, but as a weakness in the nation-State. A heap of sand, each grain individual, but bound together by propinquity and in the mass forming a great entity is no bad simile for a democracy as understood in Europe. To Sun Yat-sen, a truer Chinese than he knew, it was an epitome of weakness, lacking the monolithic character which the authoritarian empire should possess.

The overthrow of orthodoxy, of authoritarian doctrine, so essential if democracy is to be real, if the free play of ideas is to be allowed to form policy and advocate changes however sweeping, meant in China the simultaneous overthrow of moral standards. Confucianism was another monolith; ethics, morals, politics intricately bound together, inseparable, and clinging to the Empire like ivy to a tree. If Confucian doctrine was no longer sacred, then the bonds of filial obedience, of honesty and fair dealing were also deprived of sanctity; and if loyalty, the supreme Confucian virtue, were to be deprived of its object, the Throne, then no public virtue could survive.

The idea of patriotism, love of country, is not in China an ancient concept. Loyalty to the dynasty meant also, of course, loyalty to China, to civilization, and was so obvious a duty, so natural a sentiment of any thinking being, that it was not separated from its constituent ideas. The dynasty was China; China was the civilized world. No one would be loyal to barbarians rather than to China, and so the concept of patriotism lacked a contradiction and was left unexpressed.

Such were the causes which were leading the old Empire to destruction and revolution, and such were the obstacles in the way of a democratic State emerging from that revolution. It was thus inevitable that the revolution, which, once started by the changed circumstances of the Chinese world, could never be arrested half-way, must go through three main phases. First a period of increasing anarchy during which the pillars and bastions of the old order successively fell. Then a search, often enough down blind alleys, for a new pattern for society, a new theory of civilization. Finally, the search having shown that all other patterns were cut to suit very different communities, the reappearance of the fundamental concepts of Chinese society in a form fitted to the changed world.

These concepts are: a world sovereign authority, the old Empire, co-terminous with civilization; a balanced economy by which only luxuries and surplus products are exchanged, the basic industries and basic transportation being managed by the State; the establishment of an orthodox doctrine which harmonizes all the activities of the human being and provides a code of ethics, of politics, and of every other activity, including economics. This orthodox doctrine not only enshrines the aims and ideals of the Empire but also provides a means of selecting for its service the able and loyal members of the intellectual class.

In these old Chinese ideas, whether in their ancient form or in new guise, there is no place for freedom as the West understands it, no place for salvation as the Christian understands it, and no place for individualism as the Liberal would have it. But the old Chinese ideas fit very well to the new pattern. Loyalty to a doctrine, belief in the one world order which is civilization, and beyond which is either treason or barbarism, the duty to serve the sovereign authority, the importance of the clan—or the party—the subordinate role of the individual as such.

If it be true that the Chinese Revolution has ended in a new version of the ancient society, expanded beyond the limits of the Chinese Empire, embracing not Confucianism but Marxism, equally contemptuous of outer 'barbarians', and equally self-satisfied with the new orthodoxy which time has not yet proved inadequate, this is, seen in perspective, a very natural conclusion.

The Empire was forced into revolution not because the Chinese themselves were discontented with their way of life, but because outside changes, sea-power and navigation, the conquest of the steppes, altered the basic conditions of their autarchic world and made it too small to survive. Very well, the old Chinese world was too small, but nothing had happened to convince the Chinese of the inadequacy of their concept. The scale was too small; then make it bigger; the Chinese Communists, embracing a world authoritarian doctrine in place of one local to China, have enlarged the arena in which old Chinese ideas can once more be put into practice, in more modern guise, expanded to the new scale, but fundamentally the same ideas which inspired the builders of the Han Empire and the restorers of the T'ang.

CHAPTER TWO

THE EARLY REPUBLIC: 'MIN KUO' PERIOD

NOT FAR FROM Peking, in the Western Hills, there is an ancient temple, where grew a strange and rare plant. This plant flowered at long intervals, and then only at the accession of a new emperor. Then it put forth a single blossom. When the Empire fell the plant flowered again, but this time was covered with a multitude of small flowers. So, at least, the Peking people will tell you. The monks were asked to explain this strange phenomenon. To republican officials, visiting foreigners and other persons of modern cut, they said that the crowd of little flowers symbolized the rule of the many, the people of China. To the more old-fashioned inquirers the monks would say that perhaps the explanation of the miracle was that in place of one sovereign, the Empire would now suffer the oppression of many small despots.

It was under the dreary and disastrous rule of the warlords that this story become popular in Peking; at the fall of the Empire, even in the ancient capital, there was perhaps a less cynical outlook. The Republic which was established early in 1912 following the abdication of the Manchu Dynasty was, the revolutionaries hoped, to be a democracy modelled closely on those of the United States and France, the two republican countries which were most familiar to the Chinese intellectuals. In the intention of its other chief founder, the former Imperial commander-in-chief and first president of the Republic, Yuan Shih-k'ai, it was to be a brief interregnum ending in the foundation of his own imperial dynasty. The event proved that both were wrong; the Republic was destined to end neither in democracy nor in a new dynasty, but in chaos.

Between the republicans, who were led by men long out of touch with their own country, exiles who had worked for years abroad, and the vast mass of the Chinese people, there was only one idea in common: that the Manchu Dynasty was beyond reform and must go. It had been in full decline for many years, and that decline had involved the decay of China as a power, the invasion of her sovereignty at home, and mounting economic distress in the countryside. Already in 1840 the ancient pattern of dynastic decline had begun to show its well-known symptoms. The failure of the Empire to defend itself against the English in the Opium War revealed its weakness; the T'ai P'ing rebellion was the first great peasant rising caused by oppression and corruption and inspired, like many of its predecessors, by an esoteric creed. It was suppressed only after years of devastation by new armies which the Court could but imperfectly control.

Further disastrous foreign wars, the Anglo-French attack which took Peking in 1866, the war with France in 1884 which lost China her suzerainty over Indo-China, and finally the war with Japan in 1895 which lost Korea and Formosa had ruined the prestige of the dynasty. The Empress Dowager Tzu Hsi, a familiar type in history, the forceful woman of few scruples who dominates a decadent court, had arrested the fall of the dynasty at the expense of paralysing every tendency to reform. She had virtually dethroned, and actually imprisoned, the Emperor Kuang Hsu for his part in the sudden wave of reforms which were initiated in 1898 in a last attempt to imitate the Japanese restoration movement and modernize the Empire. The Empress Dowager by the force of her personality and the support of the conservatives had held China stiff and rigid in the old hierarchic pattern; beneath that mask the corpse of the Empire was fast decaying, and when she died in 1908 the swift crumbling of the Imperial power brought all to ruin.

Yuan Shih-k'ai had been the instrument which the Empress Dowager had used to overthrow the reformers and the Emperor Kuang Hsu. He had also been the last Chinese viceroy in Korea and he was the commander and creator of the modernized army, armed at least with rifles and artillery instead of bows and arrows and spears, which had been formed after the T'ai P'ing rebellion and the war with Japan. He was disliked by the Regent who took power in the name of the child Emperor when Tzu Hsi and the Emperor Kuang Hsu died, on the same day, in 1908. Yuan was then dismissed from all his posts. Four years later the revolt of the garrison of Wu Chang, on the Yang Tze, following the accidental discovery of a republican conspiracy which involved officers of that garrison, brought the dynasty face to face with a vast insurrection. The southern provinces, always anti-Manchu, and more affected by foreign contacts, rose without resistance and joined the republican cause. The north, nearer to the Throne, less interested in foreign ideas, remained passive. The only hope which remained to the dynasty was the modern army, which Yuan had created. Unless he also commanded it, it would most probably join the rebels. Yuan was recalled, given supreme command, and took the field.

Yuan certainly did not intend to save the dynasty which was in any case beyond rescue. But he was able and intended to defeat the rebels and then, the saviour of the monarchy, to usurp the Throne. His chance had come, following the pattern of past history. Such had been the career of more than one of the founders of great dynasties, and of many more transitory regimes. At first all went as Yuan expected. The rebels had fewer trained troops, mostly southerners, and less artillery. The Imperial Army gained some successes and easily held the line of the Yang Tze. China could have been divided between Monarchy and Republic, for the western rebels who had joined the Republic would have been crushed by Yuan's superior force. But one factor appeared which upset the calculations of the commander-in-chief. It became apparent before many weeks were past that the Republicans had the sympathy and support of the foreign powers, and that support meant much.

The Western powers had no cause to love the Manchu Dynasty. It had resisted them when it dared, yielded when it must, tricked them when it could, and finally, in 1900, allowed the peasant rising—called the Boxer Rebellion—to engage in large-scale massacres of foreign missionaries and attacks upon the Legation Quarter in Peking itself. It was agreed on all sides that now that the Chinese were showing themselves anxious to introduce democracy and possibly even Christianity into the old Empire they should be supported by the 'civilized world'.

Yuan, who had few modern ideas, could make a shrewd estimate of a situation. He had driven the Boxers out of Shantung, the province he then governed, and thus deserved the good will of the West. He saw that the foreigners wished the Manchus to go, but also wanted peace and order in China to promote their trade. A strong man would be to their liking. Also, the conquest of the south in the name of the Manchu Dynasty was going to be difficult. He cared nothing for the dynasty; the Empress Dowager, his old mistress, was dead, and the Regent his enemy.

He therefore betrayed the dynasty, offered peace to the Republicans, the unity of China, the abdication of the Manchus, on one condition: that he should be the first president of the Republic. Negotiations to consummate this betrayal went on, while the helpless dynasty, unable to enforce loyalty or resist treason, bargained behind the scenes for life and property. They were accorded both. The abdication agreement granted the Emperor his title, the Summer Palace for his residence, a shadow court to wait upon him and large revenues. Yuan, after all, did not want the Imperial dignity to be smirched or reduced, for one day it would be his own.

The Republicans walked into this parlour with astonishing insouciance. Sun Yat-sen, their leader, resigned his provisional presidency of the Republic. The new capital was to be in Nanking, but since Yuan delayed the transfer (with the backing of the Diplomatic Corps) and then arranged a mutiny of his troops to provide an excuse for staying in Peking, the unwary Republicans yielded on this point also. By agreeing with Yuan they hoped to gain the peaceful abdication of the Emperor, the reunion of the country, and the end of the civil war. It would not have been so easy to conquer the north, and the real fear of foreign intervention, perhaps by the Japanese on

Yuan's side and by the Tsar in Mongolia or Sinkiang, urged them to accept the terms and trust Yuan.

The Republicans mistook the widespread anti-Manchu feeling in the south for republican fervour; they believed that democracy held a virtue proof against all reaction, and that the mere adoption of a constitution based on those of the West would ensure the modernization of China and the recovery of her power. For the most part these men had little or no knowledge of government or of the Chinese political scene; they had imbibed democratic ideas in their student days abroad, they felt bitterly the contempt expressed in foreign countries for antiquated and powerless China, and they believed that by adopting the usages of Europe or America they would also secure the friendship and protection of those powers.

Nothing could have been less true. Of the foreign powers only America was really sympathetic to the republican cause, and the United States at that time took but a secondary interest in the Far East, confining her active support to words. American religious interests were enthusiastic and hopeful, American business houses followed the views of their British and European colleagues and were dubious and unconvinced. The European powers were all either covertly or actively hostile to the Republic.

Britain, then the ally of Japan, believed that the Japanese model, the reformation of the Empire rather than its overthrow, was the true and proper pattern for Oriental progress. Any wild flight into democracy could only have unsuitable repercussions in India. In so far as the new Republic might make China strong and modern it would threaten the established privileges and colonial possessions of the European powers in the Far East. In so far as it might disorganize China and breed civil war or disorder it would prejudice the trading interests of the Western powers in this region. France and Germany, then both colonial powers enriched at the expense of China, felt the same; Russia, an absolute monarchy, could not be expected to welcome a democratic republic in Asia.

Above all Japan was necessarily hostile. Japan had humbled

the Empire and seized Korea and Formosa. She had established herself in Manchuria and virtually extinguished the nominal Chinese sovereignty there. She had shared the special privileges of the West in trade and extra-territorial rights, concessions and tariffs. She was a divine empire, to whom the spectacle of a successful republic in China would be offensive and even dangerous. The rise of China would banish for ever her dream of continental empire. The Empire had been surrounded with foes or half-friends all anxious to profit from its demise; the Republic was surrounded with enemies determined to strangle it at birth.

It must also be admitted that the Republic soon confirmed the doubters and discountenanced its few friends. The Parliament, elected in 1912, was a travesty of democracy. Votes were openly sold and openly quoted on the market. The members, when they met, devoted all their time to appropriating large salaries to themselves. Without roots in Chinese history, without tradition and without honesty, the organs of democracy presented a shameful picture of irresponsibility and corruption. Truly 'a monkey had dressed up in the robes of Duke Chou'.

To the President, Yuan Shih-K'ai, the spectacle was not disagreeable. The more quickly the Republic discredited itself, the sooner would China be ready for his solution, the new dynasty. He knew that he could count on the Western powers, already alarmed at the decline of order and the evident incapacity of the republicans. He knew, too, that he could count on the main part of the older generation of officials, who would welcome a return to the system they knew and understood. He thought that he could at least count on the passive acquiescence of the peasantry who knew nothing of politics or democracy. Finally he felt sure he could count on his troops.

Preparations were soon put in order. Yuan secured a large loan from the European powers, without the consent of Parliament, and thus flouting the Constitution he made himself independent of it. The few capable republicans were either exiled or assassinated; organizations were formed to petition for the establishment of a monarchy. They were favourably entertained, renewed, and at last, after due delay, accepted. The dynasty was proclaimed, the President, Emperor-elect, performed, for the last time in history, the ancient rite of ploughing and sacrifice at the Temple of Agriculture and the Altar of Heaven, and the date of his enthronement was announced.

All had gone forward in accordance with the precedents of history: the old dynasty had yielded to the constraint of its own most powerful military commander; he had assumed full power and was now about to ascend the vacant throne, with the customary delays and polite refusals. To Yuan and to many of his contemporaries this seemed natural and right. The Republic was just an ephemeral fantasy of returned students; there was no revolution, only a change of dynasty.

And then things began to go wrong. Japan suddenly, in the middle of the First European War, May 1915, presented to China the famous Twenty-one Demands, which if accepted would have placed China under a virtual Japanese protectorate and extinguished her independence. The Western powers were now at death grips with each other; they had need of Japan. America, who could have acted, was not prepared to intervene on a large scale. Yuan temporized, accepted some of the demands, postponed others, tried to obtain foreign support to reject the most outrageous. His prestige was destroyed, the Chinese people were roused to real alarm and indignation.

Yuan got little help from the divided and hostile European powers, and earned, by exposing the scheme, the cold implacable enmity of Japan. It was in vain that Yuan now pursued his plans. He could still count on the support of his officials and his well-pruned Legislative Assembly, but the army was wavering. On Christmas Day 1915, the commander of the forces in the remote province of Yunnan rose in revolt and denounced the pretender. Other garrisons hesitated, then joined the revolt. In a few weeks it became obvious that any further attempt to establish a monarchy must mean widespread civil war. Yuan gave way, dropped his plans in March 1916, and died, a broken-hearted man, in June.

This sudden collapse of what had apparently been a natural and universally-accepted development astonished the world at the time, and still requires explanation. Three things were the main causes of Yuan Shih-K'ai's failure. Firstly his own character, which was treacherous and untrustworthy. He had already thrice betrayed those who had put faith in his loyalty: first the Emperor Kuang Hsu, whom he betrayed to the Empress Dowager; next the Regent, who recalled him to defend the dynasty, and saw him betray it instead; lastly the Republic, which had accepted his terms, made him President, and trusted him to the full. The Chinese at that period were still under the strong imprint of Confucian tradition. Loyalty is the highest of the Confucian virtues, and loyalty was conspicuously absent from Yuan's career. He might have founded a dynasty in other times; it is doubtful whether it would have lasted more than a generation; one of those transitory regimes which arise between the great enduring dynasties of China.

The enmity of the Japanese was the second main cause of the collapse of Yuan. The Japanese provided the money to finance the revolt of the generals, they sheltered his enemies and discouraged his friends. Yuan was unacceptable to Japan because they feared that he would succeed. A restoration of the Empire was to the Japanese the only conceivable way in which China might emerge from her troubles. If she did so, and became a strong modern power, Japan had no prospect of empire on the mainland. Yuan must therefore be cast down, and the chaotic republic restored so that chaos might deepen until Japan was ready to gain her ends. Had Yuan rejected all the Twenty-one Demands, made himself the leader of a national movement of resistance and accepted the risk of war with Japan, he might have anticipated history and led China forward to a new order, under a new dynasty. But Yuan was not such a man, and perhaps China was not yet ready for such a struggle. The old order had still many bastions standing, only the Throne was gone, and the basis for a national resistance was still lacking.

The third cause of Yuan's failure was the ambition and jealousy of his generals. These men suddenly found, in the confused scene of the Republic, that they, the military, were the real holders of power: the Emperor, the symbol of civil control, was gone. The viceroys and governors of the old Empire had passed away. The new governors, men without prestige or experience, were feeble barriers to military ambition and only too anxious to share with the generals in the spoils of office. Now Yuan wished to restore the Empire, to reimpose the control of a strong and lawful government, to humble the army and promote his own relatives to princely rank. It was clear to the generals that as arbiters of the factions of a weak republic they would count for more than as the obedient generals of a new Empire. Moreover, all could aspire to do what Yuan wished to do. The dynasty was fallen, so any able general could found another. Why leave this to Yuan, who was ageing, who had no capable sons to follow him; once Yuan was gone the field would be clear for all comers.

The early progress of Yuan's monarchical movement and its subsequent swift collapse alike prove how little as yet the revolution had achieved. None of the objectives of 1911 were any nearer to realization. China was weaker than before, more subject to outside pressures and spoliations. The internal situation was deteriorating; no remedy for the peasant discontents had been produced, modernization was only making superficial changes, industry was still tiny and bound up with foreign controls. The Republic had, up to Yuan's death, been merely the old Empire without the Emperor, without prestige and without sanctity. Nor was the Republic able to defend itself. Whatever causes had operated to frustrate Yuan Shih-K'ai, the sentiment for democracy and the activity of the republican party played no part in them. No one had seriously opposed Yuan except his own generals. Not one of the republican leaders had any hand in his overthrow.

Consequently, when he fell, the Republic did not recover its former position, but became the sport of the military. For several years after 1916, a succession of ephemeral cabinets occupied the ministries of Peking, assumed the name of the government of China, endeavoured to collect loans from the

Western powers, and were one and all the creatures of whatever military commander had won the last civil war. In the south, the republican party, under their leader Sun Yat-sen, established themselves in Canton, repudiated the title of the Peking government to rule, claimed to be the only legitimate government of China, and were equally dependent on the fickle favours of the local military satraps. These generals, like those of the north, were only interested in money. They supported or betrayed the government for money; they warred upon each other to secure richer revenues, they organized the opium trade, sold the official posts, taxed the people for years in advance, squeezed the merchants, and finally, immensely rich, allowed, for a last payment, their troops to be defeated, and retired to the safety and ease of the foreign Concessions in Shanghai or the British colony of Hong Kong.

If matters were so conducted in the great cities and in the capital, in the provinces things were often far worse. Under the Empire there had been few troops in the countryside. The landlords lived in their villages, the peasants paid them rent. When times were bad, the landlords remitted rent, to alleviate the distress around them. If they did not they were in danger of being burnt out or slain. The magistrate and the governor were careful not to overtax the people, lest revolt occur. Revolt might mean calling upon the Court for troops. The Court would also inquire into the disorder and probably execute the over-covetous officials.

There was a natural balance; the poor were oppressed, but not too far; they could react with success, or at least with danger to the oppressor. The troops were armed with sword and spear, so were the peasants. Rifles did not exist, machine-guns were unknown. Jack was as good as his master on the battlefield. Or nearly as good; trained troops could of course easily rout a peasant rabble, but trained troops were few.

Now the general balance of the countryside was upset. There was no Court to rebuke or decapitate a greedy official; there was, instead, a horde of soldiers, vagabonds in uniform, without discipline or pay, who fattened on the land. They were allowed to pillage, to rob granaries and slay without punishment. The landlords fled to the cities from these disorders. They left bailiffs behind to collect their rents. The bailiffs found that the only way to live, and to grow rich at the same time, was to go into partnership with the military. If both agreed to collect from some village, good times or bad, all opposition could be overcome. Those who resisted would be shot. The soldier with his rifle and machine-gun could lord it over thousands of peasants.

Throughout the period of warlord rule, from 1916 to 1925, conditions steadily deteriorated. Little was heard of the distress of the countryside in the cities or abroad. Missionaries might report what they saw, but few realized how great the change was, nor what storms were brewing. The Chinese Revolution had become an incomprehensible confusion. No principles appeared to be in conflict; no contest between democracy and tyranny was visible, no climax and no conclusion. The Western world, when it gave any attention to this scene, either despaired of China and foresaw Japanese conquest or clung to the belief that a strong man would emerge to restore some kind of order. Japan, well pleased at the rapid decline of China, continued her slow penetration and prepared for swifter and more decisive strokes.

The warlord period was, however, not without lasting importance. It consummated the destruction of two main pillars of the old order. The Civil Service, still more or less intact when the Empire fell, perished in the Age of Confusion. The older officials withdrew to retirement. The younger either joined the hangers-on of some general for a brief period of spoliation or, leaving politics aside, endeavoured to obtain a post at one of the many new universities. In the warlord period the scholar class, at least the best elements of it, withdrew from government into academic life. Government and administration were left to ignorant soldiers and self-seeking careerists.

The flight of the rich from the countryside, the prevalence of banditry hardly differing from the exactions of the military destroyed the balanced economy of the countryside, drove the peasants down further into misery, drained money away to the coast, and left the great irrigation and drainage works uncared for and in decay. Disastrous floods, famine for which no relief, unless from foreign sources, was available, the decline of inland trade, the dislocation of communications, all contributed to the ruin of the old order of society. The military rule had alienated both scholars and peasants; it had defied every moral restraint and outraged every hope of improvement; it was the direct cause of the second phase of the Chinese Revolution.

It was not generally realized in the West, which continued to proffer good advice to China and still made no sustained attempt to comprehend her problems, that in this sad period of disorder democracy and with it all that the West hoped to see flourish in China had been discredited and cast aside. It is true, of course, that democracy had never had any trial at all; had never taken root in this alien soil, and that the pitiful travesty of the early Republic was neither an example of democracy nor a proof of its failure. Yet that is how it appeared to the Chinese people. In the name of Parliament they had seen gross and shameless corruption; in the name of democracy they had seen nothing but weak and bad government, military usurpation, violation of law, every kind of oppression and national decline. By the end of the second decade of the twentieth century the Chinese people were completely disillusioned with the false gods imported from the West. They turned restlessly to some other solution.

There were many who would now have welcomed a restoration of the Empire; many who regretted even Yuan Shih-K'ai. Other attempts to restore the monarchy had been made. In 1917 one of the least progressive generals had occupied Peking and clapped the young Manchu ex-Emperor on the throne. For a week the Empire was restored—in Peking, where the shopkeepers dutifully produced their dragon flags, kept stored away for such an eventuality. The other generals, who had been manoeuvring to effect just such a restoration, but had not yet composed their jealousies nor agreed upon the division of the spoils, now combined to oust Chang Hsun and conduct the young Emperor back to retirement. Chaos returned once more.

The one effect of this comedy was to discredit still further the fallen Empire. Whatever others may have planned, or hoped to effect, there was never another movement to restore the Manchus, or to found another dynasty. The Japanese showed singular lack of understanding of China when they believed that the restoration of Pu Yi to the throne in Manchuria would reconcile the Chinese to the loss of that country.

The Chinese are not romantic, particularly in politics. No lost cause appeals to the Chinese, no fallen house receives sympathy or support. What has fallen is down and can never be raised up. There have been no restorations in China, no Jacobites, no ghosts from the political past. Under the Manchu Dynasty, it is true, the secret societies, such as the Triad, did proclaim their objective to be the restoration of the Ming Dynasty. Dr Sun Yat-sen, when the Manchus abdicated, solemnly proceeded to the tomb of the founder of the Ming Dynasty at Nanking, and announced to the august shade of Ming Hung Wu the ruin of the enemies of his house. He did not, however, ever suggest that the living representative of the Ming family, the Marquis Chu, who had with his ancestors been a pensioner of the Manchu Dynasty, should be invited to ascend the throne. In Chinese terms expressions of loyalty to the fallen Ming Dynasty were merely an assertion of opposition to the reigning dynasty, and in no way predicated the restoration of the Ming or mortgaged the political future of the opposition movement. The Ming themselves, also succeeding to a foreign dynasty, the Mongols, had declared their aim to be the restoration of the rule of the T'ang and the Sung— but had never sought out any surviving descendants of those dynasties. The mass of the people neither regretted the Empire, nor hoped for its return. They probably expected a new dynasty, they disliked what they saw of the Republic, yet in a vague way they felt that the Empire could no longer meet the need. Something was required which would suit Chinese ways and yet adapt itself to changed conditions. No one really thought that a new dynasty, encumbered by the memories of the past, would prove able to steer China on to a new course. By 1920 it was clear that Western democracy was not the solution, and tacitly it was abandoned even by the revolutionary element.

The prestige of the West in Asia, at least in the Far East, was greatly shaken by the First World War. During that struggle Japan had been allowed to gather in the spoils, and the alliance of every independent Asiatic nation had been sought for no very high motives. The corrupt and powerless Peking Government had been bullied into declaring war on Germany, with which it had no quarrel, simply so that the Allied powers might seize the German shipping which had taken refuge in Chinese ports, and close and confiscate German business in China. This affair made a bad impression on the Chinese. The Germans, deprived of extra-territorial rights, soon proved, after the war, that this was an advantage, and regained their commercial power with much Chinese good will. The day soon came when only for Germans, wearing armbands with the character for German on their sleeves, was it safe to walk the streets of Canton.

Japan, on the other hand, the ally of democracy, had been allowed not only to take the German concession area in Shantung province, but to keep it for herself after the war. China, an ally, was to be robbed for the benefit of Japan. This indecent treatment aroused in China the first real storm of nationalist feeling (May 4, 1919). Student parades demanded redress. The terrified and indifferent politicians of Peking were awakened to a sense of their own peril, if not to that of their country. The Chinese delegation at Versailles refused to sign the treaty. It was the first act of dignified self-assertion that the Republican Government had ever performed. It was due entirely to unofficial forces, the outraged patriotism of the students, backed by the less comprehending sympathy of the people. It was an event of much significance, for with it went another: the first recovery of sovereign rights from a Western power.

The Russian Revolution had not at first struck any responding note in China. The events of Petrograd or Moscow were very far away. For some years Siberia, which was close at hand, was held by Whites. But the Soviet Government gained complete control of all Russian territory in 1920 and in that year approached China with an offer to renounce not only her extra-territorial rights but her special privileges in North Manchuria, where a new and more equitable agreement was to be negotiated. This was the early age of the Soviet regime when the doctrines of Marx and Lenin were still uncorrupted by Stalinist interpretation.

A Russian envoy, Adolph Joffe, arrived in Peking, where he was boycotted by the Diplomatic Corps, but feted not only by the Chinese politicians, but still more by the intellectuals. It is certain that the Soviet could have chosen no act more calculated to promote sympathy for Communism and interest in its doctrine. The renunciation, voluntarily, of special rights and privileges which Russia under the Tsars had extorted from the Empire set a standard of friendly co-operation—whatever the long-term motive—which the Western powers were unable and unwilling to attain. Comparisons between the behaviour of the Communist power and the 'Capitalist Imperialists' as they now began to be called, were drawn, and were unfavourable to the West. Sun Yat-sen had appealed to Britain and to America for recognition of his would-be democratic regime at Canton, and assistance to overthrow the ruinous rule of the warlords. His appeal was rejected.

At the time it is probable that Sun's appeal and its rejection were incidents which hardly detained the attention of the highest levels of government in the West. China and her troubles were perennial, insoluble, remote. Europe had much more pressing problems; no electoral interest was concerned with Sun Yat-sen or his opponents. All unnoticed, the second turning-point of the Chinese Revolution had arrived, and, still incomprehending and indifferent, the West once more backed the wrong side. When Yuan first showed his hand the West might have put its influence behind its professed ideals and tried to bolster up the tottering steps of China's infant democracy.

The Republic was a weak vessel, but at least it was made in the Western image.

The powers preferred the strong man, and thus ensured the collapse and discredit of the early Republic. Ten years of anarchy taught them no lesson. When Sun Yat-sen, whose Government was certainly the legitimate one by the legal tests to which the West attaches so much importance, appealed for recognition and aid to end China's misery, they again refused. They did not get a third chance. The Russians stepped in where the West feared to tread, but it was not an act of folly.

The Western powers had their reasons, or excuses. Sun Yat-sen, a sincere idealist, was not a good administrator, his nationalism was effervescent, and at times tactless. It was far from certain that, if helped, he could re-establish the Republic or rule it with order and competence. Had there been any other visible alternative this argument would have carried more weight, but at least a fallible idealist was to be preferred to the blank folly and ruthless corruption of the warlords. The West also still feared, not what Sun Yat-sen might fail to do, but what he might achieve—the formation of a strong and nationalist China.

The European powers all had colonial territories either taken from China or from kingdoms formerly under Chinese suzerainty. A strong China would certainly reassert her ancient right and claims. Every other State which had emerged from weakness or subjection had followed such a course. Then the trading interests of the West were firmly established in China in their Concessions, fortified by extra-territorial rights, and protected against any danger of Chinese competition by tariff treaties which limited China's right to impose duties. Any proposal to interfere with this comfortable situation raised vehement protests from Shanghai and these complaints were influentially backed in the home country.

The warlords, too weak and too corrupt to care for China's interest unless it seemed to coincide with their own, did not press for the recovery of lost rights and sovereignties. They liked the Concessions which gave them safe sanctuary at every adverse turn of the political wheel. They could there invest their spoils in safety, under the protection of the foreigner's law. There, too, they could remain, plotting a return to power, safe from any danger of arrest or interference. The Concessions were neutral ground. The fact that revolutions do not stand still; that if the stream of change is dammed up by some obstacle it either finds a way around it or bursts through, this did not occur to the Western statesmen and merchants. Most of their countries were not familiar with revolutions. In France and in America, revolution was, of course, a famous, almost a sacred, memory. But this very fact inhibited the peoples of these countries, as it still does, from understanding the revolutions of Asia. The American and French revolutions were victories won in the name of liberty, inspired by classical precedents, steeped in the traditions of Greece and Rome. The Chinese had no right or claim to any such inspirations or any such inheritance. Their revolution had not restored law to supremacy, nor enthroned democracy, nor overturned privilege. It was just a travesty of revolution mouthing slogans derived from superficial knowledge of the West, but aimed solely at personal enrichment and despotic power.

These views, widespread among the foreigners in China, were backed by the consideration that if any other explanation was admitted, the results might be very inconvenient. If it was accepted that European ideals were valid in Asia, then the claims of Indo-Chinese to settle their own affairs, of Indians to indepencence, and of coloured races to equality could not be denied except by sheer force. The Western nations were unwilling to draw these conclusions, and preferred to wrap themselves in a cloak of unreality.

The ideological leadership and inspiration of the Chinese Revolution had been Western and democratic; repudiated as a sham by the West, it withered and was cast aside by the Chinese revolutionaries themselves. They turned to Communism, not at first consciously, but by way of Russian aid and encouragement, Russian sympathy and equal treatment. In 1921 Sun Yat-sen met Joffe in Shanghai. The conference ended in an agreement, by which, while declaring that both Sun and Joffe recognized that Communism was not suitable to China, Sun accepted in the name of his party, now renamed the Kuomintang or Nationalist Party, the aid of Russia and the alliance of the still infant Chinese Communist Party.

The Kuomintang was then reorganized on the lines of the Russian Communist Party, with political commissars, mass propaganda organs and strict discipline. It no longer claimed to be working for a democratic republic but for a party dictator-ship which would govern the country for several years—the period of tutelage—until the people had acquired the necessary knowledge of democracy and political skill to govern them-selves. Whether Dr Sun really believed that a people without previous experience would in some way acquire it without participating in government must remain unknown. All history was there to show him that once an authoritarian regime has been established it will never yield power except to force.

The Kuomintang therefore turned away from democracy, and after the death of Sun Yat-sen in 1925 it is doubtful whether any important leader really expected or desired the end of the period of tutelage. They often opposed the power of their own leadership, but rather in the hope of acquiring it for them-selves than with the intention of introducing democracy. It was not on democracy that the new revolutionary appeal was based, but on nationalism. It was not the evils of Chinese society which it mainly aimed to overthrow, but the power and privileges of the foreigner. The recovery of sovereign rights was the chief purpose of the new revolutionary party, the Kuomintang. Very secondary to this aim was the pro-motion of social revolution, the reform of the land system, or the introduction of a rule of law.

It is true that Dr Sun's three principles, the basic doctrine of his party, included in the third, people's livelihood, a vague and imprecise aspiration to social betterment. But whether this principle meant in practice Socialism, the Welfare State, or merely some measures of modern hygiene, better communica-tions and other accompaniments of a developed capitalist society, was left obscure. The real beliefs and ideals of the Kuomintang were more clearly expressed, many years later, by Chiang Kai-shek, in his book *China's Destiny*, in which all the evils and troubles from which China suffered are ascribed without qualification to the unequal treaties and foreign imperialism.

It is important to remember that at this time, 1921-5, Fascism was hardly known. The rise of Mussolini during these years was an event which was little remarked in China. Hitler would remain unknown for another decade. The Chinese, while repudiating Western democracy, had no authoritarian model to turn to except Soviet Russia. But the Kuomintang was not a Communist Party, and was soon to quarrel finally with Communism. The authoritarian character of the Kuomintang, not Communist, nor yet Fascist, was really a new political form, half-imitated from Russia, but without the doctrine which gave meaning to Russian Communism; half an echo of the fallen Empire, but without the sanctity and assurance of the Throne and its encompassing Confucian orthodoxy. The Chinese were beginning to seek their own solution, but as yet contempt of the past and fear of foreign influence prevented them either from turning back to the monarchy or on to the acceptance of a strange ideology.

The Chinese Communist Party did indeed already exist. It was founded, in China, in 1921, and almost simultaneously in France among the Chinese students in Paris. The first leader, Ch'en T'u-hsiu, was a well-known man of letters and Professor of the Peking National University, the premier university in China. Among the founders were Mao Tse-tung, then a library assistant in Ch'en's university, and, among the Paris group, Chou En-lai. Chu Teh, an older man, who had already served in the warlord armies and came from the landlord class of Szechuan, perhaps the most conservative in China, had renounced his military career, abandoned his opium habit, gone abroad and, in Germany, become a Communist. It is significant that none of these early foundation members and later leaders had imbibed Communism in Russia or understood Russian.

The background of these men was various, but none were workers. Ch'en was an intellectual; Chou the scion of an old official family—the son of a 'mandarin'; Chu, a Szechuan landlord and militarist; Mao, a middle peasant or yeoman in origin, the son of a farmer who owned land, employed labour, and could read and have his son educated. One other thing was common to the chief leaders, and to many of their later lieutenants. They all came from the west centre of China, from Hupeh, Hunan and Szechuan, the region where landlord-peasant relations were most dislocated, where militarism had conducted itself more foolishly and ruthlessly than anywhere else, and where the influence of the coast and Western ideas was least profound and most disliked. How far this background and, still more, twenty years of isolation in these same regions later on has formed the outlook of the Communist leadership may be argued, but it cannot be ignored.

As a result of the Sun-Joffe conversations the Chinese Communist Party was recognized, at least in the area controlled by the Canton Government, and it was agreed that Communists might enter the Kuomintang as individual members. Thus a strange and ill-defined alliance was made. The Communists concentrated their activity on the fields of propaganda and mass organization. They also succeeded in infiltrating the army. The government remained in the hands of the Kuomintang. Meanwhile the endless cycle of warlord civil wars continued in the north. For a brief time the emergence to supreme power in Peking of Feng Yu-hsiang, a general who was both a Christian (Protestant) and also inclined to the Left and to nationalist ideas, seemed to promise a peaceful reunion of China. Sun, already a sick man, came to Peking and there, in March 1925, died. Nothing came of his journey. Feng was before long ousted by the reactionary Chang Tso-lin, the warlord of Manchuria.

After the death of Sun the Kuomintang, still entrenched in Canton, and controlled by a shifting group of leaders, actively prepared for an expedition to conquer the north and destroy the warlords. Real reform, a disciplined and devoted army and revolutionary enthusiasm marked the new regime in Canton. Elsewhere these changes were but slightly considered. It was held by foreigners that the 'Cantonese' as the Kuomintang were usually called could never defeat the more warlike northerners. The northern expedition finally started, under the leadership of Chiang Kai-shek, early in 1926. The general had been sent for advanced training to Moscow by Sun Yat-sen and on his return had created and commanded the new military training college at Whampoa. From this college have come forth not only the best-known generals of the Kuomintang but also their ultimate rivals and victors, the leading generals of the Communist army. Old comradeship and early friendship may not have been without significance in inducing the final surrender of many of the Nationalist generals in 1948-9.

A year or so before the launching of the northern expedition, an event had occurred which, with the irrationality of popular response, had greatly eased the task of destroying the warlords and carrying forward the revolution. On May 30, 1925, a student crowd demonstrating against the foreign-controlled police of the International Settlement in Shanghai on the occasion of the arrest of strikers from a Japanese mill, were fired upon with some fatal casualties by the police in the Nanking Road.

It is not easy now, and for foreigners it was still more difficult then, to imagine or to gauge the violence of the reaction which this event produced. Nationwide boycotts of British and Japanese firms, individuals and organizations swept from Canton to Peking. Demonstrations which provoked or involved further violence occurred at Canton and elsewhere. A total boycott of Hong Kong, with a mass withdrawal of the Chinese working population there, nearly ruined the colony and wrecked its trade. Missionaries had to leave the interior, the Press maintained a violence and scurrility which was fortunately concealed from most foreigners by their inability to read Chinese. The foreigner, bewildered, indignant and alarmed, sought in vain to explain, to reason, to justify. No attention was paid by rich or poor, student or peasant. Universal indignation, violent hatred and ferocious threats of vengeance were the sole response.

It is extremely important to examine this strange phenomenon, which is a perfect example of what the foreigner failed to understand about China and where the Chinese lack any comprehension of the West. The Westerner, even the liberal Westerner, felt that though the police might have acted hastily, they were legally in the right. They had been assailed in defiance of a prohibition against parades. They had given the due statutory warning, they had fired first in the air, only secondly at the demonstrators. Law had been upheld by a necessary act of firmness, however tragic the consequences to individuals. Fathers who mourned their sons should have restrained rash youths from taking part in politics which they could not understand. If more discipline were shown in the home these things would not happen. Such were the admonitions, more in sorrow than in anger, which leading and well-known Westerners long resident in China offered to their critics.

To the Chinese, to all Chinese, the professor, the politician, the merchant and the coolie all this was 'wind past the ear'. It meant nothing, struck no chord, seemed a tissue of thin excuse. The Chinese viewpoint utterly ignored the law and legalities. It was simple, direct, easily understood—by Chinese. Shanghai was a Chinese city. In that city Chinese had been shot down by foreign-controlled police. Those shot were students, scholars, members of the educated élite, to whom no law should apply except the Confucian code of decorum and ethical restraint. Moreover they were patriots, they were protesting against acts of 'imperialist oppression'. The Chinese attitude to law was here most significantly displayed.

Law meant violent penalties, which could be justly applied only to criminals: it was outrageous in itself, an aggravation of the offence, for the Westerner to talk of legal justification for such an act against such persons. The legal status of the concessions at Shanghai, of the foreign police force itself, all

54

these things meant nothing at all to the Chinese people: in so far as they admitted them to be facts, they claimed that time was already long past when such anomalies should be abolished. The Nationalist policy of 'recovery of sovereign rights' received an immense impetus and mass support. For the first time since the Revolution the whole body of the Chinese people was stirred and roused. It remained for revolutionary leadership to give this great force its own goal.

It is probable that the May 30 incident in Shanghai was but a match to touch off the highly explosive material of revolution which had accumulated. The Revolution had so far failed to do any single thing to benefit China. Conditions were worse than under the Empire. No goal, no intelligible ideal was held out to the people. Democracy was discredited and no other objective recognized. At this point the manifest power and privilege of the Westerner, his claims and his wealth, his rights and his infringements of Chinese sovereignty stared the Chinese people in the face and offered a simple and compelling explanation of all their frustration. The foreigner was to blame, his aggression was the cause of all the sorrows of China. Drive him out, strip him of his wealth, seize his Concessions, abolish his privileges, and then the Revolution could go forward in the assurance of victory, of modernization and of peace.

It was clearly to the interest of the Kuomintang and the Communist Party to further this view. May 30 was a godsend to them. The militarist Government in Peking and the provincial warlords were embarrassed, abashed and alarmed. They were described as 'running dogs of the Imperialists' because they did not at once take the foreign Concessions by armed force. For what were their armies useful? They would not fight the foreigner, then what would they do? It was a telling argument which bit deep into the minds of the soldiers themselves. The Peking Government made feeble protests, rebutted by the Westerners, and derided as cowardice by the Chinese people. The Government dared neither to take action against the foreign powers nor restrain the fury and violence of the people. Foreigners spoke of the 'Spirit of Boxerdom' and demanded troops for protection before it was too late. All of which was excellent propaganda for the revolutionaries, who portrayed the foreigner as hand in glove with the militarists to sell China and divide her into colonies. The real dangers of the nineteenth century were projected into the twentieth, when at last the people were sufficiently enlightened to appreciate them.

Under these circumstances the northern expedition could hardly fail. As it went north from Canton provincial warlords bargained, resisted half-heartedly and collapsed. By the summer of 1926 the revolutionary armies had taken Wu Han, the three cities of Hankow, Wu Chang and Han Yang which together form the great urban centre of the Yang Tze Valley; they approached Nanking and were closing in on Shanghai. With them, like a tidal wave, came social revolution. The Communist organizers spread through the rural areas inciting the peasants against landlords; others stirred up the workers of Shanghai, who needed little encouragement to resent their poverty and ill-treatment.

Every class was behind the revolution. The irresistible union of scholar and peasant, the key to success in China, was at last achieved. It can hardly be doubted that had this union persisted the Chinese Revolution might then and there have been carried to its conclusion, the power of the foreigner broken, the landlords tamed, the military despots destroyed and independence truly achieved. Under what guise this regime would have ruled, by what doctrines it would have been sanctioned, and how it would have approached the further problems of industrialization and population cannot be surmised.

Yet it is important to recall that at the time of the northern expedition the great revolutionary urge was nationalist and anti-foreign, not primarily concerned with economic conditions but with political defects. Nothing can be more different than the behaviour and the spirit of the nationalist armies of 1926 and the Communist armies of 1949. Both were revolutionary, but while the former were filled with a furious and fanatical enthusiasm for their cause, careless of the obstacles and ignorant of the outside world, the Communists, twenty-three years later, were a war-hardened, perfectly disciplined, efficient and fully endoctrinated force, not swayed by passion or resentment, confident of victory, contemptuous rather than resentful of the foreigner.

The revolution of 1926-7 was an explosion, violent and evanescent; the revolution of 1948 was an avalanche, ponderous, irresistible and conclusive. In 1926-7 the revolution had no assured aim; to some it meant the simple expulsion of foreign influence and privilege, to others widespread reform, to the Communist minority, social revolution. It had no unity of purpose and therefore no certainty of operation. In 1949 the revolutionary forces were wholly under the control and leadership of the Communist Party; they worked towards an accepted aim, their operations were co-ordinated and they had come to a clear realization of what objectives were significant and what could be ignored.

In the face of the sweep and violence of the revolutionary advance, the Western powers, who had been merely irritated and perplexed by the Chinese reaction to the May 30 incident, became seriously disturbed. For the first time, perhaps, since 1900 the Chinese crisis became the immediate concern of the Cabinet. Mr Baldwin visited a room in the Foreign Office, in company with the Foreign Secretary, Mr Austen Chamberlain. They were shown the large-scale map of China. 'So Canton is down there,' exclaimed the Prime Minister, 'I always thought it was here'—pointing to the neighbourhood of Tientsin. Mr Chamberlain contributed the remark that China was really very much larger than Japan.

Having identified the position of Shanghai on the map, and appreciated the importance and political influence of the British interests there, they then decided to send a strong force of troops to garrison the International Settlement, which hitherto had no garrison of foreign troops. Ships of war were also dispatched to the Yang Tze to lie off the ports where foreign Concessions existed. These measures had in the past sufficed to impress every Chinese military commander with the unwisdom of provoking the foreigner too far.

This time matters took a different course. The Nationalist armies, undeterred by the presence of foreign warships, approached, attacked and captured Nanking. They then carried out some indiscriminate killing of various foreign residents, the main body of whom were only saved by a barrage from the warships and a perilous escape over the city wall with ropes. The Nanking incident brought the revolutionary forces to the brink of war with the Western powers. Other incidents occurred. At Hankow the mob, incited by the political organizers, overran the British Concession, plundered the homes of the foreign residents and forced them to retire to their ships which could be protected by the gunboats. At Wan Hsien even an unregenerate warlord, no Nationalist nor revolutionary, could seize British ships, resist their release by gunboats and drive these gunboats off with severe casualties caused by artillery fire. China was certainly changing. Perhaps Yang Sen's actions at Wan Hsien were the most significant of all these affrays, since neither he nor his men were animated with revolutionary zeal.

Shanghai, when the foreign garrison arrived, was still held by the warlord Chang Tsung-chang, perhaps the most ignorant and brutal of all the tribe. He had filched Shanghai, a rich prize, from his rival, Sun Ch'uan-fang, who had already succumbed beneath the assaults of the Nationalist forces. But now the army of the revolution was fast approaching the greatest and wealthiest city in China, the home of the richest merchants, the most numerous and awakened proletariat, the stronghold of foreign interests.

At the news of the coming change the Shanghai workers, organized since May 30 of the previous year as the boycott pickets, rose under Communist leadership and by a well-planned coup wrested control of the Chinese-governed part of the city from the warlord's forces. A few days later the main Nationalist armies arrived, the northern troops surrendered or fled, and the forces of the revolution were confronted, across a string of barbed wire, with the foreign garrisons.

The events of February had roused the most acute anxiety in the foreign community. All their illusions had been ruth-

lessly exposed. The confused, meaningless revolution was suddenly revealed as Communist-led and Moscow-controlled. From
the belief, held until the fall of Hankow, that the 'Cantonese'
were nothing but a rabble out for loot and incapable of coherent
operations, they now passed at one bound to the equally extreme view that the revolution was a gigantic Communist conspiracy organized and operated from Moscow. This was a satisfactory belief, and still has its devotees, because it meets the
needs of pride and sloth. If the Chinese revolution is really nothing but a machination of the Kremlin, then the old idea that
the European is always superior is still valid. For the Russians,
for this occasion, can be treated as Europeans. It avoids the un-
pleasant necessity of trying to understand China and her
problems.

It can hardly be doubted that at this point, February 1927,
war with the West, undeclared, but probably most destructive
and prolonged, was imminent. Had the revolutionary parties
held together it was inevitable. The prospect was ruinous to
the foreign merchants, appalling to the missionaries, and unwelcome to the home Governments. 1927 was a time of peace
in Europe; no one wanted a distant war in China. It was also
very unwelcome to large classes of Chinese. The merchant and
the banker, the landlord and the rentier, might wholeheartedly
join the Kuomintang to vindicate China's rights, assert her
just independence, and curb the foreign encroachment. But
war meant much more than this. It meant, first of all, social
revolution. Everyone could see that after the events of Shanghai
and the progress through South China. The war would mean
the arming of the peasants, the loss of the coast cities, the
elimination of the influence of wealth and the rise of the Communist Party and the extremists of the Left.

Chiang Kai-shek had for a long time seen that the alliance
of a landlord and merchant party with Communist revolution
was unlikely to endure. It had been necessary to ride the wave
of revolution which May 30 had set rolling. Now he was in
danger of being dumped by that wave, cast aside by more
extreme leaders. The Nationalist Government, now established

at Wu Han, whence it had moved from Canton, was very much to the Left, under the influence of Borodin and other Russian advisers. Those advisers, as is now well known, were actually urging the Communists to keep faith with the Kuomintang, believing, on Stalin's instructions, that the Communist Party could not carry forward a revolution alone but must at present merely prod the Kuomintang to go as far as possible.

The Communist Party, then completely under Russian orders, was anxious to maintain the coalition even though the country was aroused to a much more extreme revolutionary ardour. Whether Chiang and the Right Wing knew this and counted it as an element of strength for their plans or were ignorant of the facts made no difference. On March 26, 1927, Chiang struck, disarmed the pickets, slew those Communist leaders whom he could catch, and soon broke with the Wu Han Government to form his own Right Wing Nationalist Government seated at Nanking. Among those Communist leaders in Shanghai who escaped, by a remarkable chance, was Chou En-lai, who had been chief organizer of the coup of February in Shanghai.

This event, the break with the Communist Party, was to have been the 'whiff of grapeshot' of the Chinese Revolution. So Chiang hoped. At first it seemed as if he might be right. Wu Han wavered, then broke and came to heel. The Nationalist Governments were re-united at Nanking. The Communist Party was cast out, driven from power and proscribed; the Russian advisers sent back to Moscow. In the following year, 1928, the united Nationalist armies successfully drove north to Peking, expelled the last warlord, Chang Tso-lin, and removed the capital to Nanking, where it was soon recognized by the relieved foreign powers.

The essence of the whiff of grapeshot theory is that the revolution should have outlived its creative—or destructive—phase, and that stability is now the need. The small handful of troublesome doctrinaires once dispersed, peace and consolidation can ensue.

These conditions were not satisfied by the situation in China in 1927. The revolution had once more become violently active, it had swept away the militarists and begun the task of freeing China from her subjection to the foreigner. But much remained untouched or hardly altered. Even the foreigner still retained most of his Concessions—all the really important ones —and all his extra-territorial privileges. Some restrictions, such as those on tariffs, had been conceded to appease the wolves, some Concessions, such as that at Hankow and smaller ones at other Yang Tze ports had been renounced. They could not in any case be held. But the land problem, the peasants and their poverty remained virtually as before. There was as yet no new institution which promised to restore the fallen power of civilian control, there was no ideology to cement the new society, no objective beyond a distant and unreal promise of a democratic constitution and the still unsatisfied demands of nationalism.

The workers of the great cities could be, and were, suppressed. The Communists were driven from power, but on August 1, 1927, a part of the Fourth Army, one of the best fighting units, mutinied at Nan Chang and, led by its Communist officers, formed the Red Army. The revolution was not over, it had taken to the hills.

The events of 1927-8 nevertheless ended a phase, the phase of unity between peasant and scholar which had so effectively broken up the warlord world. Henceforward, for many years, that unity was lost. The peasants, suppressed and uncared for by the reaction, rallied to the Communist Party, when, a little later, that party dropped its dogma and took note of reality. The scholars, the educated class, still imbued with nationalism and believing that the Kuomintang was the party which stood for an independent China rather than subservience to Russian orders, rallied around the new regime in Nanking or at least held off from the Communists. The revolution went into second gear; the Nationalist Party, in effective control of the vast majority of the provinces, could now show what it could do for China.

CHAPTER THREE

THE NATIONALIST DICTATORSHIP: 'KUOMIN' PERIOD

ONE OF THE first acts of the new Nationalist regime presided over by Chiang Kai-shek, when it was established in Nanking, was to build near the tomb of the first Ming emperor on the slopes of Purple Mountain a vast and imposing sepulchre for the founder of the Republic and Nationalist Party, Dr Sun Yat-sen. The structure is in most respects a copy of the ancient imperial tombs; it is built, however, not of stone, brick and timber, but of concrete, and though covered with coloured tiles and a Chinese-style roof it is not well proportioned and lacks the harmony and grace of old Chinese architecture. Partly foreign in style, with a Chinese roof, using materials ill adapted to the design, the monument of Dr Sun epitomizes the regime of his successor. For all these faults marred from the first the government and administration of Nanking. The Kuomintang could never make up its mind whether its revolutionary past should impel it forward to modernity, or its nationalist chauvinism carry it back to Chinese tradition. It was shoddily modern, built with ill-considered adaptations of the West, but still strove to cloak its power in the respectable mantle of Confucius, the Chinese roof, but not made of the right material.

In 1928 the Nationalist armies entered Peking. Chang Tso-lin, the last warlord, retreated to Manchuria, where he was blown up in his train by the Japanese, who had no further use for him. The Japanese had also attempted to stop the Nationalist advance at Tsinanfu, in Shantung, but though their intervention there, wholly unjustified and pre-figuring future events, did prevent the eastern army from advancing, the western force, moving up the Peking-Hankow railway, took Peking almost unopposed. This sort of Japanese interference, which provoked the Chinese without really altering the course of events, was frequent in the early years of the Nationalist regime. It was not until 1931 that the Japanese adopted more effective tactics. After Peking had fallen and the government there dissolved, the capital was formally transferred to Nanking, and the foreign powers, with much reluctance at the idea of leaving Peking, conferred recognition on the regime which had halted the revolution in its tracks and saved the Shanghai interests.

Those interests themselves, or rather many of the foreign residents, were unable to move with such agility. They continued to distrust Chiang and his regime as 'Red' long after he was actively at war with the Communists. The fact that Chiang and the Kuomintang were sincere Nationalists and therefore aimed to reduce the influence of foreigners and curtail their special privileges was quite enough to damn him. The home Governments, informed by specialists who took more detached views, realized that Chiang was a great deal better for them than any possible alternative and that some concessions must be made.

They agreed to enter into negotiations for the ending of extra-territorial rights and other infringements of Chinese sovereignty. The negotiations were prolonged, indeed they never concluded, for ten years later, while the matter was still under discussion, the invasion of the Japanese made all such questions irrelevant. The history of the Nanking Government's foreign policy, their effort to regain China's sovereign rights and lost territories, is instructive since it reveals the main weakness of the regime and of its ideological appeal. The second revolution of 1926-7 had been borne on the wave of national fury aroused by the May 30 incident in Shanghai. It was only in part a movement for social betterment, and that impulse was crushed by Chiang's coup in Shanghai in 1927. The main motive force, which brought in the educated class and merchants, was nationalism. It was to recover the full power of the State in its own territory that the Kuomintang went to war, and it was in the belief that such a recovery was the essential prelude to any modernization and reform that the merchants and intellectuals backed it.

Once in power, how did the Nanking Government fulfil these expectations, how did nationalism work out in practice? Against Britain, France and the lesser European powers the Kuomintang was always ready to throw a stone. The lesser evils of the International Settlement at Shanghai, the Concessions in Tientsin and Canton, the extra-territorial rights of British subjects, the existence of the colony and leased territories of Hong Kong and Wei Hai Wei, these matters concerned the Chinese Foreign Office, formed the subject of protests, negotiations, popular resentment fanned by officials and constant pin pricks.

Meanwhile the Japanese were already dominating the vast and rich area of Manchuria; they were soon to annex it outright, or rather to cover such annexation in the discarded robes of the Manchu Dynasty. They then invaded Jehol province, without any effective resistance by the Nanking Government. Later still they virtually detached North China from the control of Nanking, used the Settlement at Shanghai as a base of attack, stationed ever larger forces in Chinese cities such as Tientsin and Tsing Tao, and at last openly invaded the whole country. During this long and cumulative series of aggressions the Nationalists of Nanking yielded step by step, without resistance, without listening to the clamour of the people, the indignation of the intellectuals, or the appeals of those provinces which they abandoned.

During the years when the Japanese aggressions were growing annually more menacing the Generalissimo, as Chiang was styled, devoted his time and his German-trained armies to fruitless campaigns against the Communist rebels in South China. Huge sums of money were wasted on these vain attacks, heavy losses of material, many casualties among the best-trained troops. None of these troops were ever permitted to fight the Japanese, to garrison threatened areas, or to check by their presence the more flagrant violations of China's territory in which the Japanese military almost daily engaged. During the ten years of the Nanking regime of the Kuomintang Manchuria and Jehol were lost, Inner Mongolia and North China were so infiltrated by the Japanese that only a touch was needed to capture this great region; Shanghai was made into a base for Japanese aggression in the south. This was a greater loss of territory and power, of prestige and resources, than the Empire had suffered in a hundred years of decline.

The policy of 'internal pacification before resistance to external attack', the avowed policy of Chiang during these years, really meant hunting the Communist guerrillas while yielding vital territory to the Japanese. It was ineffective, because there was no internal pacification and external attack became ever more serious. The Communists could not be suppressed; the whole force of the Government was bent to this purpose for ten years and failed. Finally it was the Communists who compelled Chiang to resist the Japanese and thus forced their policy upon the Kuomintang. So remarkable a consequence of the breach between the Communists and Kuomintang, so strange a reversal of the situation of 1927 requires examination.

When the Kuomintang, led by Chiang Kai-shek, turned upon the Communists in April 1927, the Russian advisers and still more the Russians of Moscow were taken by surprise. They had urged the Chinese Communists to keep in step with the Kuomintang, to accept slights and even put up with reactionary measures, so that the coalition might hold until the 'bourgeois revolution', which the Russians held to be the first and inevitable step, was completed.

There must be a bourgeois revolution because China was not yet industrialized and had really no true proletariat. The peasants were, of course, by Marxist ideology and Russian experience, not a revolutionary class, but 'the packhorse of civilization' as Trotsky called them. No revolutionary party could be built on the peasants. The Russians, in fact, knew no more about China than their enemies, the Western Europeans and Americans. So the Chinese Communist Party was led by its Russian masters like a pig to the slaughterhouse. Only when the axe was already falling did the Russians draw back in fright, hastily change their directives, and urge the Chinese to fight and seize the cities. It was both too late and the wrong advice.

Some of the Communist leaders fled, others were captured, imprisoned and executed. But the army was also in part under Communist influence—the Fourth Army in particular—and it was elements of this force commanded by a Communist officer, Chu Teh, which at Nanchang raised the red flag and set the Communist Party on a new course. It was at first, on Russian advice, a disastrous course. The Chinese Communists were now urged to seize cities; only in cities are there large bodies of workers, and workers must be the base and support of a Communist regime. No workers, no Communists. That was the Russian dogma.

Chu and other leaders were orthodox and obedient; they did their best. They attacked Changsha, and were repulsed with loss, they seized Canton, and were driven out with great slaughter. They failed with still more casualties before Amoy. They did not hold a single large city, they were on the run, wandering about the mountains of Kiangsi and Hunan. They fled to Chingkangshan, an almost inaccessible mountain stronghold. There they found Mao Tse-tung, a refugee from Hankow and the fallen Wu Han Government.

The meeting on Chingkangshan, now the subject of Communist legend and art, was indeed significant. Mao had civilian experience; he had been a rural organizer for the united revolutionary armies in their advance. He knew the South Chinese countryside well, for many years he had travelled in it, and he knew the peasants and their wants. He could not get any orders from the Russians or from the fugitive Central Political Committee of the Chinese Communist Party, then directed by a Russian-trained Chinese, Li Li-san. But Mao could use his eyes and his experience. He could see the peasants of these wild hills, and see in them the one hope for his party and their creed.

Mao and Chu set up a new kind of Communist regime, based on the peasants, with land reform as its main plank,

66

guerrilla warfare as its defence, avoidance of cities as its strategy, rousing the peasants as its political objective. All of which was heresy to Russian teaching. The Central Political Committee and the Russians were quick to see that, and Mao was expelled from the Central Political Committee. He was perhaps expelled from the Communist Party. No one can now prove it. Communism does not like to leave mistakes on record.

For some years the Chinese guerilla Communists were fortunately for themselves so cut off from all communication with the world that they could not receive even the censures of Moscow; they had to think for themselves. They were able men, and though they made some bad mistakes, they found the way to survive, grow and spread. At first the idea of appealing to the peasants' land hunger was crudely applied. Landlords were hunted and slain, often with great cruelty. Kuomintang officials were put to death, all opponents or non-supporters were treated harshly.

The Communists were determined to prove themselves the friend of the peasant; the best way seemed to be to revenge themselves upon the peasant's traditional enemies. These methods certainly won the party the warm and loyal support of the peasant population, who gave them information of the movements of the Nationalists, denied such information to the latter, fed and carried for the Communists, vanished or fled from the Nationalists. 'The people are the sea; we are the fish, as long as we can swim in that sea we will survive.' So said Chu Teh, and he and Mao made sure that the fish in their shoal recognized the taste of sea water.

The educated class, for the most part themselves members of landlord families, did not appreciate these methods or sympathize with the aims of the Communists. To them it seemed that Communism was just another great peasant movement, like the T'ai P'ing or the Boxers, and, as it made no attempt to win the scholars, like its predecessors, bound to fail. It is certain that in this early agrarian stage the Chinese Communist Party had only one of the keys to success, peasant support; the other, the approval of the scholars was withheld, though not

firmly attached to the cause of their opponents, the Kuomintang. Each side lacked the dual support which would give
victory.

If the Communists by their violence alienated the scholars,
the Kuomintang by its blind selfish indifference lost the
peasants. Chiang had one policy for the rural problem, and one
only: the use of force. The Communists must be crushed; the
reform of land tenure, the alleviation of taxation, the reduction
of rent or the curbing of usury, all these might be desirable,
even advisable, but could not be put into effect so long as
armed rebellion was afoot. Such policies would have shown
weakness, would have, by admitting the claims of the Communists, condoned their rebellion and thus given it new
strength. It was the familiar argument of authority faced with
insurrection. It might have had some validity if Chiang could
have suppressed by force the insurrection which, according to
Kuomintang policy, both inhibited the Government from resistance to foreign aggression and from internal reform.

Several large-scale attempts in the years between 1930 and
1934 were made to crush the Kiangsi Soviet and its offshoots
in Hunan, Hupeh and Kuang-tung. Some of the smallest Communist areas were overrun, but against the main centre every
effort failed, and these failures were damaging to the prestige
of the Government. At last the policy of slow blockade, the
gradual compression of the Communist area, began to give
results. The Communists—according to Mao Tse-tung—also
made some errors of strategy. They saved themselves by the
celebrated Long March. Abandoning the Kiangsi Soviet and
its colonies in the region south of the Yang Tze, the whole
Communist community, army and civilians alike, broke out
of the blockaded area and marched south-west to the farthest
frontiers of China.

They passed through the backward provinces of Kueichou
and Yunnan, hardly opposed by the antiquated and ill-armed
armies of the local military governors, remote survivals from
the warlord era. They crossed the upper Yang Tze in its wild
gorges, skirted the edge of Tibet, where they met many hard-

ships from hunger and cold, and finally descended through
Kansu into the northern part of Shensi province, a backward,
remote area, easily defended, and adjoining the Mongolian
steppe.

During this mass flight the Nationalists, continually announc-
ing the utter destruction of the Communist forces, followed
in pursuit, unable to judge the direction that the Long March
was really aiming for, and thus unable to intercept it. They did
succeed in imposing the rule of Nanking on the western provinces of Kueichou, Yunnan and Szechuan, which had hitherto
remained under warlord control. Much speculation at the time
was given to the reason why the Communists had chosen to
retreat to such a backward ill-favoured region as Shensi. Many
parts of South-West China through which they marched were
more defensible, richer and less accessible to the pressure of the
Nationalist Government. It is apparent that the real reason for
the Long March, apart from the pressure of blockade, was to
establish the Communist base in a position where it could
participate in resistance to, and profit from, the impending
Japanese invasion.

The Communists had already, while still in Kiangsi, issued
an empty and propagandist declaration of war upon Japan.
Empty, because they were not in contact with any area where
Japanese troops were to be found, and were indeed separated
from such regions by hundreds of miles and the Kuomintang
armies. Propagandist, because they had already sensed that the
Chinese people were alarmed and outraged by the policy of the
Nanking Government in yielding to Japan, and were demand-
ing national resistance. By coming forward as the champions of
the patriotic movement, the party of resistance, the Communists hoped to gain support in classes hitherto opposed. At the
same time, on their arrival in Shensi, they abandoned the extreme anti-landlord measures of the earlier period and tried to
reconcile all classes in support of war with Japan.

The Communist movement had thus, in the ten years between 1927 and 1937, developed from a workers' party of
theoretical Marxists, into an agrarian party of rural revolution

—heretical Marxism in fact, if not in name—and now appeared as the party of national resistance and reconciliation, with the slogan 'Chinese do not fight Chinese'. The Kuomintang during the same period had also evolved or decayed. From the early days of the Nanking Government the question which occupied the minds of enthusiastic nationalists and the intellectuals in general was, how long would the period of tutelage last, when would a constitution be drawn up, promulgated and put into effect.

Many drafts were produced; always they were discarded, or had to be rewritten, always the new draft gave more power to the executive and the President, less to the proposed popular assembly. The practice of the Government was also a steady trend to dictatorship. While draft constitutions engaged the labours of theorists, the frequent quarrels between the leading members of the party, the arbitrary arrests, exiles and executions of opponents of the Generalissimo, showed plainly enough the real character of the regime.

These disputes were not always settled without warfare. In 1930, the revolt of the important General Feng Yu-hsiang, and his support of Wang Ch'ing-wei, Chiang's chief rival for the leadership, led to the establishment of a rival Government in Peking, and a civil war of several months. Canton and the south remained dissident, sometimes in nominal allegiance, at other times in almost open revolt. The leading members of the Government were continually occupied with these intrigues and disorders; they had less time for the real problems of government, and soon the promise of unity, reform and modernization began to fade.

There were, of course, some real achievements, largely in the fields of communications. Railways were extended, roads built, and in the provinces these changes, where the Communist war was not a complicating factor, brought a certain benefit. Much more might have been achieved if the Government, arbitrary though it was, had had complete control of the country and internal peace. The Kuomintang justified its failure to do more by pointing to Japanese aggression and Communist insurrection. There was truth in this claim, but not the whole truth. Japanese aggression could not have made the progress it did if the army had been organized to resist it, instead of being consumed in drives against the Communists.

The Communist insurrection could have been contained, perhaps subdued, if the Government, in the rural areas which it fully controlled—the vast majority of the provinces—had put into effect a real policy of land reform. The reduction of rents, remission and honest collection of taxes, measures to provide the peasant with loans at moderate interest, some resettlement and some redistribution of land, all measures which elsewhere have been the surest shield against Communism, all these were possible, quite practicable, but neglected.

But there was something else which ate out the heart of the Nationalist movement: the lack of any real satisfying and inspiring ideology. Nationalism was not enough, especially when it meant in practice yielding to the Japanese. Democracy was manifestly not the ideal or the practice of the regime; it repudiated the past, yet seemed to hanker after Confucianism; it was not Christian, although many of its leaders were baptized Christians. To what end, to what vision of the future, the Kuomintang progressed, no one really knew. Not many of its members cared.

The short-term prospect, the rewards and spoils of office, the ambition of high command, all these things were eagerly sought and fiercely contested, but when it was asked where all was tending, when the provisional character of the Government would end, what ultimate shape it would assume, all was uncertain. Government propaganda and school indoctrination confined itself to a narrow and unintelligent nationalism more often concerned with criticism of the Western nations than of the Japanese. The Chinese are a highly intelligent people; it is not possible to enlist their co-operation in this way. The intellectuals withdrew from politics; the careerists controlled the party and strove to secure the favour of the Generalissimo, upon whom all depended.

The Chinese people are not averse to the personal rule of an

71

autocrat; they had accepted the Empire for thousands of years. They now accept the 'leadership', as it is euphemistically called, of Mao Tse-tung. But with this acceptance goes respect; it is necessary for the autocrat to show plainly that he knows his job, that he is the master of the Empire, not merely the manipulator of intrigues, the arbiter of factions. Chiang Kai-shek never really controlled China; he could not prevent Japanese infiltration, he could not crush the Communists, he could not discipline the Kuangsi generals nor keep Canton loyal; he juggled with the factions of the Kuomintang, but only ruled by playing one off against the other. A military ruler to command respect must be successful in war; a civilian autocrat must, like Stalin, construct an instrument of government both efficient and loyal. Chiang was an unsuccessful general; his party was neither loyal nor efficient.

Under the Kuomintang the worst evils of the warlord era were reduced, or eliminated. The internal situation did not seriously deteriorate, but it did not improve. The external situation changed for the worse. Instead of the limited encroachments of the Western powers, anxious for trade openings, for profitable concessions and special rights, but not at all anxious to take over the immense task of conquering and governing China—in place of these gadflies, the Kuomintang faced Japan, who did in fact intend to conquer China and to incorporate the whole Empire in her own.

The Kuomintang never faced this danger or made a policy to meet and counter it. They refused to see that to oppose Japan, which really did threaten, it was wise to conciliate the Western powers who did not. They failed to understand the change which the first world war had wrought in the West. The European powers were now faintly ashamed of their aggressions of the past. Their active Left parties were openly critical of 'imperialism'. These nations were now no longer any danger to China; it was not a question of whether they would seek new rights and concessions, but of how long it would be before they gave up what still remained to them.

Moreover, the West was now aware that democracy was on

the defensive; it was prepared to encourage, even to aid in resistance to totalitarian aggression. America was no longer the aloof self-contained country of the early Republican period. America was already moving towards that contest for the Pacific which Japan also foresaw. The true policy for the Kuomintang was to place themselves unequivocally on the side of the democracies; to introduce those reforms which would convince the West that China had the same faith, and to show such resistance to the Japanese as to bring close the danger of a widespread war. The West was anxious to maintain peace; the prospect of a war throughout China, and one which might perhaps engulf the Eastern possessions of the West, would have stimulated the European and American leaders to take active steps to restrain Japan.

Instead, the obvious trend in China towards Fascism, the preference for German advisers in the military sphere, the weak yielding to Japan which gave no promise of national survival, and the continued covert hostility to the Westerner which the Kuomintang constantly displayed, these traits cooled the interest of the West, and induced the widespread belief that China was doomed to succumb to Japan, that there was no sense in engaging in a quarrel which China would not support, and that neutrality was the best policy for the Western nations. When the war came, China was left alone.

The Kuomintang was, of course, to a large extent the prisoner of its own past and of the still-decaying ancient Chinese social system. It strove to arrest the course of the revolution, to stabilize society while the necessary basis did not yet exist. The attempt to modernize China without interfering with the land system, the endeavour to fit some rags of Confucian doctrine to a party dictatorship, which itself was supposed to be temporary, to deny the practice of democracy and still pretend to be preparing the people for it, to proclaim and teach nationalism, and yield to the national enemy, this medley of contradictions could not form a coherent policy which would win mass support. The Kuomintang failed for lack of vision, for lack of any long-term policy thought out in terms

73

of reality, and thus became a prey to selfish ambitions, to corruption and to nepotism.

In 1936 it was clear that a crisis was approaching. The Communists had completed their Long March, they were plainly not 'exterminated' and they were safely ensconced in North Shensi. They were also appealing to the nation for unity against the Japanese. In Europe the rise of Hitler and the disunion of his opponents threatened a new war, and wholly inhibited the democratic powers from hindering or opposing Japan. The Japanese were soon to inflict public humiliation on the British inhabitants of Tientsin without evoking anything more than protest from the British Government. They were to sink an American warship in the Yang Tze and escape the consequences. Given these circumstances, and the Japanese military mind, it was obvious that within a few months Japan would make some further sweeping advance in China, expecting no intervention from without, and very little opposition from within. Peking and North China had been virtually detached from the control of Nanking by the Ho-Umetsu Agreement in 1935.

The protests of Chinese patriots had been silenced by imprisonment and censorship. The Government, still pursuing the will-o'-the-wisp of internal pacification, was deaf to the cries of the outraged citizens of the north, heedless of the Japanese threat to what remained of China.

In December 1936 Chiang Kai-shek was planning one more 'extermination drive' against the Communists in Shensi. The base of operations was the city of Sian, capital of the province. The army facing the Communists there consisted of local Shensi forces and the North-Eastern Army—the troops of Chang Hsueh-liang, son of the warlord Chang Tso-lin, and ousted ruler of Manchuria. His men, like himself, were natives of the Manchurian provinces, exiles, who saw little hope of return, and less point still in fighting the Communists, who were, so they said, anxious to fight the Japanese. There had been comings and goings between the nominally hostile armies. There was, in fact, a virtual armistice in operation.

The Manchurian troops were in no mood to continue attacks upon the Communists. When the Generalissimo heard some rumours of this disaffection he decided to proceed to Sian to deal with the situation and press forward the offensive.

He arrived in that city with his staff by air on December 7. On December 12 when at a hot-spring resort outside the city, he was surrounded and made prisoner by the mutinous troops of Chang Hsueh-liang and his Shensi colleague. Thereafter, well treated but held prisoner, the Generalissimo was forced to listen to the arguments of his captors. These arguments were in favour of peace with the Communists and resistance to Japan. The Generalissimo was at first adamant. He would never pardon rebels. Soon it became clear that if that were to be his attitude he would never have the opportunity to pardon or to punish. Meanwhile in Nanking, intrigue and alarm were woven in an intricate pattern. The family of Chiang were utterly opposed to measures against the rebels which would endanger his life; others were not so solicitous. There was a conflict between those who wished to uphold the policy of the Kuomintang at the risk of Chiang's life, and those who wished to save his life at the cost of throwing over his policy.

In Sian, while this debate continued, and preparations for an attack both by land and air went forward, the Generalissimo had had to see another visitor, one most unwelcome to him: Chou En-lai, the Communist leader who had organized the Shanghai uprising, and narrowly escaped with his life when Chiang carried out his counter-revolutionary stroke. Chou had several talks with the leader of the Nationalist Party. He at last convinced him of two things; firstly that only by accepting the terms which the rebels and Communists proffered could he save his life, for, unless he accepted, the rebels would put him to death. Secondly, that if he accepted these terms the Communists would acknowledge his authority as head of the State. The terms were amnesty for the rebels; an armistice and peace pact with the Communists, and a united front to oppose any further Japanese aggression. Chiang accepted.

By these agreements the Communist Party undertook to

abolish its titular independent State, which was renamed the Border District Administration. It also undertook to suspend land distribution and confiscation, but insisted on rent reduction in its areas. It finally agreed to abolish the name of Red Army and call its forces the Eighth Route Army of the national forces, under the supreme strategic direction of the Generalissimo, whose authority and government were also acknowledged as legitimate. These were big concessions, even if some were more nominal than real. They aroused the scorn of Trotskyist Communists, the wonder of ordinary Chinese. The Communists henceforward had a fascination for the Chinese educated class; could it really be that here was a party ready to sacrifice its own interests for the good of China? That may not have been in fact, as will be shown, what the Communists were doing, but the appearance was very valuable to them and won them wide support.

The 'face' of the Government was saved by these terms, so skilfully combined to give Chiang 'face' and the Communists the substance of what they wanted. The long war was over; the internal pacification had at last been achieved, now the Government could with good grace go forward with the policy of resistance to external pressure. But in reality, as every thinking man could see, it was Chiang who had yielded, and Chang Hsueh-liang and the Communist Party who had forced him to throw over the policy he had followed for ten years, and adopt that which the Communists had made their own.

The internal pacification had been achieved not by conquering the Communists, but by making peace with them; the resistance to the Japanese was their policy, forced upon Chiang Kai-shek. The 'face' which Chiang comforted himself with was also poor coin compared with the reward in public esteem which the Communist Party won for ending the civil war and compelling the Government to resist Japan. Hitherto, since 1927, the Communists had lacked the support of the great mass of the educated class. Now they won back all and more. Their Yenan university in the Shensi hills became the resort of the active and enterprising students from all over China. The

Communists were respectable; members of the united front, patriots; perhaps only 'agrarian reformers', a harmless name, which they cunningly allowed to be given currency.

The object of these manoeuvres by Mao and his colleagues is now clear. They had adopted, for several years already, a new long-term programme, which should make possible the ultimate triumph of Communism. War with Japan was essential to that plan. War would mean the speedy defeat and retreat of the Nationalist armies, which, however well they fought, had not the equipment to resist Japan for long. The Japanese would overrun wide stretches of China, but while they would root out the Nationalist regime, destroy its administration, drive away its officials, and substitute their own, or puppet rulers, they could not garrison the countryside and still have the troops to conquer all China. Either they must advance far and wide, leaving the villages alone, or they must intensify the occupation of a restricted region, which would mean that the war could not be fought to a conclusion.

The Japanese counted on the surrender of a defeated China. They might get that from the Kuomintang, or they might not, but the Communists, who had ten years of experience in guerrilla warfare behind them, could be sure of being able to keep the field, for years if need be, till they, and they alone, represented Chinese resistance. One day they would win, and they would be automatically the rulers of China—Communist China.

Whether Mao expected a total Japanese conquest, and thus the disappearance of the Kuomintang, or a surrender to Japan, and the discrediting for ever of the Kuomintang, or a stalemate in which, as happened, the Nationalist Government was deprived of three-quarters of its territory but managed to defend the remainder, in any case the Communists would win. They were the fish, the people were the sea, and the people of China were in every village, Japanese-occupied, Kuomintang or 'liberated'. It is probably true to say that Chiang Kai-shek also saw this prospect. The reluctance to accept peace with the Communists, or to oppose the Japanese, came from this cause.

War could only be fatal to the Kuomintang unless it were won for China swiftly, by powerful allies. But China had no allies. Yet Europe was on the brink of war, and world war offered to the Kuomintang its one chance of victory and survival.* In the belief that general war in the Far East would soon precipitate a wider conflict the Nationalist Government was prepared to take the inevitable risk and in the words of one of its more able military leaders 'sell space to buy time'.

Both Chinese parties thus concluded the truce, which ended the civil war and prepared for the national war against Japan, with mental reservations. The Communists saw the way to ultimate triumph through the disasters which war must surely bring to China. The process of levelling the old order would be greatly accelerated by the universal ruin and impoverishment which invasion must bring. They thought they could afford to be the ally of the Kuomintang because that party would perish and the Communists would be their heir.

The Kuomintang entered the war with less hope; yet for them also there was some prospect of advantage. National resistance under the leadership of Nanking, if at all effective, would do much to restore the fallen prestige of the Kuomintang. It might win sympathy abroad; it could look forward to the support and alliance of the great democratic powers, who would not want the Communists to be left as the sole defenders of Chinese independence. If Japan could be held—at whatever sacrifice of space—then time would bring the succour of the West, ultimate victory, and the Communists could be cast aside and if necessary crushed by force. Since neither side was sincere mutual accusations of treachery are equally irrelevant and equally justified.

The course of the war fulfilled the expectations of both parties—with a twist. The Japanese made all the mistakes which the most fervent Chinese patriot could have hoped for. They advanced far into the interior, only holding key cities and lines of communication. They sought to destroy the Chinese field armies, those of the Kuomintang, but neglected to search out

* As it does today.

and scotch the beginnings of guerrilla resistance. They continued to cherish the hope that the capture of this or that city would bring the capitulation of the Chinese Government. They permitted their troops to treat the population with great brutality and disgraced their army by the ferocious sack of Nanking, the wanton attacks on universities and other cultural institutions, and the slaughter of prisoners. They alienated all foreign sympathy or tolerance by open disregard of the rights of foreign nations and ill-treatment of their nationals. They could not have adopted policies more calculated to rouse the Chinese people to enduring opposition.

In the early stages of the war the Japanese easily took possession of North China, which they had already infiltrated. Only a symbolic resistance was offered by the provincial armies of that area. The attack from Shanghai—using the International Settlement as a base—was, however, very firmly opposed by the main strength of Chiang's modern army, and held for three months. This defence of Shanghai won the Chinese the respect and wondering admiration of the world. No one had thought the Chinese armies capable of such steadfast courage and endurance. The Kuomintang gained much prestige by this action, and still more by the battle of Tai Erh Chuang, in Shantung, in which a Japanese force, moving imprudently southward, was caught and totally routed by the Kuomintang General Li Tsung-jen.

Up to the end of 1937, and even far into 1938, the Kuomintang seemed to be making the better show of resistance, and the Communists gained little praise or consideration. For one thing, while the battles fought by the Nationalist forces took place in the coast region, where foreign correspondents operated, and where well-known places were involved, the Communist forces fought in the mountain zone of North-West China, and they engaged from the first in guerrilla rather than positional warfare. Their effort was thus not spectacular and passed almost unnoticed.

In 1938 and 1939, while China still fought unaided and alone, the picture began to change. The Nationalist Government had been driven from its capital, Nanking, at the end of 1937. In the latter part of 1938 it also lost the temporary capital, Hankow, four hundred miles farther up the Yang Tze. Canton, its last link with the coast, was captured by the Japanese with so little resistance that talk of treachery and cowardice was everywhere repeated. The Kuomintang was now driven to the western mountain region of China; all the coast was lost; all the North China plain; all the middle Yang Tze Valley. These are the richest, the most populous, and the most developed provinces of China. They contained all China's heavy industry, all the railways, all the navigable rivers except the difficult Upper Yang Tze. They also contained, in the big coastal and river cities, all the modern-minded and foreign-educated Chinese who had given the Nationalist movement its leadership and its strength.

Many of these indeed chose to follow the Government into the western mountain provinces; the universities, to their great honour, did the same, abandoning their buildings, their libraries and often much of their laboratory equipment and taking refuge in ancient Buddhist monasteries far from any contact with the world of learning. Much equipment with truly Chinese patience and labour was carried away in small boats, on the backs of men, and on pack animals. In the far west the Chinese intellectuals bore hunger, neglect and insanitary and unhealthy conditions for six years, but did not abandon their intellectual pursuits or their standard of scholarship.

The Nationalist Government, from the end of 1939, never made any further military effort to recover lost territory; it sat patiently in Chungking, the wartime capital, waiting for the world war to alter the whole scale of the conflict. It held the passes and defended, with some success, the rice-producing area of Hunan, which was very necessary to the victualling of the army and the swollen population of the west. It did not engage to any serious extent in guerrilla warfare behind the Japanese lines.

This task was left to the Communists who had set about the infiltration and organization of the so-called occupied areas.

They sent in their trained forces in small units, collected and reorganized the scattered bands of former soldiers, or patriots who were in arms against the Japanese, installed themselves in the more inaccessible hill regions, set up a civil administration, collected taxes, reduced rents, associated the population of all classes in the administration of these 'liberated areas' as they were now called, and waged a skilful but limited guerrilla war against the Japanese. It was not much publicized, but gradually it became an important factor. The Japanese at first ignored these activities as 'banditry'; presently they found that whole regions were slipping into the hands of the 'bandits', and had to take 'punitive' measures. Villages were burned, peasants slain, but the elusive guerrillas were not brought to battle. All that the Japanese gained by such expeditions was a firmer resistance and more widespread hatred.

It may be asked why the Nationalist Government did not from 1939 onward organize its own resistance, send in its own guerrilla units, and keep alive its claim to be the Chinese Government of the occupied provinces. Some small and unco-ordinated attempts to do this were indeed made, but they were half-heartedly supported, left without proper supervision and gradually were either taken over by the Communists or liquidated by the Japanese. The real reason for the failure to expand Nationalist guerrilla activity was the jealousy of army commanders for irregular formations, and above all the fear that the Government entertained of arming and rousing the peasantry.

It was the prospect of social revolution following the war, the fear that the armed peasant who had been a guerrilla would never become once more a docile tenant, this very real danger inhibited all Kuomintang support for the guerrilla resistance. The failure to follow the revolution through, to carry it to the villages, and complete the task, was now shown to be the fatal error of the Nanking Government, and the ultimate cause of its downfall.

During the years between 1938 and 1941, the Nationalist Government was divided into factions favouring continued resistance or negotiated submission to the Japanese. Germany, seeing the danger of Japanese aggrandizement on the one hand, and of her entanglement in China on the other, tried to induce Chiang to make peace, and even obtained considerable modification of the more extreme Japanese demands. It must always be held to Chiang Kai-shek's honour and credit that he rejected these tempting offers, and refused to follow what seemed the easy way out. Wang Ch'ing-wei, his chief rival, was a weaker man, and took what he deemed to be his chance. He fled from Chungking by way of Indo-China, and accepted the Japanese post of nominal head of the 'Chinese Government' in Nanking. Wang's flight was not copied by other prominent Kuomintang leaders. The ruling policy still remained to 'sell space for time', and wait and hope for Japan to become embroiled with the democratic powers.

In this the Chinese were, as is well known, justified. Japan had a programme of aggression and empire which required the expulsion of the Western nations from the Far East. The conquest of China would not have deterred her from those plans, and the failure to conquer all China did not modify them. It is true that for China the prospect in 1940 appeared dismal. The Western powers were going down in defeat before triumphant Germany. America was neutral; so was Russia. Had Japan then attacked Britain and France their participation in the war against Japan could have done China no good. It must also be credited to the Kuomintang leadership that they had long-term faith in the cause of the Allies, and counted on changed fortune in the future. Here, too, they were right. Japan could not fulfil her aims without war with America, war between Japan and America was China's chance, and worth more than any offer which Hitler could induce the Japanese to make. The Chinese saw America's danger from Japanese attack, and Japan's fate as a consequence of such an attack, more clearly than either Washington or Tokyo.

The Communists had less to hope from foreign intervention. Their only real foreign friend was Russia, who was careful to give the Japanese no grounds for displeasure, and was not yet at war with Germany. The Russians, moreover, still eyed Mao Tse-tung and his party with a cold and questioning glance. The united front was, of course, a policy approved by Moscow, but the united front against Japan did not at that time fit Moscow's foreign policy. The past differences of the Chinese Communists with Moscow were not forgotten, perhaps by either side, and the Russians remained very dubious of the real strength and potentiality of the Chinese Communist Party.

Late in the war, in 1945, Stalin could say to Harry Hopkins that he did not regard the Chinese Communists as a serious factor, and recognized only Chiang's Government as that of China. It may, of course, be doubted whether Stalin was sincere. He may have intended to lull American suspicion, he may at the same time have reassured Mao. Yet it is also true that many incidents, to be related later, show that Russia did not appreciate the real position in China, and was as much surprised by the outcome as the Western powers.

On the other hand the Communists in China had not much to expect from victory won by foreign arms. If the Kuomintang was saved by America the future of the Communist Party would at best be uncertain, at worst, in jeopardy. The longer the war went on, the more the Communist control of the so-called occupied areas deepened and intensified. An abrupt end to the war would interrupt this process. A long inconclusive war was Mao's interest, swift victory was Chiang's hope. Both were to be disappointed. The first result of Japan's aggression upon American and British possessions in the Far East was the rapid collapse of the Western powers in that region. Years were to pass before American strength could repair these disasters and pass on to final victory over Japan. When that victory was attained it was too late to suit the Kuomintang, but, since it still survived, it was this regime alone that the victorious powers recognized as the legitimate Government of China. The Communists were treated as dissident forces who should properly submit to the authority of Chiang Kai-shek. Their claim to share in the surrender of the Japanese, or to administer the provinces in which they had maintained resistance for eight years, was not accepted.

One reason for this situation was the growing dissension between Chungking and Yenan, the Communist headquarters, in the years following 1940. The truce came to be almost a dead letter. The obvious success of the Communists in organizing guerrilla warfare and resistance in the north and east contrasted painfully with the failure of the Kuomintang in the later years of the war to maintain the spirited resistance of 1937 and 1938. Their inactive armies, short of food, of munitions, and of low morale, made no warlike moves. In fact, in many places, a clandestine trade with the enemy was not unknown. Corruption, encouraged by the rapid inflation of the currency, spread through the officer corps from the generals downward. The Chungking Government saw with alarm that their cause in the occupied areas was going by default and that the Communists were becoming identified in the minds of the people with the Chinese resistance.

When the Communists showed signs of organizing fresh and large guerrilla forces, not in North China, but in the south-east, regions which though now occupied by the Japanese were the normal stronghold of the Kuomintang, dissension flamed into actual hostility. The New Fourth Army, as the Communist formation was called, was attacked by the Nationalist forces as it crossed the Yang Tze, and suffered very heavy losses. The Communist attempt to organize large-scale guerrilla warfare in South-East China was thus frustrated. This affair left very bad blood between the two parties. The Nationalist army stationed in South Shensi, adjoining the Communist base area of Yenan, imposed a blockade upon the Communist region which cut it off from the only source of foreign aid from the West, the air lift to Yunnan from India. Not merely war supplies, but even medical supplies expressly contributed by sympathizers in the West were prevented from reaching the Communist regions. The Communist penetration of the north and east of China could not be prevented. But by successfully preventing the infiltration of large-scale Communist guerrilla forces into the south-east, the Kuomintang was able to regain control of the rural areas of the Japanese-occupied provinces south of the Yang Tze.

From 1941 to the Japanese surrender in September 1945, there were really two wars in China. The Kuomintang positional war, mainly passive defence, in the south, and the Communist guerrilla war in the north and north-east. These two forces maintained to each other an attitude of suspicious and armed neutrality. No co-ordination existed between them, no exchange of plans, no co-operation. In Chungking the Communists had a delegation, which was treated with the reserve usually accorded to the diplomatic mission of an unfriendly power. The civil war, if not in actual operation, was manifestly merely in cold storage; Japanese invasion alone restrained the two parties from open warfare, and even that menace was not always sufficient.

In 1945, although early in the year Germany had capitulated, and Japan had been driven from the Philippines and from Burma, few people in China believed that the end of the war was in sight. It was thought that the Japanese army in China and the still more powerful force which garrisoned Manchuria would continue the struggle even if the home country was invaded. The expectation of a large-scale American landing on the East China coast, which would be the prelude to a vigorous and prolonged campaign of liberation, was general, and was indeed the alternative plan of the Allied Command. The other alternative was the atomic bomb, the best-kept secret of modern history, which no one in China could, of course, anticipate. The two Chinese parties in the summer of 1945 were thus planning on the assumption of American landings in the autumn. These landings would be on the south-east coast, a region in which Communist guerrilla strength was slight. The advance would be directed to the lower Yang Tze Valley and the capture of Shanghai. Thus the Kuomintang could expect an early restoration to its home provinces, the lower Yang Tze region. The Communist area to the north would, on the contrary, be the scene of the subsequent campaign, and the Japanese could be expected to secure this region, their immediate rear, in great strength. It was a prospect unfavourable to the Communist cause.

Before these plans could be realized the atomic bombs on Hiroshima and Nagasaki, coupled with a much greater decline of Japanese strength than was known to the Allies, brought Japan to surrender. The invasion of China never took place; only in Manchuria, the Soviet, hastily fulfilling her engagements after the atomic bomb had been dropped, invaded and rapidly occupied the whole of the Japanese puppet empire of Manchoukuo, except the province of Jehol. The Japanese army was in control of all the cities in Northern and Eastern China, and of those along the Yang Tze as far as Ichang. The first question that arose was the fate of the cities held by the Japanese in the midst of Communist guerrilla country.

The Allied High Command had allocated the China Zone to the supreme direction of the Chinese Government—a very reasonable and normal provision. This meant in practice that Chiang Kai-shek could decide upon the military dispositions in Chinese territory of all Allied forces. He promptly claimed his right and required the US Air Force to lift his troops to the occupied areas and thus obtain the surrender of the Japanese to the forces of the Kuomintang, not to those of the Communists. Further, the Japanese and their puppet Chinese formations were ordered to hold all posts against Communist attack and only surrender them to Kuomintang forces. These orders were carried out; Peking, Tientsin, and all the great cities of North China and the Yellow River Valley, situated in areas where Communist guerrillas controlled the countryside, and where Nationalist forces had not been seen for eight years, were handed over by their Japanese garrisons to Kuomintang forces flown in by the US Air Force. Puppet Chinese forces were allowed to declare for the Kuomintang, and added to the Nationalist army.

Once again, as in 1925, the Western conception of legality had come into conflict with the Chinese principle of compromise. To the West these proceedings were the only legiti-

mate course of action. Chiang Kai-shek was not only the legal
head of the legitimate Government of China, the Allied power
which all States recognized, but also the Zone Commander-
in-Chief. The Communists were a Chinese party which had in
1937 pledged itself to abide by the strategic decisions of the
Nanking Government, and recognize that Government's title
to legitimate rule. Nothing, legally, had happened since to
upset this situation. It might be that the Western powers
thought Chiang unwise, a bad ruler, or imprudent. That could
not alter the legal position. What else could or should be done?
Were the Communists, in defiance of the legal Government's
protests, to be allowed to participate in the Japanese surrender
as an independent power? That meant a denial of Chungking's
sovereignty over North China. To deny the use of the air
force might have been possible, but would have appeared both
unfriendly and partisan—and might be construed as a violation of the agreement on zonal command.

The Chinese, not only the Communist Chinese, saw the
matter in a different light. Chiang was not only the head of
the Chungking Government, he was the leader of the Nationalist Party, a corrupt dictatorship which had grossly deteriorated
during the war. He wished to regain power over the north
so as to crush the Communists and halt the land reform movement which was rapidly spreading through the liberated areas.
The Communists were the actual liberators of millions of
Chinese in the north; to deny them the cities they had so long
encompassed meant the certainty of civil war, for they would
never accept this decision.

The Kuomintang Government was extinct in North China
and to put it back by American aircraft could only destroy the
one hope of internal peace, which all thinking liberal Chinese
desired. If the Communists occupied all North China they
would be too strong for Chiang to crush. He would have to
compromise, there would be a coalition Government which
would eliminate the worst features of Kuomintang reaction
and restrain the most extreme manifestations of Communist
revolution. Such was the view and the hope of the Chinese

educated class, now almost entirely alienated from the Kuomintang, but not yet by any means wholly gone over to the Communists.

The realization that a new civil war must, whatever the outcome, finally ruin the existing economy and society, must destroy all that war had left of Chinese industry and commerce, these things seemed to the Chinese mind infinitely more important than legal niceties. They could not believe that America was really animated by such academic ideas, and therefore heeded the Communists who were quick to claim that the 'imperialists' were backing Chiang for their own sinister motives. The sense of public opinion was so strong against civil war, the reoccupation of the north by the Kuomintang so inevitably meant civil war, that the force of opinion was swung over very strongly to the Communist side. Many who did not approve at all of Communism felt that the Communists were this time being provoked and attacked. The reoccupation was felt to be deliberate sabotage of internal peace and the hope of coalition government, which all suspected was anathema to the Kuomintang, but was the only solution which at that time had mass public support.

These opinions did not prevail; the reoccupation proceeded, and the Communists retaliated by at once, and finally, cutting all railway communication between north and south, and interfering perpetually with such lateral railways as existed in the north. The Kuomintang garrisons in the north could only be reached by air; they were more isolated than the Japanese from whom they took over, and they and the cities they occupied were dependent on foreign supplies of food sent in by air also. If this situation was to continue, the loss of the cities and their garrisons was certain; if the Government attempted to relieve them, large-scale war was inevitable.

The only possibility of peace lay in the reconciliation of the Kuomintang and the Communist Party. Alarmed at the threatening prospect the United States sent one of her most able citizens, who had personal knowledge of China, to mediate between the factions. General Marshall's mission was, however, a tacit acknowledgment that the Communist Party was now an equal force, which could not be ignored. China was no longer one country, but two; Communist China had arisen during the war and Kuomintang China had withered in that wintry climate.

CHAPTER FOUR

THE TRIUMPH OF COMMUNISM: 'JEN MIN' PERIOD

IN THE CHINESE language the term coined to mean republic is Min Kuo, meaning literally 'People's State'. This term was used for the early years of the Republic until, after the rise of the Nationalist Party, the variant form 'Kuo Min' was used to mean 'Nationalist', the word for 'State'—'kuo' now coming before that for 'people'—'min'. This was a significant though possibly not an intentional indication of the relative importance of State and people in a democracy and in an authoritarian regime. The Communists, needing a word to mean 'people' in the sense of 'masses' and yet one which would be distinct and unassociated with the terms used by the Nationalist and bourgeois republicans, invented 'Jen Min', in which the force of 'min'—'people' is reduplicated by adding before it the word 'jen' which also means 'mankind'. The expression 'State' thus falls out and the new name for the Republic, the 'Jen Min Kung Ho Kuo' leaves the term for State, 'kuo', at the end of the phrase, well qualified by the expression 'Jen Min'— 'people's' and 'Kung Ho' which literally means 'public harmony'. Associated with the word for State this is now used to render 'republic'—with more resemblance to the Latin origin of that term.

It is also perhaps not without significance that the new expression 'Kung Ho' is not really new at all, but very ancient, since this phrase was used in antiquity to describe the only short period in which China had no sovereign, the interregnum in the Chou Dynasty which is one of the earliest accurately dated events in Chinese history. In a country where terminology is and always has been very important, these things serve to indicate the trend of thought.

The purpose of General Marshall's mission to China in 1946

was to induce the two Chinese parties to form a coalition Government and thus avert civil war. Almost everyone in China and abroad wished this project well; yet it failed. It is worth considering, since this initiative and its consequences are still much in dispute, why the Marshall mission failed, and whether it could have succeeded. To form a coalition of opposed parties is in a democratic country a possible, but never an easy, task. The country needs to be faced with a grave crisis, usually a foreign war, before party feeling can be quelled, and a minimum programme, usually victory, can be agreed upon. A coalition Government also assumes that each of the coalescing parties recognizes the other's legal right to compete for power, and accepts the fact that if one of the parties disagrees profoundly with the policy of the Government it may withdraw from the coalition and resume legal opposition.

These assumptions hardly fitted the Chinese scene. There was no constitutional Government, no organ of power other than the cabinet appointed by the Generalissimo and dismissed, individually or collectively, at his will. Neither party had ever received a mandate from electors. Both counted their support not in votes but in divisions. Political power in China since the fall of the Manchu Empire was identical with military power; a party without an army could not exist. This had been demonstrated, even when General Marshall was still in the country, by the fate of the Democratic League, a party formed among the intellectuals and university professors, which professed, sincerely, a programme of democratic ideals. The Democratic League counted among its members most of the best brains in China; it was a party of Liberals who genuinely believed in the democratic system and wished to see it put into practice. Despairing of the crude authoritarianism of the Kuomintang, the Democratic League tried to turn back, with more knowledge and experience, to the original democratic republic of 1913.

It had a wide following among the educated class, and would, no doubt, in a general election, have gained the support of millions of voters. But there was and could be no election; the

Democratic League had no armed forces of its own, and was not backed by any general who had. Chiang Kai-shek, while still negotiating under General Marshall's auspices for coalition Government, had some of the Democratic League leaders assassinated, others driven into exile, and when Marshall left China the Democratic League was proscribed and destroyed. Its remnants finally took refuge with the Communists and joined the nominal coalition Government of the Peking People's Republic.

The Chinese situation was in fact revolutionary; in a revolution, which is by definition the overthrow of constitutional government, force alone counts. Coalition government as understood in the West was impossible in a situation where parties were armies and no right of legal opposition tolerated. But there might have been, if not coalition in the constitutional sense, then agreement as between equal and rival powers, a revival of the truce of 1937. That truce had been the consequence of the direct and imminent threat of Japanese invasion, a temporary and, in the minds of the truce makers, strictly limited agreement, from which both hoped to profit at the expense of the other. The proposed agreement to form a coalition in 1946 was, on the contrary, intended to provide a permanent settlement of China's governmental crisis and bring the Chinese Revolution to a close. The Communists were by no means ready to agree to any arrangement by which their revolutionary activity, now backed by the vast mass of the peasantry, would be diverted from its goal; the Kuomintang would agree to nothing which threatened its hold on power or permitted the spread of social revolution on the land.

The Communists demanded sufficient control of the Government to ensure the spread of Communism and its land policy; the Kuomintang were determined to retain power to prevent revolution. Both demanded the reduction of the armed forces of the other and their evacuation of contested points. Both sides committed breaches of the precarious truce which had been set up to make negotiation possible. The Communists resented the reorganization and re-equipment and training of Kuomintang armies which continued under wartime agreements with American advisers. The Kuomintang complained that the Communists continued to interrupt railway and road communications, and spread their land reform in the rural areas.

Had the internal situation been easier and the conflict of the parties less violent, the external situation in itself would have made agreement very difficult. The war had brought vast changes in the alignment of power in the Far East. America had stepped forward to the front place, the dominating position, master of Japan and arbiter of China. Britain had receded; the Concessions and extra-territorial rights which had been the subject of contention for so many years had been seized or abrogated by Japanese invasion, and then, when no longer operative, resigned by treaty to China (1942). Hong Kong was still British, and the subject of Kuomintang sniping, even when the Nationalist regime was *in extremis*. France counted for nothing in post-war China. Russia remained enigmatic as ever.

The Russians had occupied Manchuria, in the 'nine days' war with Japan, and were thus in a position to hand over this vital territory, the most developed industrial region in China, intact to the Chinese Communists. Had Russia adopted this course it would have in effect decided the civil war without fighting, since the Communists, who already dominated the rural areas of North and Eastern China, could, with the Manchurian war potential at their command, have overthrown the Kuomintang at will.

This was not the policy which Russia followed, and her actions in respect of Manchuria do not support the simple belief in a world Communist conspiracy planned years ahead, and foreseeing every turn of the world situation. Russia's post-war policy in the Far East, like that of her rivals the Americans and Western democratic powers, suggests inadequate knowledge, shortsighted measures of supposed national advantage, and improvisation in face of a rapidly and unexpectedly developing situation.

The Russians, in accordance with their obligations as allies

who recognized only one Chinese Government, the Kuomintang regime, evacuated Manchuria stage by stage, handing
back the cities to Nationalist troops flown in to take them over.
Even Harbin was for a brief period handed over to Kuomintang rule, although troops were never sent so far north. But
the countryside was at the same time infiltrated and occupied
by the Chinese Communist forces from North China. The
Russians certainly did not prevent this; it is by no means
certain that they could have done so even if they had wanted
to, for the guerrillas were innumerable, omnipresent and indis-
tinguishable from the peasantry.

At the same time as they gave back the cities to the Kuomintang and abandoned the countryside to the Communists,
the Russians systematically stripped the Manchurian industrial
plants of their equipment, carrying off machinery, rolling
stock and other movables, and thus destroyed, or very greatly
diminished, the industrial potential of China's most valuable
provinces, which could have been handed over to the Communists as an intact and very powerful base area. Thus as a
matter of historical fact the Chinese Communists were denied
the North China cities by American aid to the Kuomintang,
and denied the Manchurian cities by Russian selfishness and
acceptance of the Kuomintang's claims.

Two explanations of Russian policy in Manchuria are possible. It may be that the Russians were merely just as stupid
and lacking in foresight as the Western powers. They had
seized Manchuria from the Japanese; they could not keep it for
themselves, but they could loot it to replace Russia's huge
losses in industrial power. This plan would also deny such
power to the Kuomintang, and so to an American ally; as for
the Chinese Communists, the Russians believed them to be too
weak and too deficient in technicians and skill either to hold
Manchuria if it was given to them or to work its industries if
they acquired them. At this time Stalin was assuring Harry
Hopkins that he did not regard the Chinese Communists as a
serious competitor for power, and only recognized one Chinese
Government.

Russia had been fully absorbed in the life-and-death struggle with Hitler; the Far East was as much a sideshow to Stalin as to Churchill; the high Communist command in the Kremlin had not had the time to consider the China problem nor study the reports of the experts on the spot. Unless one is to subscribe to the belief that Communism is divinely inspired, or diabolically clever, and that the Kremlin can make no mistake, this explanation is perfectly possible and contradicts no known facts.

There is, however, another which gives the Russians greater credit, at least for foresight. By handing over the cities to the Kuomintang, but allowing the Communists to occupy the rural areas in Manchuria, the Russians induced Chiang Kai-shek to over-extend his military power and engage in a hopeless campaign in Manchuria which could not be supported by land communications. The Kuomintang strength was thus consumed in the far north-east and the Communist triumph in China proper made possible. By looting Manchuria of its potential, Stalin made sure that the triumphant Chinese Communists would be dependent on Russia and could not break away and stand on their own feet. Mao had once shown independence, even heretical tendencies; these had proved successful and so won Russian approval; but he must not be allowed the industrial strength to show such traits again.

This explanation also contradicts no known facts; only it does not explain what the Russians should have done. If to yield the Manchurian cities to the Kuomintang was a trap, to deny them to Chiang would have been a hostile act favouring Communism. To allow the Communists to infiltrate Manchuria was a crime; but can it really be expected that the Russians should have resisted their entry by force, when even the Americans were not opposing the movements of Communist forces in China itself?

It would seem more probable, and more consistent with historical experience, to suppose that the real motives of Russian policy were the mixture of folly and cunning which have at all times and places been the mark of political action.

The war and industrial potential of Manchuria was a prize which Russia coveted. To hand it intact to the American-dominated Kuomintang was unwise; to hand it over intact to the Communists, a risk; they might be neither strong enough to hold it, nor loyal enough to use it to Russia's advantage. To carry it off, let the Communists have the Japanese munition dumps in the country, and the Kuomintang the stripped cities, was a compromise which kept Russia to the letter of her engagements to China—the Kuomintang—and still gave the Communists a helping hand. If they were what they claimed to be they now had a good chance to win the war—which would in any case leave China still weaker and still dependent on Russia. If Chiang could take Manchuria that would prove that he was really strong, and it would be a mistake to quarrel with him; if he could not, then Russia could not be blamed for his failure, and the Communists would need every foreign friend they had, and could not blame Russia either—openly—for stripping Manchuria.

Both Russia and America doubted the competence of the Chinese side which they backed; the Americans knew Chiang was weak, his regime corrupt, his economy unsound; but it might be that the Communists were, after all, only a peasant movement incapable of taking and ruling cities. The Russians knew that the Communists had a purely agrarian background, that they had no support from the few industrial workers in China, with whom they had long been out of touch. They had no experience of positional warfare, and their Marxist purity was at least somewhat suspect, since Mao's peasant policy had been the foundation of his power. Chiang was no doubt weak, too, but he might not be too weak to hold on for many years yet. The Chinese Revolution was not cut to a Russian pattern and so might not be the real thing; best to treat it with caution until the situation clarified.

In Peking there was current a story, said to come from Communist sources, that after the war in Europe was over Stalin sent Mao Tse-tung a Russian book on partisan warfare, the fruit of Russian experience during the German invasion. Mao read it, and showed it to Lin Piao, his best military commander, and the greatest expert on guerrilla warfare in China. Lin remarked: 'If we had had this as our textbook we should have been annihilated ten years ago.' Whether founded on fact or not, it is certainly true that Russia did not appreciate the meaning of guerrilla warfare as the Chinese Communists practised it.

To the Russians the partisans acted in conjunction, and in advance of regular army formations for whom they did the scout work, the sabotage and the infiltration which prepared for an offensive. The Chinese Communists had no regular formations in this sense: all their forces were guerrillas, all their strategy based on mobility, the absence of fixed bases, the reliance for supplies on the countryside and the co-operation of the people. The Russian armies of Stalin were the armies of a national State; the Chinese armies of Mao Tse-tung were the forces of an armed revolution. The Russians, thirty years after, were not able to recognize all the signs of revolution, when it differed in pattern from their own.

The democracies were also unable to realize the scale and significance of events in China after the war. They had for so many years been accustomed to the Chinese Revolution; it rumbled and exploded from time to time like an active volcano, but every burst of activity had been followed by long periods of quiescence, of incoherent and seemingly purposeless confusion, in which no principles were at stake, no recognizable development apparent.

The Press of the West could not be expected to cope with this sort of news. It did not make sense; the names were difficult and hard to remember; the places unfamiliar. When Shanghai or Peking was involved, the Press, with the relief of a swimmer who touches bottom, seized upon the passing event, wrote it up, and then as nothing intelligible resulted, let it drop. So, in the years after the war, the crisis of China's Revolution came unexpectedly upon the world, capitalist and Communist alike. The preliminary rounds, which were in fact decisive, were fought out in the deep interior, far from correspondents, in strange places, in an unfamiliar and unsatisfactory (from the news angle) fashion. Guerrilla war is not sensational.

Seen in retrospect it was obviously hopeless to expect that this revolution could be stopped, turned overnight into constitutional coalition Government, and kept apart from the deadly rivalry of Communism and democracy. Internal factors, the ruin of the wealthy and middle class by war and inflation, the corruption and decay of the Kuomintang, the disappearance of all but Communist government from vast rural areas, the hunger of the peasant for his land and the long-awaited opportunity to take it, all these made peace impossible.

The rising hostility of America and Russia also made peace impossible; the Kuomintang relied on that hostility to make America give arms and aid to 'resist Communism'—and therefore compromise was silly; the Americans would always play in the end, only let them get a little more frightened and they would pay up, reforms or no reforms. The Communists could also, as they began to succeed, rely on the support of Russia. The cold war was on, and in China Communism was scoring its greatest victory; Russia would have to support her fellow doctrinaires, unless she was prepared for a great psychological defeat for world Communism. The Chinese Communists also, for their part, could make the foreign friend dance to their tune, and disregard his advice.

Late in 1946 General Marshall gave up his mission as hopeless, and left China after uttering a judgment on the situation which clearly recognized that neither side would agree to the essential basis of conciliation. Both Communists and Kuomintang were equally condemned. General Marshall pointed to the Democratic League as the only group in China who understood and wished to implement democratic government. But at the very time he made this statement the Kuomintang was destroying the Democratic League and driving its leaders into exile. The Kuomintang was the Government of China, with which the American Government had a wartime alliance, and with which agreements for the training and arming of troops had been made. General Marshall condemned that Government as weak, shifty, unreliable and insincere; yet the American agreements were not abrogated and the American supplies, arms, aircraft and gasoline continued to reach the armies of Chiang Kai-shek. Those armies were now, in the early spring of 1947, deployed in an all-out campaign to conquer the Chinese Communists and impose the unreformed Nationalist dictatorship on the whole country.

The course of that obscure campaign can be easily explained by attention to its main features. The Communists held all the rural areas in the north and north-east of China. They had cut all the railways connecting North China and Manchuria with the Yang Tze Valley, and they continually interrupted the lateral railways which connect the east coast with the western mountain provinces. They also occupied the rural areas and all but the main and largest cities in Manchuria. The Kuomintang controlled all China south of the Yang Tze River, except for a few small and isolated guerrilla areas in the southern mountains. The Kuomintang also held large parts of the north-western mountain region, all the major cities on the coast, and all the large cities in the north and north-east, including those of Manchuria. With these they could only communicate surely by air, or more uncertainly by sea to the North China ports and thence by the often attacked railway from Tientsin to Mukden. They had no land communication between North China and the Yang Tze.

Chiang's objectives were thus to re-establish communication by rail with North China, to take and control the provinces through which the Peking-Tientsin-Nanking railway and the Peking-Hankow railway pass. Secondly, to establish his hold in Manchuria on a wider basis and drive the Communists there and in North China from the plains to the hills, where they could be starved out or surrounded. The Communists had to prevent this inter-communication between the Kuomintang areas, and later to seize the cities and destroy the isolated Kuomintang garrisons. Chiang first, in 1947, tried to conquer Shantung, so as to open the Peking-Tientsin-Nanking railway; he also concurrently tried to expand his control over Manchuria. In the opinion of his American advisers the second objective should have followed the successful achievement of the first; they held that Chiang lacked the power to hold Manchuria and conquer North China at the same time. They were right.

It must be said that the Kuomintang had reasons for the double attempt. If Manchuria was left alone it would be wholly lost. Once lost it would become the Communist base, too strong to retake, and menacing the Kuomintang in North China. The history of China, first with the Manchus, later with the Japanese, had shown that if a strong hostile power occupied Manchuria the loss of North China, and thus general invasion of all China, must follow. It was all or nothing; China cannot be divided. The Americans failed to understand this, and Chiang was not aided to the degree necessary to make the double conquest of Manchuria and North China. He was not sufficiently convincing as an ally, and the cost was too great. American troops probably, the US Air Force certainly, would have had to have taken part in massive strength. The danger of Russian intervention could not be ignored. It was the choice repeated a few years later in Korea, and it was inescapable.

In 1947 Chiang's best armies failed to conquer Shantung, the key to North China. They were in fact very heavily and disastrously defeated there, although no real publicity was given to these events. They also failed to expand in Manchuria, after some initial progress, and were forced on to the defensive. By the end of the year the Manchurian railways also had been cut, and the Kuomintang held only large islands of territory around the major cities. Chiang saved his face, or tried to, by the vain and useless success of taking Yenan, the Communist wartime capital, which was evacuated after Chiang's forces had penetrated into this remote region, no longer of strategic importance.

The war was won in 1947, by the negative result of the Kuomintang failure to establish communication with the north or expand control of Manchuria. In 1947 the Kuomintang were forced on to the defensive, at first passively, by the blockade of their isolated North China areas and their Manchurian zones, later actively by the opening of the Communist counter-offensive. That counter-offensive opened in the summer of 1947 with a sudden swift movement southward into the Ta Pieh Shan mountains which form the northern watershed of the Yang Tze Valley. This had been an old Communist area, in the pre-war period, and in it the Communists now established a new base, threatening the lower Yang Tze Valley and placed on the flank of any further Kuomintang effort to conquer the north.

Chiang's counter to this deadly stroke was a further and futile effort to break out of his blockaded Manchurian strongholds. The best Kuomintang troops, the armoured divisions, the American-trained forces which had served in Burma, were sent north by sea to land upon the coast of Manchuria and free Mukden from its siege. Shantung, Honan and South Hopei, the keys to the conquest of the north, were virtually abandoned. This insistence on the conquest of Manchuria, now hopeless, is one of the puzzles of the Kuomintang strategy. Perhaps the belief that success there would involve Russian intervention, and thus entrain American intervention on the grand scale, the one hope for the Kuomintang, was the secret motive for these ill-starred ventures.

The Communists, who had established their new head-quarters in South Hopei, some two hundred miles south of Peking, had now to decide their strategy. It is of interest and significance that although North Manchuria and the great modern city of Harbin had been in Communist hands for over a year, and Yenan their old base lost, the Chinese Communist Government and military headquarters were not established in this safe territory but remained in the guerrilla areas of North China. Had the Chinese Communists been the puppets of Moscow as portrayed in Nationalist and later American pro-paganda, Harbin was the obvious site for the Russian satellite regime. Had the Chinese Communists been the accepted and loyal allies of Russia they might have chosen Harbin also—the fact that they were neither compelled to go there nor wished to do so suggests that relations with Russia were not yet wholly clear. It also suggests that Mao Tse-tung preferred independence to too close proximity and understood the vital importance of North China for his cause.

In July 1948 a conference was called in South Hopei to determine the strategy which the Chinese Communist movement should adopt in the approaching autumn campaign season. Peking and Tientsin, with a narrow ribbon of land around the Peking-Mukden railway as far as the Great Wall, were all that remained of Kuomintang North China. Isolated points in Shansi, the industrial city of Tai Yuan, and the strategic gate in the Wall at Kalgan, with precarious railway communication with Peking, still held out. The guerrillas occupied the rest, and even these areas at night. Communication between Peking and Tientsin was interrupted two or three times each week. At night aircraft had to be flown off the West Field because the Communist guerrillas infiltrated at dusk to the very walls of Peking.

In Manchuria, Mukden with a huge army of over 100,000 men had been besieged for a year. Food was short, the garrison precariously fed by a constant airlift, the civilians liable to starve within a matter of weeks. Changchun, another 'island', was smaller and less well defended. One by one all other Kuomintang garrisons in Manchuria had fallen or withdrawn. The Communists controlled Shantung, apart from one or two large cities; they had occupied rural Honan, and isolated the Kuomintang there; they had advanced into the Yang Tze Valley; Shansi was in their hands; the Kuomintang had been fought to a standstill.

If the military situation of Chiang Kai-shek's regime was thus bad the economic situation was far worse, and the political prospect catastrophic. Inflation, uncontrolled, fantastic and calamitous had destroyed the value of the national currency, forced the population to rely on clandestine holdings of silver dollars, American currency and gold bars, ruined trade, corrupted the Civil Service, discontented and disheartened the soldiers. By means of a rigged exchange, personal monopolies, shameless appropriation of so-called 'enemy property'—in fact very often Chinese property which the Japanese had seized during the occupation—a small handful of the top leaders of the Kuomintang, the 'Four Families', Chiangs, K'ungs, Soongs and Ch'ens, had grown rich beyond the wildest fables of a fairy tale. Private enterprise was at the mercy of these combines, foreign trade was milked by the exchange control, every sort of corrupt practice flourished, and the middle class, the intellectuals and the officials—unless corrupt—were ground down into poverty equal to that of the coolie.

Such misgovernment, so little regard for the citizen, so little care for the country, had finally and fully alienated the educated class. The universities were suffering the heavy hand of the 'Te Wu', the special secret police of the regime. Sudden and secret arrests, mysterious disappearances, assassinations, a covert reign of terror prevailed in academic circles. Students were suspect, professors watched, freedom of thought, of publication and of speech suppressed. In so far as the choice between totalitarian and democratic government was concerned, it did not exist; the Chinese people groaned under a regime Fascist in every quality except efficiency. The Kuomintang had long lost the peasants; now they had cast away their only asset, the support of the scholars. The educated no longer feared the victory of Communism; what they feared was a continuation of civil war. An end, any end, was what they hoped for. Only one end was now possible.

The Chinese Communists, when they assembled to debate their future course of action, were well aware of this situation. They had received within the last two years a constant stream of recruits from the students of all the Chinese universities, their underground movement was effectively organized in every Kuomintang area, and their secret supporters placed in every organization. They had accurate information about every Kuomintang unit and could appreciate the political and military possibilities with small risk of error.

Yet to this conference came one of their leaders, who had

just returned from Moscow, with the views of Stalin upon the Chinese situation. Stalin urged through Liu Shao-ch'i that the Chinese Communists continue guerrilla war and refrain from pushing their victory to a decisive conclusion. He argued that the Berlin crisis, then at its height, would not in fact lead to world war, and that therefore it was important to waste America's strength by prolonging her useless aid to the Kuomintang. No real danger existed, said Liu, of American intervention by armed force, such as might be feared in the event of world war.

The contrary thesis was argued by Chou En-lai, one of the ablest Chinese Communist leaders, and the one who as negotiator for the Communist side had lived in Nanking, met the Americans and contacted the outside world. Chou said that China was now ripe for the final act of the Revolution; the moment for which the party had worked and suffered for twenty-two years was now at hand. One strong offensive, one determined effort, and the Kuomintang house of cards would go down in ruin. A single campaign would give the Communists at least half of China, two campaigns would end the war. This conclusion was the more necessary because he did not feel so confident that world war would be postponed. The Russians could be mistaken, the Americans could act more forcefully than they supposed. If war came, America would openly enter the Chinese Civil War and give aid to Chiang on a massive scale. The Communists would be driven back to the hills, to endure perhaps many more years of hunted guerrilla warfare, while China perished. If the civil war was won before the world war broke out, then they, the Communists, would be the arbiters of China's fate. They could carry on that war as they chose; they would stand for China, and they alone.

News of this debate, though not of its outcome, was soon heard in Peking. The city was then riddled with Communist sympathizers, party men of the underground, and contacts between these and the foreign Press correspondents and others were not unknown or impossible. The opinion of Mao Tse-tung, the supreme authority of Communist China, was not known. The event soon showed, indeed, what decision was reached and whose policy had been adopted. Within a few weeks the Communist offensive swept away the last strongholds of the Nationalists in North China. Tsinanfu in Shantung fell in September, the great offensive towards the Yang Tze opened in October, and the end of the Kuomintang in Manchuria came with startling suddenness on October 31.

If the Russians really meant to advise the Chinese Communists to confine themselves to guerrilla war and leave the great cities in Kuomintang hands, they must have been singularly ill-informed of the true situation in those cities, more especially in Manchuria. Mukden had been surrounded for more than a year. The very large garrison, once among the best of Chiang's troops, had rotted in idleness and on low rations. Their morale was low; the hope of relief had faded, winter was approaching, and in Manchuria winter is not just a change of season. The civil population of this great city was already near starvation level; whether the Communists attacked or not, if they maintained the blockade, the fall of Mukden was certain before the coming winter ended. The situation of Changchun, the other remaining stronghold of the Nationalists in Manchuria, was, if possible, worse. The area defended was smaller, the garrison very large, the climate more severe.

The pick of the Kuomintang troops, once engaged on Chiang's fatal gamble for Manchuria, were now confined in these two cities, and unless relieved before winter their end was sure. Once they were eliminated a huge Communist army would be freed to invade North China, and push irresistibly south to the Yang Tze. When Chiang Kai-shek is blamed for his last desperate endeavour to save Mukden these facts must be remembered; inaction would have only delayed the ruin which failure brought more swiftly.

The North China cities, Peking and Tientsin, with their isolated outposts at Paoting, Kalgan and Tai Yuan, were only slightly better off. The outposts were already for the most part under blockade; Peking and Tientsin could still communicate with the sea at Tang Ku, but the railway connecting these two cities was constantly interrupted, the countryside within a few miles was under Communist control, and the military situation of this distant 'island' nearly hopeless. Chiang therefore came to Peking in October 1948 to make a last attempt to save Manchuria and thus North China.

This last attempt was made by landing the Kuomintang's best armoured division with supporting infantry on the coast of South Manchuria, with the intention of thrusting toward Mukden in conjunction with a sortie of the garrison. This should clear the railway to the Great Wall and Tientsin and re-establish land communications. The armoured division landed, pushed inland to Chin Chow, a town upon the railway, and was there surrounded by the Communist forces. After a brief resistance the entire Kuomintang force surrendered. The Mukden garrison unwillingly set out on its sortie, moved a few miles into the country, met a very large Communist army and laid down its arms. Mukden and Changchun then surrendered. In a brief campaign of a few weeks Chiang had lost half a million men, but very few were killed.

The collapse of the Manchurian strongholds involved the fall of North China. Chiang left Peking at the end of October, when Mukden fell; he never returned. Indeed, his hold on the Yang Tze Valley was already threatened. Concurrently with the Manchurian campaign the Communists had opened the great southward attack which in the course of November and December destroyed the last strength of the Kuomintang in the battle of Hsu Chou. By the end of the year the Communists stood upon the north shore of the Yang Tze, close to Nanking. Meanwhile North China, left to its own defence, had slipped into their hands with very little fighting.

Peking had been the centre, for over a year, of intrigues motivated by the Left Wing Kuomintang, the political opponents of Chiang within the party. To these dissident elements, who hoped to oust the Generalissimo and bring a coalition Government to power, many intellectuals gravitated in the same hope; the last chance of the Nationalists, of all who were not Communists, was the expulsion of Chiang and a negotiated settlement of the civil war. As early as the summer of 1947 elements of the Peking garrison had made tentative efforts to rally support for this policy. Communist sympathizers, foreign Liberals, Chinese scholars of non-party outlook, had been entertained by these officers to sound opinion and prepare the way. Nothing came of these manoeuvres, since they were detected, the officers concerned either arrested or fled to the Communists, and the garrison commander changed.

The hopes of the Liberals then attached themselves to the figure of General Li Tsung-jen, a well-known Kuomintang officer of the Kuangsi faction, who before the war had often opposed Chiang Kai-shek. During the war Li had won fame by his victory over the Japanese at Tai Erh Chuang, in Shantung. He was well known to be in disagreement with the extreme wing of the Kuomintang, and when in Peking in the early part of 1948 had publicly entertained a number of persons of all shades of opinion who were opposed to the Kuomintang. In the same summer he successfully stood as candidate for the Vice-Presidency, defeating the candidate backed by the Kuomintang machine. Since the electors were none other than the handpicked National Assembly convened by the dictator himself, this demonstration of independence and non-confidence in the Government made a deep impression. In the summer of 1948 Li Tsung-jen, with the prestige of this political victory behind him, returned to Peking and started secret negotiations with the Communists.

The proposed terms of agreement were the expulsion of Chiang Kai-shek and his close associates from the Nationalist Government, an armistice and then a definitive end to the civil war, which would be followed by the formation of a coalition Government including the Communist Party. Upon these general lines both sides were in agreement, but the realization of this programme was not so easy. The followers of Li Tsung-jen had first to expel Chiang Kai-shek; all else followed upon that decisive act, and the Communists insisted on waiting for its consummation before carrying out their part of the bargain. The negotiations might conceivably have made progress and led to results, had they not been exposed and published by the correspondent of a foreign Press agency in Peking. Both sides then formally denied the truth of the story, firmly declared their intention of fighting the enemy to the last and dropped all intercourse.

The fall of Mukden, the collapse of the Kuomintang hold on the Yellow River Valley and the evident progress of the Communists towards the Yang Tze and Nanking reawakened the hopes of the Liberals and the courage of the conspirators. North China was then under the military and political command of General Fu Tso-yi. Fu was not an original member of the Kuomintang; he was a northerner, a native of Shansi, and a former officer of the warlord of that province, Yen Hsi-shan. Twenty years before, in 1928, at the time of the Nationalist advance on Peking, Fu had distinguished himself by the long defence of the small city of Cho Chou. During the early period of Japanese aggression, in 1936, he had won national fame and respect by firmly opposing the Japanese and their Mongol puppets in Inner Mongolia, where he had suppressed a Japanese inspired revolt and retaken the rebel stronghold. This act at a time when the Nanking Government was yielding on all sides to Japan had made Fu a national hero, and had not recommended him to Chiang Kai-shek.

In 1947 the position of North China was already so weak, the local troops so poor and the danger of defection so great, that Chiang was forced to invite Fu, then commanding in Inner Mongolia, to take over the defence of Peking and Tientsin. It was the first time the Kuomintang had allowed a northerner to command in the north; it was a sign of weakness rather than a change of heart. Fu was popular in Peking. He kept his own troops in order, he did something to relieve the peasants, he was personally honest. But he had only a limited control over the civil authorities, who were appointed by Nanking, and whose quality was very inferior. When it became apparent that North China was wholly isolated, that reinforcements from the south could never be expected and that the fall of Manchuria had released for the invasion of

North China a vast and highly successful Communist army, then Fu was at last willing to listen to those who pointed out that defence was hopeless.

Li Tsung-jen was now in the south, at Nanking, but others of his faction and views were still in Peking. One of these, General Wei Li-huang, had been the Kuomintang garrison commander at Mukden, from which city he had escaped by luck at the last moment. He attributed its loss, and that of Manchuria, to the blind obstinacy of Chiang Kai-shek and had come to despair of his leadership. Wei had been a cadet of the Nationalist Military College at Whampoa, near Canton, back in the days when the Nationalist revolution was in full surge and the northern expedition against the warlords about to begin.

One of his fellow students was Lin Piao, who became a Communist, revolted with Chu Teh at Nanchang in 1928 and had since risen high in the ranks of the Communist movement. He commanded the Communist army in Manchuria, and it was he who had brought about the fall of Mukden. In spite of these opposite histories, Lin and Wei had not lost all memory of early comradeship. When Lin and his forces approached the Great Wall at Shan Hai Kuan, the pass which is the key to North China, Wei induced Fu to let him open a secret negotiation with his old comrade.

Wei met Lin Piao near Shan Hai Kuan in November 1948. Negotiations were carried swiftly forward and an agreement reached, which had two parts, political and military. On the political side it was agreed once more that Chiang Kai-shek must be forced from power, and that Li Tsung-jen, the Vice-President, would then take over, and call for an armistice and the formation of a coalition Government to end the civil war. This time, as befitted the improved situation of the Communists and the weakness of the Kuomintang, certain cessions to the Communists were required. The army was to be 're-organized', in fact, that is, to be brought gradually under the control of the Communist Party.

The military side of the agreement was to be put into

practice before Chiang fell, and involved the withdrawal of Fu's troops from the vital passes of the Great Wall (or rather, in modern terms, of the range of high mountains along which the Wall is built) and the peaceful entry of the Communist army into Hopei and the North China plain. One Kuomintang army, which was not under Fu's direct command, and which occupied Tientsin, was to be left there to surrender or to be destroyed by the advancing Communists. Peking was to be evacuated and left an open town; Fu's own troops were to withdraw to Inner Mongolia.

The terms were accepted, and late in November the military side was put into effect. Fu's troops gave up the passes and fell back on Tientsin and Peking. Li Tsung-jen, however, as before, failed to muster sufficient support to drive Chiang from office. At this point also, unexpected factors intervened to upset the plans for a peaceful solution, even in North China. Chiang Kai-shek had consistently refused to supply Fu Tso-yi with any of the equipment and arms which he continued to receive from America. In vain the American advisory group officers urged upon the stubborn Generalissimo the danger of North China, the consequences of its loss, the weakness of Fu's armament. Fu was not in the inner ring; he was not an old Kuomintang man, he was a northerner, he was not trusted. At last, almost by their own act, the American advisers succeeded in getting a ship loaded with mechanical transport, artillery and munitions diverted to Tientsin for Fu's army. This belated succour reached Tientsin soon after the agreement for peaceful surrender of North China had been secretly made. It wrecked everything.

In the first place the garrison of Tientsin, a Nationalist army, were not Fu's own northern troops, but men from the south under their own Kuomintang general. Fu was determined that the arms from America should not fall into their hands. He also did not wish them to go straight to Lin Piao and the Communists. It would greatly increase his bargaining strength when 'reorganization' came if he had those arms for his own men. Fu therefore delayed the implementation of the agreement until he could get the arms unloaded, and sent up to Peking by rail. His retreat was slowed down, his evacuation of Peking postponed. Lin Piao was not long in noting this change, and soon discovered the reason. Secrets were not well kept from the Communist Party. He came to the conclusion that Fu was betraying his word, and, tempted by the prospect of the American arms, was about to resist. Lin Piao decided to strike first.

It was early December; Fu was gradually drawing in his troops on Peking, preparatory to his later withdrawal. The arms were being loaded into trains at Tientsin, six trains. The Communists, already inside the Wall, were slowly advancing towards Tientsin along the railway, encountering only token resistance. In the north-east they had also passed through the mountains, and were about fifty miles from Peking. Suddenly they fell upon one of Fu's brigades as it came down through the Nankou Pass. The attack was wholly unexpected and completely successful. The brigade was destroyed, the railway to Kalgan cut, and Fu left with about seventy thousand of his troops in Peking. For a few days, extremely indignant, he defended the northern approaches, to give time for his trains of arms to reach Peking.

On the night of December 12 Lin Piao moved his troops around westward of Peking in a wide turning movement, carried out by one of those 'long marches' of over forty miles, at which the Communist guerrilla-trained armies excel. Early on the morning of the 13th his advance guards were in the suburbs of the city. The railway junction at Feng Tai, a few miles from Peking, was taken without resistance, and in the yards, intact, were captured the six trains of armaments from the American shipment to Tientsin. Fu's own headquarters in the suburb outside the West Wall were overrun, he narrowly escaped capture and his staff papers and records were lost, Peking, indeed, was almost captured by a trick. A train was seen approaching the railway gate; the signalman at the last box realized that it was not a scheduled train, and halted it to get confirmation from the army. The occupants, realizing that they were suspected, tried to rush the gate, but were fore-stalled. They were Communist troops who might but for this alert signalman have taken Peking by a *coup de force*.

Fu retired into the walled city of Peking, an oblong enclosure measuring fourteen miles, and in this medieval fortress pre-pared, in the twentieth century, to stand a siege against an army provided with heavy artillery. His garrison numbered about seventy thousand men, the civil population exceeded two millions. In all the records of modern warfare no other such improbable operation as the siege of Peking has occurred to enliven the task of the historian. Yet for six weeks, from December 13, 1948, to January 22, 1949, this strange siege continued.

The defenders fired off great numbers of shells into the sur-rounding countryside, and were at all times ready to open up upon foes real or imaginary with machine-guns and rifle fire. The Communists rarely fired a shot, and never used their artillery. They closed in on the city, taking the outer suburbs beneath the walls, occupying the south airfield (Nan Yuan) and thus interrupting Peking's communications with the outer world. The defenders then prepared an emergency landing strip inside the city on the open space which had formed the glacis of the old Legation Quarter. On this rough and perilous ground some planes alighted, and took off, for the higher ranks of the Kuomintang hierarchy and their 'Te Wu' or special secret police had no desire for martyrdom.

The defenders had been left without any air support, since the Nationalist Air Force had flown off to Shanghai on the first approach of the Communists, first selling its stocks of petrol on the black market. As the Communist forces, other-wise now well equipped with captured American arms supplied to the Kuomintang and Japanese weapons from the Man-churian dumps, had no aircraft, the war remained in this respect also somewhat archaic. The Communists did not press the siege, because they had no intention either of damaging an historic city which they intended to restore to its ancient place as the capital, or of getting a bad name by injuring the inhabitants. No possibility of relief existed. The nearest Kuo-mintang forces, except the besieged defenders of Tientsin, were more than five hundred miles away in the Yang Tze Valley, and still retreating. The siege of Peking must end in one way; it was only a question of time and of 'face'.

Fu Tso-yi had been infuriated by what he regarded as Lin Piao's treachery; Lin Piao felt that Fu was not to be trusted. Between these two offended commanders no further com-munication was possible. So the siege dragged on. No doubt the exact difficulty was not appreciated at Communist head-quarters, which had on its hands the final stages of the great and decisive battle of Hsu Chou. When, perhaps, Mao Tse-tung and Chu Teh could give the Peking problem their attention, it was easily solved. Lin Piao was sent with his troops to press the siege of Tientsin, and his place as com-mander of the forces surrounding Peking was taken by Nieh Jung-chen, the long-established Communist commander of the guerrilla region adjacent to Peking, who had been in those parts since the beginning of the war with Japan, yet still re-tained his colloquial knowledge of French and a St Cyr cut to his uniform. Nieh, like many others, became a Communist in Paris, not Moscow.

Negotiations between Fu's chief of staff and Nieh were speedily settled. On January 22 Peking was in fact surrendered under a nominal 'peace settlement'. The closing stages had been hastened by the bombardment, by a very light piece of artillery, of the area in which the Kuomintang special secret police had their headquarters. The accuracy of this fire gave much satis-faction to the citizens. A curious incident had meanwhile taken place outside the city. On their first approach to Peking the Communist forces had occupied the two universities of Tsing Hua and Yenching, situated about ten miles from the city. When it was found that Fu refused to surrender, Lin Piao had seriously envisaged carrying the city by assault, and as this would involve breaching the walls—immensely thick and sixty feet high—artillery would have been necessary.

Before deciding on the point to be breached the Communist

command asked Professor Liang Ssu-ch'eng, of Tsing Hua, the leading architect and archaeologist in China, whether the place the military favoured was objectionable on historical and aesthetic grounds. Professor Liang thought it was; he said that the spot chosen, a gate in the west wall of the south city, was one of the few pieces of unrestored Ming military architecture surviving, and it would be a great loss to art and archaeology if it were destroyed. He suggested, in turn, another place, also opposite a vacant space within the walls, where bombardment would neither slay the citizens nor damage an historical monument. The Communist command accepted this change, but fortunately the surrender of the city obviated the need for any bombardment.

Tientsin had fallen on January 15, to direct attack, after a brief siege. The fall of Peking, swiftly followed by that of the few remaining smaller places in North China, closed a chapter. From that date the Communists, who had passed from guerrilla to large-scale positional warfare in 1948, were no longer a mystery force lurking in the interior, enigmatic and obscure. They became at once the rival Government of China, established in the ancient seat of Empire, with the chance to prove what they could do when called upon to govern, and to show whether they could carry the Chinese Revolution through to its end and give the country peace.

On February 3, 1949, a day of swirling duststorm, the Communists entered Peking in strength, in battle array. The long columns of artillery, mechanical transport, cavalry and infantry took all day to pass through the great south gate, the Ch'ien Men, and then file—deliberately—through the old Legation Quarter, to humble the last shreds of the foreigner's pride. The parade was exceedingly well controlled and carried out in perfect order. The troops, veterans, instantly recognizable to all who saw them as real soldiers, not the ruffians in uniform who had so long disgraced the name in China, were under a firm and rigid discipline. Their weapons were well kept and clean, and they were of Japanese or American make in almost equal proportions. To the surprise and disappointment of some observers, who had fixed ideas on the subject of Communists, no Russian weapons and no Russians were to be seen.

The fall of Peking and the defeat of the Kuomintang before Nanking brought a lull to the civil war. Chiang Kai-shek withdrew from the presidency, under pressure, but did not leave China, did not relax his secret control of the machinery of Kuomintang Government and Party, and so hampered all the activities of his nominal successor, Li Tsung-jen, the Vice-President. It might have seemed that none the less now was the time for Li to make his long-cherished scheme of coalition a reality. Now he could freely negotiate with the Communists. He did indeed negotiate. From February to April the negotiations dragged on; no real fighting took place. The Communists controlled all China north of the Yang Tze, the Kuomintang still held the south and west.

Towards the end of April the Communists were confident that Li Tsung-jen was about to accept their terms, terms which they subsequently made public. The days of equal bargains had now passed. The Communist terms of April 1949 were in fact surrender terms. The Kuomintang had to accept coalition on conditions which would have made the Communists supreme in the Government; they had to accept the surrender of their armed forces and their reorganization under Communist control. For this they were offered some participation in the government, some legal right to exist as a party. It may be that the Communists, as they claimed, really hoped that these terms would be accepted. They would have gained at once, by assimilation of the recognized legitimate Government of China, that complete international recognition and acknowledged status which they have subsequently sought in vain. They would have occupied China's seat at UN. There was not much else that the surrender, as opposed to the conquest of the Kuomintang, could have given them. The participation of Kuomintang politicians and officials in government was a disadvantage to the Communists.

At the last moment Li Tsung-jen, as it is said under threat of assassination by the 'Te Wu' of Chiang Kai-shek, refused to sign the agreement and fled from Nanking. The Communists, who were ready for any eventuality, thereupon gave the order to cross the Yang Tze and began the rapid conquest of South and Western China. It was on this occasion, near Nanking, that the Communist troops crossing the river and their supporting artillery became involved in the clash with the British sloop *Amethyst* then on her way to Nanking.

What was almost certainly originally an accidental encounter was soon inflamed into a serious clash. Other British warships which tried to come up river to the assistance of the crippled *Amethyst* were fired upon and driven back with loss. The Chinese Communist troops, long taught that the 'capitalist imperialists' were the friends of the Kuomintang and the enemies of the Chinese people, easily believed that the British were assisting the Nationalists to repel the crossing. The incident was eventually smoothed over, but it is improbable that British ships of war will ever again sail on the waters of the Yang Tze.

The fall of Nanking, a few days later, the precipitate retreat of the Nationalists, their speedy loss of Shanghai and the main provinces of the south, even their brief sojourn in Canton until the summer rains were over and the Communists reorganized for the *coup de grace*, all these swift disasters were but the aftermath of the decisive battles of the previous autumn and the failure of the peace negotiations of the spring of 1949. The Kuomintang preferred to go down in defeat and to take refuge in Formosa. The Communists passed on to total victory and to the establishment of a new regime owing nothing to the support, or to the surrender, of the Kuomintang or any of its factions. The period of nationalism, 'Kuo Min', was over, and the People's Republic, the 'Jen Min' era had arrived.

In this last phase of the Chinese Revolution the ancient rule of Chinese history had been once more proved true. Only with the support of both the peasants and the scholars can revolution in China succeed. The original Republican revolution of 1911 was the work of a small number of Western-educated men, with the passive acquiescence of the mass of the people. Since it lacked any active support from the peasants and failed to retain what it had had from the educated, it failed and ended in military tyranny. The Kuomintang revived the hopes of the scholar class, and in 1926, with the Communists in alliance, roused the peasantry also. Success was swift and sweeping until the breach between Right and Left drove the Communists into opposition, and with them went the support of the peasants. The Japanese invasion once more united the two main forces in Chinese society, and made possible the resistance to Japan, so hopeless in cold calculation.

In 1945 the only hope for peace was in the agreement of the two main parties, but that agreement was impossible so long as one party worked for revolution and the other for reaction. The scholars were lost to the Kuomintang through its corruption, nepotism, misgovernment and inefficiency. They were won by the Communists, who in a long period of exile and hardship had learned to practise moderation, to govern honestly and to build a disciplined army. The Kuomintang had lost the road to democracy, and the Communists had travelled far from the pattern of the Russian Revolution. Thus the scholars and the peasants found they could give support to the Communists, and could not survive under the Kuomintang.

Neither party offered the Chinese people democratic government. The ideals of 1911 were forgotten. The Chinese people looked now for a Government which could govern, which knew its mind, had power and purpose, a theory and a practice which fitted together—in fact for a modern version of the government under which they had lived for so many centuries. The totalitarian aspect of the Communist regime does not dismay the Chinese people: the Empire was also totalitarian, though the word was not then coined. It was absolute, and so is Communism; it was hierarchic, ruling through a chosen group of specially trained men, the Confucian 'Mandarin'. So is Communism, ruling by its party, who are brought up on Marx and form a class apart. The Empire had its doctrine, its total explanation of philosophy, politics and economics; the teaching of Confucius. So has Communism, for which Marx as interpreted by Lenin, Stalin and Mao Tse-tung explains all and justifies everything.

So the Revolution went full circle, the old order fell, chaos followed its collapse, until from the fundamental forces of Chinese life and thought a new order, borrowing forms more than ideas from abroad, but claiming modernity by virtue of its foreign dress, has arisen to restore the Chinese Empire in the form of the People's Republic. As ever in China, form does not matter, but content is all important.

CHAPTER FIVE

CHRISTIANITY IN THE CHINESE REVOLUTION

WHEN CHRISTIAN MISSIONARIES of the European nations first penetrated into Western China they found, in the city of Sian, the ancient capital of the T'ang Dynasty, a stele on which was recorded the rise and prosperity of the Nestorian Church in China during the seventh and eighth centuries of the Christian era. Princes had been enrolled in that church; great ministers had contributed to its funds and restored its shrines. In the eighteenth and nineteenth centuries nothing else remained. No trace of Nestorian Christianity was to be found among the Chinese, no literary evidence of its existence, no tradition, no memory. At first the missionary scholars were inclined to doubt the authenticity of so dismal a monument of regression. But the Nestorian tablet is genuine enough; other evidence, painfully assembled from texts, and some few traces of inscriptions, crosses and other Christian emblems, have been found to substantiate the fact. The Arab historians confirm it. In the T'ang period Nestorian Christianity flourished in China, then waned and vanished away.

This uncomfortable fact needed explanation. The most ready, and the most soothing, was to emphasize the fact of Nestorianism rather than Christianity. Nestorius was a heretic; the Catholic Church had cast him and his followers out, to proselytize, if they could, among the Oriental nations beyond the Roman frontier. The Protestants had accepted, centuries later, the Catholic condemnation of their own forerunners, the great heresiarchs of the early church. Thus both Catholic and Protestant missionary could agree that Nestorius was a heretic, and his followers not true Christians. Their failure in China was explained and need not prejudice the hopes of the Western missionaries. The Nestorian failure was fortunately complete, it had left no heretical church in China to dispute with the upholders of purer doctrine. China was a free field with no favour, and it was the greatest opportunity Christianity had found since the conversion of the Roman Empire.

In many ways it seemed to be a similar opportunity also. In China there was no established faith, fanatical and traditionally hostile to the Christians as in the Islamic world of Western Asia. Nor was there an all-embracing religion, entering into every detail of life and moulding society in its pattern, as in Hindu India. The Chinese world resembled the European classical world in that the ruling class were philosophic pagans, more interested in ethical doctrine than in religious beliefs, and the mass of the people polytheists who had no theological prejudices, but merely worshipped their gods with traditional rites. This seemed a very fair prospect for Christianity. Yet it has proved the most frustrating of all the mission fields, the great blind alley of Christian endeavour.

The early Catholic missionaries, perceiving the resemblance to pagan Rome, and realizing that the emperor was the font of Confucian orthodoxy, saw that to convert the Throne, to make a Chinese Constantine, was the swiftest and surest road to success. They concentrated on the court. They used their scientific skill as astronomers, engineers and even as artillery-men, to win them acceptance; they gained a foothold in official circles, they made some conversions among men of influence, and they themselves became accomplished Chinese scholars. In fact, among the early French and Italian missionaries it became a question whether China was not converting the missionaries faster than they were converting the Chinese.

The ready acceptance of Chinese customs, the conformity to Confucian ideas, and the erosion of European concepts which took place in the missionary to Peking soon alarmed the Vatican. Certain practices, such as firing off crackers when celebrating Mass, were forbidden. Still more serious, the easy tolerance of reverence to ancestors and what were in fact religious rites to ancestral tablets, which the Jesuits had admitted, were now rigidly condemned. The result was a swift loss of imperial favour, the ruin of the Trojan horse which the early missionaries had skilfully constructed, and the persecution of the church. The high level attack upon the Throne had failed.

In the middle of the nineteenth century the Protestant nations, following in the wake of British military and naval power, forced the Chinese Government to admit them to the Empire and permit their teaching. This second Christian offensive was thus from the first bound up with the political power of the seafaring nations, and was made possible only by their success in defeating the Manchu Empire in war. As such it was and remained suspect and unwelcome to the Chinese educated class. The Protestants paid no attention to the court, and tended to ignore the official class also. They endeavoured, by translating the scriptures into Chinese, by street corner preaching, and by evangelistic tours to win a wider audience and convert the people. Protestantism had always come up from below, and the experience of Europe should be valid in China.

It very nearly was; some years after the first Protestant missionaries had worked in Canton, and made a partial translation of the Bible, this work fell into the hands of a Chinese of the educated class, but a failed candidate for the Civil Service, named Hung Hsiu-ch'uan. Hung was also a Cantonese, or rather a Hakka, a member of a community descended from northern immigrants, but long settled in Kuang Tung. Disappointed and ill, Hung came upon the Gutzlaff translation when on his sick bed. He had already had visions; these seemed now confirmed by his reading of the Bible. Hung rose from his couch a religious leader, a divinely inspired prophet, and before long was at the head of a religious sect, which soon became a rebellion.

The T'ai P'ing rebellion, or the Great Peaceful Heavenly Kingdom, as Hung called his movement, was in some ways yet another great peasant upheaval, coming, as before, when the dynasty was in decline, and using an exotic creed as its rallying point and inspiration. The Yellow Turbans had done the same nearly two thousand years before. The difference was that this exotic creed was not some variant of Taoist magic or esoteric Buddhism, but a form of Christianity, and thus open to the influence of the West. Hung taught his followers the Christian religion as he knew it. He further claimed to be divinely inspired, by visions in which he had conversed with Jesus and with God. He took the title—so offensive to the missionaries—of 'Younger Brother of Jesus Christ'. By this it would seem he meant no more than that he, the prophet and instrument of the Deity, was adopted as the brother of Christ, just as the Emperor was the 'Son of Heaven', the adopted son of the Supreme Deity, appointed to rule the earth.

The early success of the T'ai P'ing movement was sweeping. They overran much of South China, took Nanking and there established their capital (1853). They narrowly failed to take Peking also. They penetrated into West China and everywhere overthrew the government of the Manchu Dynasty, destroyed the temples of the Taoists and the monasteries of the Buddhists, and tried to establish their own new religion. Here, it would seem, was the great chance for Christianity; here at last was the Chinese Constantine, who would subdue the whole Empire to the true faith. The assistance of the Christian powers of Europe would have made his victory swift and certain.

The Christian missionaries did not see the matter in this light. To begin with, the missionary body was at least half Catholic, and the Catholics regarded Hung, whose inspiration was Protestant, as a heretic, and a menace to the faith. The Protestants were in a more difficult situation. Hung was certainly inspired by their work; they did not quarrel with much of his creed, which was their own. But he had never been baptized. He had not received any direct instruction from a foreign missionary, his doctrine was defective in some points, and inadmissible at others. To admit Hung as a prophet was to add sweeping and far-reaching tenets to the Christian faith, beliefs which the churches at home would be slow to accept, would in fact indignantly reject. Yet nothing short of this would meet the situation. Hung was clearly not going to renounce his creed and his visions, accept baptism from a missionary and listen to his teaching. Such a course would have destroyed his influence with his followers, would have been unthinkable to a man inspired, fanatical and convinced of his own divine mission.

The Protestants temporized, sent emissaries to inquire, doubted and debated, and finally rejected the T'ai P'ing prophet as an impostor, and so lost their share in the only Christian movement which ever had a chance of converting the mass of the Chinese people. The Protestant powers, England and even America, were ready to lend arms and officers (including General Gordon) to the Manchus to repel the assault of the Christian T'ai P'ing rebels. The French, although not at that time under a Government much influenced by the church, were even more ready to crush a heretical Protestant rising which threatened to build a strong China. The T'ai P'ings had no friends.

The powers had just made a very satisfactory treaty with the Manchu court (1860), by which concessions, tariff privileges and the virtual foreign control of the Chinese Customs had established their trade in a sure and sound position. Their naval power dominated the China coast; any further trouble from the Manchu court could be dealt with expeditiously and firmly. The prospect of the fall of the Manchu Dynasty, and the rise in its place of a strong new regime, claiming to be Christian, yet admitting no foreign direction in its religion, willing to modernize China, and doubtless before long asserting its rights and its equality with the West, all this was not welcome to the statesmen of nineteenth-century Europe.

The Christian European States thus assisted the pagan Manchus to crush the Christian, if heretical, Chinese T'ai P'ings. They were utterly destroyed. Their leader took his life, his followers either perished at the hands of the executioner or fled into hiding. The fallen faith was forgotten, the T'ai P'ing movement had no successor and no survivals. Thus ended, in effect, the Protestant offensive to convert China to Christianity. This fact would be strongly denied, was not admitted, and was never even understood as a possible truth. For another ninety years the Protestant churches have poured money and effort into China. Missionaries gave up their whole lives to the work; Chinese pastors have carried it on, some prominent men have been converted; but the mass of the Chinese people has never responded.

The only mass reaction which came from the peasant population, as in the Boxer Rising, was strongly hostile to Christianity, and for the significant reason that it was 'foreign'. 'Primary Devils' were, for the Boxers, the Christian foreign missionaries; 'Secondary Devils', equally deserving of death, the Chinese converts. The open expression of this attitude died with the Boxer rebellion: the inner conviction, the unexpressed belief, continued to restrict and hamper the progress of conversion.

Other psychological obstacles opposed the Christian missionary. Some of these were of his own making, others deep rooted in Chinese tradition. The aims of the Catholic and Protestant missions were not identical, and their methods conflicted; this led a peasant and rural Chinese to treat them as two conflicting religions, the one supported by the power and money of England, the other by the influence and wealth of France. The fact that not all Protestant missionaries were British, and not all Catholic missionaries French was either never generally understood or simply ignored. The belief was firmly held, even by those not inimical to the missions.

The vague but persistent idea that to become a Christian was in some way to become a dependent of the foreigner, to cease to be fully Chinese, also acted powerfully. This was not a new idea. The Chinese Moslems, a small minority in most provinces, were in part at least, on the paternal side, descendants of foreign mercenary troops and Central Asiatic tribesmen. They had long intermingled with the Chinese and spoke only the Chinese language. Yet to the non-Moslem they were not 'Han Jen'—Chinese, but 'Hui Tze'—Moslem, a different race as well as an alien faith. Much of this attitude was transferred to Christian converts.

The Protestant missionary, often a fundamentalist, believed

in the approach of Armageddon, and the doctrine of the Elect. He thought that what was most urgently required was to bring some knowledge of the Gospel to all Chinese, among whom might be, indeed certainly were, some of the unrecognized Elect. He therefore tended to diffuse his activity over as wide an area as could be covered from the mission station base. Social work, although undertaken by many missions, was by some regarded as a side issue, not really worth the main effort or the diversion of funds which should be used more properly for evangelistic work.

Other Protestant missions did consider medical and educational work to be very important, but also with the basic idea of reaching by these means a wider audience. The Protestant missionary was true to the doctrine of individual salvation and believed that such saving of souls, rather than conversion of the masses, was his duty and his proper work. The Protestant also brought to China some of the prejudices which work in his home country had instilled. Drink was an evil; the slums of Victorian England proved the fact. Therefore prohibition of the use of wine in China was a Christian duty. The stage in Europe was, or might be thought, free and even licentious. Therefore the Chinese drama must be forbidden to the Christian convert. Other minor habits, such as smoking, were frowned upon, and many little foibles of the European Reformed Churches erected into basic dogmas of the Christian religion.

The Catholic missionary approached China in a very different way. Christianity in his view was a way of life, as well as a doctrine for salvation. What was needed in China was the same method which had succeeded two thousand years ago in the Roman Empire: the slow creation of small Christian communities, separate and close-linked cells of the new faith, who should in time spread and grow, imperceptibly if possible, by adapting as much of Chinese culture as could be easily accepted by the Christian, and slowly changing the rest. There should be no sharp break with the past, but rather a conservative transformation from within.

It followed that mass movements must be superficial and not to be trusted; individual conversions were a necessary step, but only a step; the building of the Christian family, not the salvation of the individual soul, was the real aim. When the community was Christian the individual would be automatically brought up in the faith; this mattered much more than the conversion of old women, men at odds with their fellows, or those of deeply religious temperament. They could all come in, but the birth of Christians was more to be desired than the conversion of those past childbearing.

The missionaries of both the Reformed and the Catholic churches found that the greatest obstacle to their progress was not the fanatical devotion of the Chinese to some pagan creed, but their tolerance. It was not the refusal to worship God or acknowledge the divinity of Christ, it was the readiness to add these acts of faith to the worship of idols, the belief in Buddhism and its Boddhisattvas, the reverence to ancestors and the sacrifices to their tablets. The Chinese people did not reject the Christian faith, but they were unwilling to grant it the exclusive title to belief which to the European seems so natural.

'Three ways to one goal' the Chinese proverb says, meaning that Buddhism, Taoism and Confucianism are all admissible philosophies, all tend to civilize the human race and discipline the passions of the heart. But the 'goal' is not salvation, not the life after death; it is the good life, the right conduct, here on earth. The conception of a unitary religion which excludes all other faiths from any claim to truth or trust, the idea of the 'infidel'—meaning one who holds another faith as tenaciously as one holds one's own—these ideas have never found a place in Chinese thought. Consequently the basic assumptions of the Christian religion were alien to the Chinese and found no welcome.

With this went another idea, strange to the West, but deeply set in the Chinese mind—the view that all religion which had supernatural sanction, all belief in God or gods, was in some way backward, illiterate and uncivilized. A well-known Chinese writer of the present age once remarked: 'In China

the educated believe in nothing, the uneducated in everything.'
Underlying this just observation may be seen the constant
opinion of the educated that nothing is worthy of 'belief' in
the dogmatic religious sense, and that such belief is the mark
of the undiscriminating illiterates.

For ages past the Confucian scholars had mocked and upbraided the Buddhist religion, denying power to its gods,
rejecting its relics and its miracles. The Taoist polytheism was
also regarded as only fit for the 'stupid people'. The fact that
the Imperial Government found it wise to subsidize temples
and maintain monasteries only underlined the contempt which
the scholar felt for such religions. They had to be humoured
to keep the people content. That religion is the opiate of the
people—Trotsky's phrase—would have been warmly endorsed
by the officials of the Empire—only they would have drawn
from it a different conclusion.

When the Sung philosophers recast Confucianism in more
modern form in the tenth and eleventh centuries A.D., they
tried to prune away all the numerous evidences of religious
belief and divine powers which survived in the texts of an
earlier and less sophisticated age. They themselves repudiated
any idea of a supreme god, substituting the more abstract
Moral Law. 'There is no man in heaven judging sin,' said Chu
Hsi, the greatest Confucian of the later ages. It was this abstract
morality free from supernatural sanction and 'superstition'
which so much appealed to the European scholars of the
eighteenth century who first became aware of Chinese thought.
It was also this which was the greatest obstacle for their more
devout descendants, the missionaries of the next century.

The approach of both Catholic and Protestant failed to meet
any real need in the Chinese mind. The sacrifices which the
Protestant demanded, wine, theatre and tobacco, seemed irrelevant and merely quaint to the Chinese. They compared them
with the equally peculiar and, to them, meaningless, Moslem
prohibition on eating pork. The individual approach, the
doctrine of salvation for the soul, but not necessarily for the
community, which might be doomed to Armageddon; this

seemed to the Chinese socially irresponsible and dangerous. The Protestant failed to ask for the right renunciations, or to gear his demand to the level of the whole society. The Catholic did not ask for enough.

The Catholics would have accepted the Empire, unreformed, so long as it became Christian. They did not want to educate the people to a new culture, but to convert them to what the Chinese thought of as a new superstition. The aim of individual salvation, the Protestant panacea, seemed anti-social, the Catholic objective of converting the faith of the populace without altering their economic condition or changing the structure of society seemed pointless. Why change men's beliefs, what did it matter what they believed, so long as they acted in accordance with the Confucian virtues?

The antithesis of salvation and damnation, the prime motive for Christian conduct and orthodox belief, was absent in the Chinese mind. The people could never really understand that this was the motive of Christian mission teaching. To travel abroad and live among strangers, not for profit or advantage, but merely to alter their religion and substitute another, equally steeped in the supernatural, and thus to the educated, equally unsophisticated, seemed a most improbable explanation. It was much easier to believe, with the mass of the people, that the missionary was the agent of some foreign power.

If the missions failed with the conservative scholars and the people for these reasons, they had, for a time, a certain success with the discontented and progressive element among the educated class. To those who saw the weakness and decline of the Empire, and had come to doubt the efficacy of its orthodox doctrine, the idea that Christianity was inseparable from modernity, that the foreigner's religion and his material power were in some way connected, came as a new hope. If the Chinese became Christian they would also acquire these powers and make this material progress. Some missionaries, more simple-minded than insincere, gave colour to these ideas in their teaching.

That such converts as they made came to Christianity for

things it should not offer, and would bring to it things it did not want to accept, these fears did not occur to them. To some converts of this type the adoption of a new religion was welcome because it automatically discharged them from observing the obligations of those that they renounced. To become free from prejudice and 'modern', that is, no longer bound by the rules of the old society, was an attraction for those who had found the rules hard to observe.

There was also the restless but sincere idealist who was appalled by the misery of the poor, the antiquated character of law and government, and had become convinced that democracy and liberty could only exist in a Christian background. These potential revolutionaries tended to join the Protestant churches. They expected a new order of society to arise from the conversion of the Chinese people, and they became discontented with the slow progress of evangelistic work, and doubtful of the appeal to the individual. Many of these later drifted into the ranks of Communism.

In the early period of the Republic the missionaries and their Chinese converts were alike convinced that the Chinese Revolution was the great opportunity for Christianity. The Throne had gone, and with it the stronghold of Confucian orthodoxy. Once this barrier was down it should be possible to sweep forward to success. The founder of the Republic was a Christian. Dr Sun, indeed, did not make the conversion of the Chinese people one of his political objectives, but he gave an example. The new universities founded by mission societies, the returned students who had been converted abroad and were now sure of the best positions and the most influential academic posts, all these things should carry Christianity forward to victory. Buddhism was manifestly a spent force, Taoism a hocus pocus in which only the most ignorant believed. Confucius was dethroned. There was no obstacle left to conquer—except the Chinese mind.

There were in fact contrary tendencies of the greatest power operating on that mind. Many students abroad might become Christians; many more found that Christianity in its native lands was not taken at the value the missionaries put upon it. They found the Left anti-Christian on the Continent, and the intellectuals in all Western lands at least unenthusiastic. They came to see how divided Christian churches were, how little science and learning conformed to the dogmas of those churches, and how few among their teachers believed that the adoption of Christianity was the solution for China's woes.

They found, too, that many Europeans took the same view of religion as their own conservative scholars. The vision of a Christian republic soon faded. The Republic was dominated by warlords who were not Christians, and the one that was—Feng Yu-hsiang—showed a very unchristian aptitude for treachery, and a cold-blooded ferocity in disposing of his enemies. Above all, the First Great War and the Russian Revolution dimmed the hopes of Christian success.

The war did great damage to the prestige of the European peoples in Asia. This was illogical, since the Europeans had always practised war and had gained their position in Asia not by peaceful means but by force; but they had seemed to act together, or at least to avoid, in Asia, the worst evils of their dissension. Now they had destroyed each other, eagerly employed and cajoled Asiatic peoples to take their part, and worst of all, weakened themselves. The whole philosophy of Western Europe was called in question. Democracy suffered, and Christianity could not escape. The East, the Chinese, could and did make war, they could and had practised upon each other all the cruelties of racial and political hatred. But so now had the West; if in the name of Christianity these things were also done, why become Christians? What virtue was there in the foreign religion? To the Chinese there appeared to be little to gain from such a change. They looked elsewhere for the new doctrine. Christianity had not the answer.

The positive side of the Russian Revolution, the doctrine of Marx, the theory of Communism, had effects in China which will presently be considered. The negative side had also powerful consequences. The Russian Revolution overthrew the

Christian church in Russia. It proclaimed its atheism, denounced and exposed the superstitions of the church and undertook an active campaign to deride its doctrines and uproot its beliefs. The Chinese saw this with interest. It seemed as if now one European power was drawing aside the mask which had covered the true face; and exposing the real character of Western religion and its link with imperialism.

Not all the Russian anti-God propaganda could strike a responsive note in China, but much of it was only a modern version of what the Confucian scholars had said of Buddhism since the T'ang Dynasty. Now the Russians were saying it about Christianity. At this time Russia was very popular. She had renounced her extra-territorial rights and special privileges. It was widely believed that her exposure of the plots and ambitions of the powers in the East, made from the Tsarist archives, were all too true; so was, perhaps, the exposure of the Christian church. It cannot be doubted that this Russian propaganda had a great effect among the young Chinese scholars of the new generation.

The prospect of a rapid extension of Christianity in China as a result of the fall of the Empire thus proved illusory. The rise of the Nationalist Party and the Second Revolution confirmed the trend away from Western ideals and consequently from Christianity. The Second Revolution was in its early stages openly hostile to the missions. The foreign nationals of those powers which profited from unequal treaties were all alike subject to the deepest suspicion and made the victims of hostile attacks. Most mission stations along the Yang Tze and in South China had to be evacuated; there was a demand for the renunciation of the privileged status of missions and missionaries, and with these demands many of the more thoughtful missionaries agreed.

It was realized, too late, how deeply the work of evangelization had been compromised by the fact that the missionary enjoyed extra-territorial rights and had his country's armed power behind him. These rights and this power had seemed necessary to the missionaries of the nineteenth century, who otherwise doubted whether they could have entered China at all. In the twentieth century they were branded as marks of 'imperialism' and served to inflame nationalist opinion against the missions rather than to protect the missionary.

In spite of these setbacks, Christianity could count certain notable conversions as signs of success. Dr Sun was indeed dead, and even in his later lifetime had seemed to drift away from his Christian beliefs towards Nationalist ideals. But shortly after the break between Chiang Kai-shek and the Communists, the new leader of the Nanking Government himself announced his conversion. With Chiang there were also his brothers-in-law, T. V. Soong and H. H. Kung and their influential wives. The Kuomintang higher leadership was strong in Christian converts.

Even at the time, fresh from the disheartening experience of the evacuation and anti-Christian tide in the provinces, many missionaries felt dubious about the value to their cause of these Nationalist leaders. They doubted, with good reason, whether the practice of Christian virtues was always as prominent as profession of the faith. They could not ignore that whatever the beliefs of the leaders, the conduct of the Kuomintang Government was not marked by virtue of any sort.

With the passage of years, the increasing signs of dictatorship at Nanking and corruption in the administration, the hope, held only by a minority, that the Christian leaders of the Kuomintang would lead the country as a whole towards salvation and conversion, was quietly abandoned. It was only too plain that Christianity in China was fighting, not a victorious campaign under this leadership, but a difficult and losing battle in the provinces against the Communist guerrillas, then very hostile to the missions, and in the universities and schools an equally hard fight against the appeal of Marx. The Nationalist Party, putting its nationalism before the Christianity of its leaders, insisted on vexatious regulations concerning the teaching of religion in the schools. Pressure against missionary schools and activity was kept up, in various ways, by both sides. Open hostility from the Communists, more insidious opposition from many elements on the Nationalist side. Christianity was now on the defensive.

The Chinese people as a whole had lost interest in the question of Christianity. The decline of Christian influence in the European lands, the falling away of large classes of their people from active belief and worship, the rather old-fashioned theology and unrepresentative religion of the later missionaries, all these things had caused a widespread belief in China that the missions no longer represented the vanguard of Western civilization and modernity, but were in their own countries somewhat in the position of the Buddhists in China.

The rise of modern secular education, the spread of knowledge of Western languages derived from lay institutions, and the establishment of many Government and private universities had broken the early monopoly of Western learning which the mission colleges had once enjoyed. Still more, the revolutionary situation of the country prompted reformers to look for a creed which embraced all aspects of the problem, political and economic as well as spiritual, and thus the limited objectives of the missionary, as they seemed, were disregarded.

Yet it must be recognized that Christianity and the missions accomplished many things in China, though not the thing they most desired to do. They broke into the closed world of Confucian learning, and sowed there the seeds of scientific knowledge, of Western political thought, and of Western economic theory. They started the first hospitals in China, and the whole Chinese medical profession owes its origin to their teaching. They opened the Chinese mind to the consideration, though not in this case to the acceptance, of a different ideology, an alien but yet ancient orthodoxy which China had ignored.

The Christian missions, staffed by men of different sects and various nationalities, showed that it was possible to have a world-wide faith, a system of values which was applicable in many countries. All these were new ideas to the Chinese. It may be said that Christianity stormed first into the breach in the Confucian citadel; it was repelled and overcome; and on

its back the ultimate victor, Communism, mounted to the assault.

It is sometimes suggested that the original inspiration of Communism came from Christianity, that the ideals of the brotherhood of man, of the rights of the humble, and the community of property, were first expounded to mankind by the Sermon on the Mount, and were unknown, or at least not practised, before. If this is so, and Communism is the last offspring of that teaching, neither parent nor child are willing to acknowledge the relationship. Yet in organization and discipline, in the system of control and selfless devotion of the rank and file it is obvious that Communism has borrowed wholesale from the church and the monastic orders. The Chinese Communists took these things at second hand, from the practice of the Russian Party, but in other respects they sought to imitate the work of the missions, and have at long last, in the fullness of power, acknowledged the debt.

Any close observation of the Chinese Communists reveals the strong resemblance between them and a religious organization. The single-mindedness, not to say fanaticism, the devotion to duty, the complete belief and unquestioning acceptance of a dogmatic creed, the sense of sin, absent before in China, and the practice of confession, all these things are familiar to the European from Christian experience, but were strange to the Far East. The insistence of the Chinese Communists on rigid and even pedantic honesty in money matters is reminiscent of the Puritan horror of blasphemy and bad language. Corruption has become as repugnant to the Chinese Communists as foul language was to Cromwell's Ironsides. It is hard to doubt that some of these characteristics come from Christian examples, not only from the manners of the Russian Communist Party.

This seems the more probable as the Chinese Communists during their formative guerrilla years, a whole generation, were never in touch with Russia, and hardly in relations with the Russian Party. They were, however, in the deep interior, in contact with the missions, and with men who had firsthand knowledge of their work. It is true that in the early years the Chinese Communists treated the missions as imperialist outposts, harried the missionaries, put some, principally Catholics, to death, and drove others from the country.

In time they came to see that the missions had some things to their credit. They had fed the hungry and nursed the orphan. The best of them had tried to instil a sense of human equality and decency into the relationship between rich and poor. The idea that every man and woman has a soul, and an equally valuable soul, though not a Communist belief, leads also to the better treatment of man by man. The Communists were hard to the Catholics, very often because of the unwise concentration of land in the hands of the church. The Catholic mission had often become a large landlord and as such the missionary was in Communist eyes a 'class enemy' and treated as such. Some at least of the Protestant missionaries whom the Communists made captive and held for months came back to speak moderate things about their captors and did not deny the virtue of some of their practices.

The period prior to the war with Japan in 1937 was nevertheless one in which the Communists were professedly hostile to Christian missions, and in the areas in which they operated drove the missionaries away. After the Long March and the truce between the Communists and Kuomintang, active persecution of religion ceased, and subsequent policy has been to grant toleration. This was made explicit after the Communist victory by Article 5 of Chapter 1 of the Common Programme of the Chinese People's Political Consultative Conference, adopted on September 29, 1949. This article guarantees to the people the freedom of religious belief. Freedom of belief had in fact been permitted in Communist areas since the truce of 1937.

Yet the truce did not save the missions from further disasters. A new and far more formidable enemy was about to take the field. The Japanese army was not only indoctrinated with its Shinto paganism, not only hostile to Christianity as such, but treated the missionaries at first as suspects, later as open enemies. When the conflict broadened out into the Pacific War in 1941 most of the missionaries became 'enemy aliens' to the Japanese and their puppet regimes. As such they were interned, and their mission stations either closed or left to converts.

It was not only the numerous British and American missionaries who suffered this fate; most of the European countries were under German occupation, and their subjects also were treated as enemies. Dutch, Norwegian and Belgian missionaries suffered equally. The Germans had for some years been forced to withdraw or hand over their activity to others owing to the Nazi policy of restricting funds to foreign missions. Among the Catholics the position was a little different. Many of the Catholic missions were either staffed by Spaniards, who were neutral, or Italians, who were allies. These the Japanese had to leave alone.

This favour did not help them in the end. The Chinese Communists gained control of most of the rural areas in the so-called Japanese-occupied provinces; they occupied, also, the vacant mission stations, and while treating any missionaries who managed to remain, if Allied subjects, as friends, they grew very hostile to the Catholic missions run by Axis and neutral missionaries, whom they accused of co-operating with the Japanese. This issue of co-operation with the enemy was later used to drive out almost all the Catholic missions which survived in the North China countryside.

By the end of the war the combined hostility of the Japanese to the Allied missionaries, mostly Protestant, and the opposition of the Communists to the Catholic missions, mostly Axis or neutral, had virtually rooted out all the missions in the interior of the northern provinces. Those in the large cities, which the Japanese occupied and the Kuomintang took over at surrender, were able to return after the war, but the countryside, once in Communist hands, was never reoccupied by the foreign missionaries.

During the course of the civil war which followed the breakdown of General Marshall's truce negotiations, the distinction between Catholic and Protestant missions and churches became sharper in the political sense. The Protestant churches in China had gone a long way towards autonomy; the missionary still worked where he could, but the direction of the church and many of its higher offices were now in the hands of Chinese Christians. The war, and the internment of most Protestant missionaries, had hastened a process which had been in action even before the war, since the great anti-foreign movement of 1927.

Wherever the Chinese Protestant Christians formed a compact and numerous community they were thus able to claim the benefit of the religious toleration proclaimed by the Communists, and were allowed to enjoy it. Where, in the deep country, the mission had made but slight progress, and was later closed by war, the Christian community tended to lose identity and its rights. Churches were closed or used for other purposes, mission stations taken over by local organs, when they had not been destroyed by Japanese or Chinese forces during the war.

The Catholics, however, under the general opposition to Communism which the Vatican had endorsed, tended to the support of the Nationalist cause. The leading members of the Chinese hierarchy were openly on the side of the Kuomintang. The foreign missionaries who, as among the Protestants, no longer occupied most of the highest posts, were also strongly anti-Communist, and although not great admirers of the Kuomintang, still felt that from the point of view of religion it was the cause to back. Not all foreign Catholics agreed with this attitude; many would have preferred neutrality, but the church as a whole came to be regarded as one of the few non-governmental organizations which supported the Kuomintang. This did it great harm in the years that followed.

The Communist victory in 1949 has now faced the two churches with a new situation, one which requires a wholly new approach. Communist policy has been made clear, at least in respect of the Protestants; and in respect of the Catholics it would appear to be also fairly plain. The two religions are not to receive the same treatment, this can be assumed from the fact that the policy announced by the new regime was specifically confined to the Protestant churches.

In June 1950 the leaders of the Chinese Protestant churches were summoned to a conference in Peking, called by the Government, to announce and discuss the policy of the regime towards these churches. Only Chinese Christian leaders were invited and no foreign missionaries attended. The meeting was held, in the Communist manner, at night, and the Premier and Foreign Minister, Chou En-lai, presided. Chou was very friendly to the delegates, and the conduct of the proceedings was intimate and informal.

The Communist leader began by saying that the Communist Party had come to recognize that the Protestant churches had contributed, by their social and educational services, to the well-being of the Chinese people. The party, he added, appreciated that fact and respected the churches for this work. It was work which they alone had undertaken, and which, limited though it necessarily was, was yet of great value and merit. Sooner or later, he said, the party would take over such social services, and as it would have behind it the resources and the power of the Chinese State, it would do these things on a larger scale, and better.

In the meantime, however, the State was not yet ready or able to do this work as it would wish to do it. Personnel had to be trained, the necessary finance provided; the reorganization of the economy was still far from complete, and the State had too many other pressing matters to deal with. When the State was ready to go into this field it would wish to do it on the grand scale, and would not want to make only a small beginning. Therefore the Government wished the Protestant churches to continue their social work, and if possible to expand it. They would do so with the full favour of the Government, and could rely on its support.

The Prime Minister then added, with a chuckle, that of course the party realized that the churches would not wish to confine themselves to social work only; they would desire, they would probably insist, on the right to continue their evangelistic work also. They wanted not only the right to worship God in their way, but to persuade others to do the same. Now, he said, the Communists regarded Christianity as a superstition; they considered the preaching and teaching of superstitious beliefs to the people to be wrong and reactionary. Yet unless the churches were to be allowed to continue such teaching, they would discontinue also their social work, which the party wished to see continue.

The Prime Minister smiled; and leaning forward intimately, said: 'So we are going to let you go on teaching, go on trying to convert the people; provided you also continue your social services. After all, we both believe that truth will prevail; we think your beliefs untrue and false, therefore if we are right, the people will reject them, and your church will decay. If you are right, then the people will believe you; but as we are sure that you are wrong, we are prepared for that risk.'

Then he added that this only applied to Chinese Christians; if the Chinese wished to follow this faith they might do so, but they must have no foreign aid. No further missionaries would be admitted to China; those who left, whether on retirement or on leave, would not be allowed to return. Those who remained, provided they obeyed the laws, could stay till they died or retired. Only such individuals, doctors or teachers, whose services are useful in those other capacities, not as missionaries, would in special cases be allowed to return, but not to undertake any evangelistic or religious duty.

The policy has been accepted by the Protestant Christian churches in China. They had no choice, or rather the only choice was between acceptance and closure. Thus the policy of China under the People's Republic has come back full circle to that of the Empire after the Jesuits failed. The Chinese may be a Christian if he wishes, but he must not have support or instruction from abroad. A somewhat later pronouncement, not so official, but emanating from the new Bureau of Religions, states that China will admit missionaries of foreign faiths on a strictly *pro rata* basis. So many foreign missionaries may come to China, if an equal number of Chinese missionaries are permitted to enter the land from which the foreigners come. What faith these Chinese missionaries would preach is not specified, but can easily be predicted. Nor is it likely that the Christian countries who formerly sent the missionaries to China will be willing to accept a quota of Chinese Communist propagandists in return.

Towards the Catholic Church no such explicit policy has been announced, but that restrictions still more severe will be imposed cannot be doubted. The Catholic missionary is equally for ever excluded in the future. Those who remain can stay, but in recent months there has been a trend to persecution which is clearly intended to eliminate the foreign Catholic missionary. Accusations of offences such as black marketing, ill treatment of children in orphanages, sabotage or espionage for the Americans or for other 'imperialist powers' have been lodged against Catholic priests and nuns; and these charges, always followed by convicuons, have resulted in a large number of expulsions. That the purpose of this campaign is to eliminate the foreign priest is clear. The Protestants, to avoid such troubles, and in the belief that the churches can and should stand on their own feet, have now decided to withdraw their missionaries. In a few years the missionary to China, so long an important figure and a prime source of knowledge of the country, will be a thing of the past.

In the opinion of many Chinese who are not Communists, this policy of cutting off the supply of missionaries has been undertaken in the firm belief that they were not only the source of Christian teaching, but the essential support of the churches. The Communists are said to believe that once the missionary has gone—within a few years at most all will have either gone or died at their posts—the Christian movement will wither away, like a plant whose root has been cut. The Communists, and many other Chinese also, think that Christianity will strike no permanent root in China by the activity of Chinese converts alone. They expect that the history of Nestorianism will be repeated, and that in a century or less, only some monuments will remain to attest the story of the Christian missions.

They may not be wholly right in this expectation; China is no longer, even under Communism, as isolated as the T'ang

Empire. There are perhaps larger numbers of Christians, about four million, than there ever were in that time, and even the proportion of the population, small though it is, may well be greater. Yet it would seem very probable that the Chinese church, living under a Communist Government, cut off from close contact with the Christians of the West, will undergo a considerable change in character. Chinese Christianity will become more Chinese, less Western, perhaps also less Christian. It will try to adapt itself to the Chinese environment, and under the revived orthodox and exclusive State, the Empire of Communism, this must mean conformity, and conformity to things very alien to the Christian tradition of the West.

The prospect for the Catholic church in China is darker yet. The leading Chinese members of the Catholic hierarchy, men who had made their support of the Kuomintang obvious and open, have left the country, and are either still with the Kuomintang remnant in Formosa, or abroad. The leading foreign bishops and priests are under direct persecution, which is intended to end in their expulsion. Whether the Vatican can replace them and the Chinese bishops by others acceptable to the Peking Government would seem improbable. Those acceptable to the Government would not be so to the Vatican; those whom the Vatican might wish to send would not be admitted by the Chinese Government. If this is what must happen, then the Chinese Catholics will be left, before long, either without bishops, or with such as the Peking Government may force upon them. In either case they will be brought under the firm control of the Communist regime, in circumstances dismaying to those who are now Christians and discouraging to all who might be inclined to baptism.

It can be said, as a certainty, that in the foreseeable future China will be on the whole hostile to Christianity, will admit it only on hard terms, and will try to isolate all Chinese Christians from the West. Christianity has not provided the inspiration for the Revolution, nor the spiritual force which moves masses of mankind. Once, under the T'ai P'ing leader, it might have done so; it would not have been the Christianity that Western Europe knew, nor that of Rome nor the Oriental churches. It would have been a new force, a new religion in fact, a heresy to the orthodox of the old forms, but perhaps the spiritual sustenance of a new and revived form of the Chinese monarchy and culture. That did not happen, and the initiative was never recaptured by foreign-taught Christianity. The missions did indeed exert great influence, but not in the way they hoped to do. They became object lessons in social service, in modern ways of living and hygiene, but their spiritual mission was on the whole, by the vast majority, unheeded.

The Communist Party has found its own new creed, and has provided the Chinese people with a new orthodoxy, a new vision of the Chinese World Empire, this time expanded to the scale of the globe, and with Marx as its prophet. From Christianity it has undoubtedly borrowed much, sometimes with no acknowledgment, sometimes with a nod of recognition such as Chou En-lai bestowed upon the Protestants. But the essence of the new orthodoxy, as of the old Confucian one, is that all must believe, and all must obey.

Confucian scholars tolerated Buddhism and Taoism because these were the religions of the people, and kept the people quiet. The Communists have claimed to be the people; to rule in their name, and to equate the scholar and the worker. There can be no toleration of 'superstition' because it is fit only for the people; that would be treason against the sovereign mass. Christianity cannot hope for the refuge which Buddhism found for so many centuries. Christianity is not a religion of recluses and mountain retreats; it is social and bound up with the community; therefore it must be a challenge to Communism.

CHAPTER SIX

REVOLUTION AND ORTHODOXY

'THOSE WHO DO not occupy the seats of authority should not concern themselves with the government.' This succinct expression of the non-democratic outlook is an old proverbial Chinese saying. It embodies the characteristic authoritarian point of view, the theory upon which the Confucian Empire was governed. The *chün tzu*, the 'aristocratic man', or as some translators have put it, the 'superior man', reserved to himself the functions of administration and the full exercise of political power. As servant of his prince, who in turned ruled by virtue of the Mandate of Heaven, the superior man was educated and trained to govern. No other occupation was worthy of his special talents, no other class was entitled to share his burden or participate in his privilege.

The Empire was overthrown by the republican revolution; the ideals of democracy were introduced to China, misused, abused and cast aside. The Communists triumphed in the civil war, and set up their regime. On that occasion they published a pamphlet giving relevant documents concerning the foundation of the Communist State, and among these, acting as a commentary upon the provisional constitution, is the speech which Mao Tse-tung delivered on the twenty-eighth anniversary of the Chinese Communist Party. Mao in his speech answers his opponents, first fairly stating the criticism which non-Communists made of his party and policy.

'You are autocratic' (say the critics). 'My dear gentlemen, you speak truth; we are indeed; . . . having been called upon to put into effect the authority of the People's Democracy, which is the dictatorship of People's Democracy, we shall deprive the reactionary party of the right to speak and only allow that right to the people.'*

* *The Chinese People's Republic. Documents upon the foundation of the State.* Speech of Mao Tse-tung on July 1, 1949: 'On the dictatorship of People's Democracy'.

143

Once more the superior man is in high honour, and once more his critics may not criticize, since they may not occupy the seats of authority. But the modern superior men are not Confucian scholars, they are 'the people'. This term, however, is neither vague nor all embracing. Those who are to have the right to speak and govern are very clearly defined. Mao Tse-tung does not allow his hearers to go away with any illusions, for orthodoxy is once more enthroned, and doctrine must be plainly proclaimed.

'Who are the people?' says Mao, and answers: 'In China, and in present circumstances, the people are the working class, the peasant class, the small capitalists and the national capitalists. These classes, under the leadership of the working class and the Communist Party, have united and risen to set up their own State, and chosen their own Government which will exercise authority, autocratic authority, even oppression, upon the running dogs of imperialism, the landlord class, the bureaucratic capitalists and the reactionary party of the Kuomintang which represents these classes. We shall not allow them to speak or act wildly; we shall keep them under strict control.'*

The comparison between the proverbial expression of the power and authority of the old Empire and the specific claims to similar authority made for the new Communist Republic reveals both the basic similarity of the two systems and their more superficial differences. The Empire was old, long established, universal (in Chinese eyes) and assured. It was not necessary to specify the nature of its enemies. It was the accepted government of the Chinese world. Opponents must either be barbarians who had not yet understood the benefits of civilization, such as the northern nomads, or criminals who sought to overthrow authority in order to enrich themselves. No 'class' of enemies was recognized because it was assumed that every honest and civilized person would naturally accept the rule of civilization, which was that of the emperor.

The Communists live in a wider world, and in a post-revolutionary age. They cannot yet assume that their system

* *op cit.*

144

and their regime will be accepted as inevitable, natural and right. They must still preach their doctrines, repress their enemies, and stigmatize them with opprobrious names so that all may know who are the enemies of the 'people'. But if allowance is made for these temporary expedients of propaganda, it is clear enough that to the Communists, as to the Confucians, there is one truth, one doctrine and one class. This truth alone may be published; this doctrine alone must be the basis of all instruction, and this class alone is entitled to govern.

The new doctrine is of course expressed in terminology which is alien to China. The words of Mao are the language which Stalin uses and which Lenin taught. The Chinese Communist leader recognizes and proclaims this fact. It is made very clear to all that Marxism is not Chinese, but universal, that Lenin is the prophet, and that Lenin was a Russian. The Russian Revolution is the starting-point of the new world, the message of Lenin and Marx came to enlighten the darkness of the Chinese and show them the way out of their troubles. Mao answers his critics who accuse him of inclining to the side of Russia, by openly proclaiming that he does so, must and will do so, because it is from Russia that Communism has come to China, and therefore Russia is the only true friend. Confucianism was a Chinese doctrine, evolved in China to fit Chinese conditions. Marxism is universal, with a strong Russian colouring, and it is not at first sight apparent that it will fit China or Chinese conditions.

When the dogmas of Marx are applied to China it is necessary to make some unadmitted compromises. 'In China and in present circumstances,' Mao is careful to say, and thus tacitly admits that in China and under present circumstances things are not what they were in Russia, or in Western Europe in the time of Marx. The working class, as understood by Europeans, is very small, and very little representative of the nation. So intellectuals, 'brain workers', must be admitted to be workers, and can claim the rights of the sacred working class. This enables the Communist Party to recruit students and literates, essential to the workings of government and to the spread of education and propaganda, but in fact very far from 'working class' in origin.

The peasants, who in Russia proved obdurate opponents of the Communist regime, are the real foundation and chief support of the Chinese Communist Party. So they, in alliance with the 'working class' which means in practice with the intellectuals, are to be among the elite. This again is strange Marxism. But 'in China, and under present circumstances', it is very good sense and wise policy. Still stranger, among the ingredients of the people, the all-wise and virtuous people, are small capitalists and even 'national capitalists'. It is true that these classes are not quite admitted to equality. They are not fit to occupy posts of real authority nor take direction of the Revolution. Mao explains why: these classes, though necessary at present because China's industrialization is still so slight and her economy so backward, are unfitted for executive power, because, rooted in their capitalist rank in society, they lack the qualities of courage, foresight and enterprise which only 'working class' Communists can possess. Then he makes a naïve admission: 'Moreover many of them fear the masses.' In other words they do not believe in Communism.

Here, too, one of the principal differences between the new orthodoxy and the old is revealed. The Confucian system was stabilized and admitted no need of change. It looked backward, in fact, rather than forward. The rule of the sage kings of the remote past was the ideal and all modern government at best an imitation of that ancient model, at worst a degeneration from it. The Communists on the contrary preach change. The present circumstances are but a passing phase. New democracy must be transformed into Socialism and then into Communism, and far off, in the future, lies the true golden age, the classless society, when the party itself and all the organs of the State must perish and give way to 'the higher form of human society'. It is this Messianic quality, this striving towards a distant goal, that mainly differentiates Communist totalitarianism from its Chinese predecessor, the Confucian Empire.

It may well be that therein lies the greatest contribution which contact with Western Europe has brought to China, the reversal of the ancient backward-looking philosophy, which made stability its aim, and the institution of an outlook which sees change as a good, and conceives its ideal as lying in the far-off future. It is certainly not the form which the Western teachers and missionaries expected to see triumph in China. Neither the religion nor the political system of the West could find a secure lodging-place in the Chinese mind, but the idea of progress, of advance towards a new society, thought of in terms of perfection, this very Western idea has taken root in China and become the inspiration of the new regime.

It is often argued in the West that the Communist doctrine of a future classless society, when the power of the State will wither away, is unreal, a mere form of words to cover the actual establishment of a police State. It is always possible that this doctrine, like that of the millennium which it so closely resembles, will be honoured in words and never realized in practice. But it would be probably as inaccurate to suppose that the Communists of the present age are insincere in their profession as to think that the early Christians did not really believe the second coming to be imminent. Whatever may be the present state of belief in Russia, it is obvious to any observer that in China the Communist doctrine has established itself as a religion, and that a great part of its success is the appeal which it makes to men of religious temperament.

The reasons why Communism, as interpreted by Mao Tse-tung, is more successful than was Christianity, even as interpreted by Hung Hsiu-ch'uan, the Heavenly King of the T'ai P'ings, are worth consideration. Under the Empire, in the old Chinese society, there was no institution which ministered to the psychological needs of those who are by nature inclined to rate future bliss more highly than present comfort. The Confucian ideology preached obedience to the ideal of the distant past; Buddhism promised Nirvana to the individual, but saw the world as 'illusion' and as evil. To the former society was degenerate, to the latter irremediable. The Chinese who saw the evils of society, hoped to cure them and planned for a brighter future for posterity got no encouragement from either of the prevailing ideologies. This gave Christianity its opportunity, but it failed because with the Christian doctrine went other things incompatible with Chinese traditions and habits of thought.

The educated classes in China had grown accustomed for many centuries to deride belief in the supernatural as unsophisticated and crude. They could not accept the Christian dogmas, and at the same time were disappointed at the Christian indifference to the world. The world for the Chinese has always mattered more than heaven. It has always been what to do about the government of mankind rather than what to do about the individual soul which has seemed to them important and urgent. To the very many and increasing numbers of Chinese who saw that the world was falling to pieces and that Confucian orthodoxy had no remedy for the catastrophe and no plan for the future, it became necessary to find a doctrine which should speak with the tone of authority and conviction that the Chinese expect from orthodoxy, which should prescribe positive measures for putting the world to rights, and which should not base itself and its claims upon supernatural sanctions and beliefs which the Chinese educated class could not share.

These conditions have been fulfilled by Mao Tse-tung's Communism. The new religion proclaims its own infallibility and the perverse wickedness of its opponents. It makes no pretence of democracy or free will, it does not permit any other view to share its power or dispute with its authority. It announces a programme, taking many years to achieve, which promises a steady improvement in the condition of human life, ending in a paradise: and this paradise will exist here on earth, not in some imagined heaven. This programme is not dependent on the favour of gods but on the efforts of men, and above all on the guidance of the elect, the Communist Party, the incarnation of the leadership of the working class, the most vital element in human society.

This doctrine seems unsatisfying to most Westerners. The ideal of an earthly paradise in the remote future, which will never be seen by those now living, but only enjoyed by posterity, seems unattractive to men who have been brought up to appreciate individualism and the value of the human personality. Many Europeans will not welcome the promised independence from divine protection, even if they could believe that God did not in fact inspire the universe. To most Europeans the suggestion that one group of citizens, because of the nature of their occupation, and irrespective of their moral qualities, are alone entitled to assume leadership and political power is a contradiction of historical experience and a most undesirable ideal. Whether the ruling group are to be workers or landed gentry, the West would not in modern times accept the concept of divine right, and regards any such doctrine as a reversion to more primitive forms of social organization.

It is therefore difficult for the West to believe that the Chinese people can have voluntarily accepted Communism. It is hard to credit the free support given to a regime which denies freedom to some and only hands out a very qualified form to others. And yet there is no real doubt that the new system has obtained the support of the people, has satisfied the aspiration of the literates, and has won to itself the devotion of the men of religious temperament. The Communists in China are dedicated men, selfless and sincere, blind to any criticism of their belief, narrow and devout, hard working, incorruptible and self-assured. They have learned a doctrine and understood its teaching; they practise its virtues, they have no conception that it can have defects. They are fanatics.

As understood in China the Communist doctrine makes the people sacred and sovereign. The people can do no wrong, the people are the source of all power and authority. The Communist Party is merely the agent. Just as the Emperor was the agent of heaven sent to rule the earth, so the Communist Party is the instrument by which the supreme people rule themselves. Heaven was a convenient symbol or fiction which authorized the actual autocracy of the Throne. The sovereignty of the people, a notion as intangible as the authority of heaven, equally serves to justify the retention of power by those who claim to rule on the people's behalf.

But towards those members of the people who can be seen and encountered the Communist must practise the virtues which his faith upholds. The people, and the individual member, must be treated with kindness and consideration. The Communist must not assume that because he is the appointed ruler he can treat the people like subjects. At least in the present phase of Communist power in China this distinction is valid and important. Over the whole nation the party exercises an autocracy as absolute and much more efficient than that of the Empire. Towards individual members of the people the Communist is kindly, courteous, helpful and indulgent. The fact that these virtues have been instilled into the troops, who not only pay for their requirements but have been trained to behave with exemplary discipline towards the people, is well known, and can be explained by the need to gain the support of the masses. The fact that examples of real kindness and sympathy can be observed when only individuals are concerned and no supervision by party members or officers is possible cannot be explained away.

No one who has observed the Chinese Communists in their daily treatment of the poor and simple peasantry will deny that a very different and wholly new spirit has been shown, a spirit which in other circumstances would be claimed as an example of Christian conduct and a product of Christian teaching. The corollary of the absolute faith in the doctrine of Marx and Mao Tse-tung is the actual practice of virtues which this faith commends. The religion of the Communists is not all one-sided; with belief goes performance, and the nature of the Communist good works is as closely related to the central doctrine of their faith as Christian charity is to the Sermon on the Mount.

When high-ranking Communist officers, driving by in their staff car, came upon a peasant whose cart had slipped off the embanked road into a ditch, they stopped, took off their coats, and pushed and pulled in the mud till they got the cart back on the road. When the policeman helps an old man to push his heavy barrow across the tram tracks and holds up the motor cars and trams till he has finished, these acts, which are praiseworthy in any country, have a deeper significance to those who perform them. They were helping a man of the people, proving to themselves and to him that they were good Communists, that their beliefs were real and that they lived up to them. To help the people is more than an act of kindness, it is almost a religious rite.

The party member is indeed the priest of the New Order. He expounds the doctrine which guides his own conduct; he lives a life apart, at the disposal of the party, maintained by them in austere poverty, at their orders to depart to some distant place at once, making no contacts beyond the party, entertaining no friends, renouncing all mundane ties. That is to say all ties beyond the party. Within that select order he may marry and relax. He may make merry and indulge his personal tastes. The Communist system in China imposes many restrictions on its members and demands many renunciations, but these restraints are not those which a Christian pastor or priest accepts, nor are they adopted for the same motives. It is not to discipline the individual soul and purify the character that the Communist renounces normal life, but to promote the ends of the party. This is a religion not of personal salvation but of collective improvement.

It has been assumed in the West that the promotion of virtue and the establishment of canons of right conduct were inseparable from belief in God and the practice of religion. It was thought that although atheists or free thinkers might behave with perfect morality this was because they still accepted the standards which Christian teaching had laid down, were in fact merely Christians who had renounced the beliefs but not the ethics of the faith. It is also often claimed that the virtues of the Communists, in Russia or elsewhere, are of the same order; that these virtues are really Christian or religious, and may be expected to decline when the generation which was formed in a Christian atmosphere has passed away. The Chinese Communist movement provides a test of this theory.

— It must first be observed that the influence and knowledge of Christianity in China was slight. It is not the case that the Chinese Communists are largely recruited from former Christian converts. For the most part they had no direct contact with Christian teaching. The leaders of the party were brought up in the Confucian tradition, and although they have renounced that doctrine as 'feudal' it is probably from that source that the secular character of Chinese Communist ethics derives. Confucian ethics were also divorced from belief in God and supernatural sanctions. Though traces of earlier beliefs remained imbedded in the classical literature, the Confucian scholar, since the Sung period, was in fact an agnostic. The Chinese literate class which as a whole 'believed nothing' as one of them put it, retained for several centuries a strict moral code inspired only by the ethical teaching of Confucius and his Sung interpreters.

Confucianism was not, however, a dynamic creed. It looked back in a half-antiquarian spirit to a supposed golden age in the distant past. It did not attempt to arouse enthusiasm, to inspire the mass. It was quite content to let the 'stupid people' worship any manner of god as and how they wished. The Communists being by definition the party of the people must make a religion which will satisfy the people, but which must be no more 'superstitious' than the ethical system which used to be the privilege of the scholars. The people have no reason to think that they were happy in the remote past, any more than today, so the new heaven must be cast into the future, to which all may strive, even if few will see it come to pass.

The gods must be overthrown, since they promised nothing in this life and the Communists are only concerned with this world, to them the only reality. The people must also be aroused, given purpose and hope, simple ideas and clear manifestations of the improvements which the Communists seek to bring about. This is achieved by making the mass, the indefinable innumerable people, into a God. The people are themselves God. They can do nothing wrong, because by their doing it it becomes necessarily right. They cannot be identified with any one or two fallible human beings; even the party, the chosen instrument, may make a mistake, may fail to do the will of the people. The fact that it has made a mistake is itself evidence that it has not done the will of the people, just as its triumph is evidence of the 'correctness' of its line. 'Correct', the word most on the lips of the Chinese Communists, means to them what 'righteous' meant to the Christian. To be correct is to be in line with reality, to do what is going to succeed, for what succeeds must be what the people want. Nothing against the will of the people can ultimately triumph.

The only limitation upon the power of the divine people is its own ignorance and the wicked machinations of the class enemies, who play the role of the devil in the new theology. The party, acting as the prophet of the people, must lead the nation towards the promised land, the triumph of Communism, and the ultimate heaven of the classless society. Just as Satan in the Christian theology is in the end powerless before God, a figure of tragic failure doomed to pursue an illusion which can never succeed, so, to the Communists, the capitalists, landlords or imperialists are fated only to enjoy their power for a space. Their end is certain; they may be troublesome now, but as their activities are noxious to the people they can never prevail. Happier than the Christian Satan, they are not immortal, and members of these accursed classes can be redeemed. This, indeed, is a very necessary article of faith, since Mao himself, many of his collaborators, and the prophet Lenin, were all born into that class of capitalists which Mao says has neither the courage nor the vision to lead the people.

Every dogmatic religion is open to philosophic criticism; the rise of Islam and the Reformation of the Christian Church appeared to opponents as senseless exhibitions of mistaken fanaticism; it may indeed be legitimately doubted whether these movements have made the peoples who followed them happier or wiser than they were before. Much suffering and destructive wars have been the usual consequence of every great spiritual upheaval, but when the centuries have passed it is always found that things are much as they were before, the human animal continues to behave with as much or as little wisdom, and the great surge of change breaks upon some distant shore, where conditions are so different to the homeland of the new movement that the inhabitants are not impelled to overthrow their own form of society. Islam failed to conquer Europe; Protestantism was rejected by the Latin countries. Communism finds scant support among the democratic nations of Anglo-Saxon culture.

The criticism of enemies is never listened to nor taken into account by the devout. The Moslems were not deterred by Christian comment upon their theology; the Puritans paid no heed to Catholic invective; both sides accused the other of every vice of authoritarian oppression, both sides persecuted those who did not accept their doctrine, to both sides their own was the 'free' world. If such critics are listened to the hearer must wonder why those of the opposite opinion, presumably sane men, can possibly accept and submit to doctrines described as an atrocious perversion of the values of human existence. But the credulous listener would get this same impression by accepting the criticism of either side.

When Chinese Communism is examined it is easy to see the characteristic defects of a dogmatic religion and a totalitarian system, but this in no way shakes the faith of the Chinese in their new regime, and in no way explains how it came to exercise its present authority over the minds of men. The political revolution which changed China from a monarchy to a republic and then from a Nationalist to a Communist authoritarian State was paralleled by a literary and cultural revolution which had an equally profound effect on thought. The military success of the Communists would have been in itself insufficient to secure the new regime had it not been accompanied by a conversion which has aligned the great majority of Chinese intellectuals behind the Communist movement. This has been the greatest triumph of Mao Tse-tung and his party, and assures to them a basis of support far stronger than that enjoyed by the Communist regimes of Eastern Europe, where political revolution was not associated with widespread intellectual support for Communist doctrine.

When the Empire fell it was inevitable that the old standards of literary criticism, the old style of literature itself, and the long-established traditions of historical and philosophic writing should be shaken and overthrown. In the early days of the republic the younger generation of Chinese scholars already realized that the educational system of the Empire and the prevailing literary fashion were inadequate and outmoded.

The Chinese language is written in an ideographic script, of great antiquity. This system has not all the disadvantages which are often ascribed to it, for although it involves a severe strain on the memory and takes much longer to learn than alphabetic scripts, it has two great merits. Firstly, being independent of sound, it is not affected by dialect differences, and can be equally intelligible to men who cannot speak the same language. The Chinese system, like the Arabic numerals, uses symbols which denote ideas, not words. '5' is not pronounced, or if sounded the word used differs in various languages, but '5' remains equally intelligible to French, Slav or English speakers. This system which is familiar to the West in the restricted field of numerals is used throughout the Chinese written language.

Secondly being independent of sound the Chinese script is largely independent of time. An ancient document, provided it is still legible, is no more difficult than a modern one, if written in the same style. The Chinese Dynastic Histories, written at periods between the first century B.C. and modern times, use the same style and are equally intelligible to an educated man. It is only when documents of high antiquity are in question that stylistic differences, archaic forms of the ideographs, and the obsolete use of some of these, require special study to be understood. Even so it is probable that a Chinese scholar finds less difficulty in reading the oracle bone inscription of the Shang period, fifteen hundred years before the Christian era, than a European scholar will find in reading the *Anglo-Saxon Chronicle* or a mediaeval charter.

Independence of time and independence of sound had the effect on Chinese style of rendering it extremely concise, lapidary and, to the uneducated, obscure. All that was needed was to convey the sense to the eye, the ear was not involved. The use of ancient phrases and expressions which no longer convey any meaning when spoken was common. As the Chinese spoken language is an old one it had long since shed almost all grammatical terminations, inflexions, parts of speech, tenses and genders, and become a monosyllabic speech with a high percentage of homophones, distinguished by tonal emphasis. In common speech it had long been the practice to combine two monosyllables of similar meaning to make the sense plain. Thus in colloquial speech one does not say 'chin' for gold, because many other words sounded 'chin' exist; 'huang chin'—yellow gold—is the colloquial term, which identifies the 'chin' in this phrase. But in writing it was not necessary to use two words; only the word of primary meaning was employed, and thus a page of the classical style read aloud became a wholly unintelligible string of homophones.

In the remote past, at the beginning of the Christian era, it is probable that the Chinese language still retained sufficient distinctions between the sound of words to be written nearly as it was spoken. The style which then came into general use, in the Han period, may have been as close to speech as literary English or French is today. Certainly many words then retained consonantal terminations which have vanished. The fate of the word Buddha, introduced into China with the religion in the third century A.D., is illuminating. It must be assumed that the early Buddhist missionaries taught the Chinese to say 'Buddha' as it is still sounded in the Indian and cognate languages. The Chinese have a habit of shortening any word which requires two sounds, and thus in transliteration two characters, to one, using the first only. 'Mei Kuo'—America—is commonly spoken and written with only the first word 'Mei'. So Buddha was shortened down to Bud. It would seem probable that the character still employed for the first syllable of Buddha was sounded something like Bud as late as the eighth century. Today this character is read in the standard Chinese dialect as 'Fo', and it is as Fo that Buddha is known to his Chinese followers. Yet this word Fo is nothing but the first syllable of Buddha changed by time and uncontrolled by an alphabetic script.

When such far-reaching changes in pronunciation are possible it is easy to understand that the original sound of the Chinese language has wholly disappeared; the style of the Han period, which may have been near to that speech, now no longer bears any close relation to spoken Chinese. But as that style is elegant, contained the gems of Chinese thought and literature, was perfectly intelligible by virtue of the ideographic script and thus never changed, it became and remained the usual medium for all literature, right up to the revolution of 1911. This meant that the educated man, who had not only been taught to read three thousand and more characters, but also to understand what was in fact a dead language, could read any literature, ancient or modern, Korean or Chinese, Annamite or even, usually, literary Japanese, with equal ease. The uneducated man, or the poor man with a slight knowledge of characters, or an imperfect education, could not read any literary work, could not understand one if read to him, and could at best use his slight knowledge to keep accounts or write simple letters.

The combination of an ideographic script and a dead literary language made education difficult, expensive and exclusive. It was an instrument perfectly designed to retain power in the hands of a special and limited class, the 'scholars' who when in office were known to the West as the mandarins. This situation was repugnant to the new generation of Chinese who had seen the West and appreciated its widespread literacy, its easy intellectual communication, and realized that these facilities were essential to democratic institutions. It was obvious that no system of popular education could be constructed on the basis of the literary style of old China. The number of ideographs which the child must learn, the obsolete usage of the old language, the complexities of its style, the use of obscure literary allusions which presuppose a wide reading, all these things make the old Chinese literature the preserve of scholars. Two reforms were essential; it was necessary to write Chinese as it is spoken, and it was necessary to find some means of simplifying the script.

Some extremists despaired of both; they urged the abandonment of the script and the adoption of the Roman alphabet. As this is often suggested it is worth examining the objections. The Chinese language is monosyllabic, and although in colloquial speech words are combined to simplify meaning, tone still plays a very important part in the differentiation of words of similar sound. The mere transcription of Chinese into Roman letters, as is done when teaching the language, cannot render a long or medium passage of Chinese intelligible. Certain modern romanizations do this better than those formerly in use, but are still inadequate to convey the meaning. If some elaborate alphabetic system were devised which took account of tones, it would still mean that only the one main dialect of Chinese would be available and that all other dialects, and all regions where tone values differ, would be forced to use what would be in fact a new language. Their plight would be no better than when the old literary language was in use.

There can be no doubt that the unity of the Chinese Empire and nation has been due in very large part to the use of a common written language which transcends all dialects and connects ancient and modern times. This unity would be very largely destroyed by the abolition of the ideographic script, and the whole corpus of ancient and recent literature would become a dead language, confined to the attention of specialists who would be as detached and small a group as the students of Egyptian hieroglyphs. When it is realized that some seventy to one hundred million Chinese speak the dialects of the south, which are mutually unintelligible and wholly so to the Mandarin speaker, it will be seen that the abolition of the script would make the Cantonese, Fukienese, Hakka and Amoy speakers into foreigners, and sever the cultural connection between them and the rest of the Chinese people, and between the various dialect speakers themselves.

The Chinese people, like the Japanese, to whom the Chinese script is much more of a hindrance, since it does not fit a polysyllabic language well, have shrunk from the sacrifices which such a change would imply. They sought, and found, other means of bringing their script and their literature into line with the requirements of modern popular education. Two movements neither of which were either political or officially inspired in origin arose independently to solve the problem. The Chinese Renaissance Movement, starting in Peking National University in the years 1919-21, was concerned to break down the classical tradition in literature and to make the use of the colloquial language acceptable and popular. The fact that there already existed a restricted literature in the colloquial, the great novels, was of great assistance to the movement. The novels, which had first appeared in the Ming Dynasty, about five hundred years before the Revolution, were developed from the precis of storytellers, and consequently retained the popular vernacular style which was used in these stories.

The novels were also, for the most part, rather subversive in tone, dealing with the extortion of officials, the wrongs of the common people and the intrigues of official families. For this reason also they were popular with the new generation, just as they had often been banned by the Imperial Government. This literature, immensely popular and universally known, written in the colloquial style and rather revolutionary in tone, was just what was needed to give a firm basis for the new movement. It could not be said that this movement was wholly foreign when it took as its model the novels of the Ming Dynasty. Yet it was also 'modern'—an essential quality for success at that time, because it was eagerly absorbing foreign influences and ideas. The combination of the revival and expansion of a native literary style hitherto despised and neglected with the latest influences from the West assured the Renaissance Movement of support and understanding.

This movement was started by two men whose subsequent

history has been very different. Hu Shih, later Ambassador to the United States and President of Peking National University, has withdrawn to America and become the leading Chinese intellectual of the anti-Communist exiles. Ch'en T'u-hsiu, his old colleague at Peking National University, and co-worker in the early days of the Renaissance Movement, became the first leader of the Chinese Communist Party and, later falling from grace, died in a Nationalist prison. Yet the fact that both trends in modern Chinese thought, the democratic and the totalitarian, combined to promote the literary revolution is significant. It was, as in politics, not the division between re-volutionaries and conservatives which counted, but the later division between Nationalist and Communist revolutionaries.

The Renaissance Movement, closely associated with modern Chinese literature, and divided later between the Communist and anti-Communist wings, could never be divorced from politics. It would in fact be true to say that political divisions and parties came from the literary world itself. The influence of Russian and Left Wing European writing on modern Chinese thought was profound. From the period following the First World War and particularly from 1920 onwards, when Russian Communist literature began to reach China in transla-tion, the whole significant trend in Chinese literature was to the Left. The ideas of the European Liberals were already cast aside long before the political scene reflected this change. Lu Hsun, the greatest of modern Chinese novelists, and now the idol of Communist writers, died in 1936 and most of his work was done in the years 1918-30, some time before the Com-munist Party had become a significant factor. Other novelists, who were not Communists and still would not be admitted as such, were deeply influenced by Marxist thought and Left Wing opinion. The new medium which made possible the use of dialogue and colloquial speech also made possible the novel of the people, which was directly concerned with the suffering and misery of the poor. Under these influences the Chinese cultural revolution moved rapidly to the Left and had become impregnated with Communist thought at a time when the

Communist Party was still struggling for survival in the guerrilla war.

This partial conversion of the intellectuals, particularly those of the younger generation, was a great source of strength to the Communist Party, and was stimulated by the Japanese occupation in the war years. The Japanese and their puppet Governments attempted to suppress all modern trends in literature and to revive the old culture, which they hoped would prove subservient to the Imperial traditions of Japan. The result was to drive many of the younger and most intelligent Chinese into flight to the Communist guerrilla areas, where they were received and welcomed. The anti-Imperialist emphasis of Communist ideology fitted in well with the patriotic resentment against Japan, and the still-active opposition to the encroachments of the Western powers. It became very difficult for a Chinese intellectual to defend the policies of the Right, which too often had been first ineffective, then subservient to Japan, and lastly identified with the decadence of the Kuomintang and the rise of American influence.

While the Renaissance Movement had been from the first the battleground of political theory, the second great modernizing force in the cultural revolution was quite untouched by political controversy. The mass education technique called the Thousand Character Mass Education Movement originated in France, among the Chinese coolies who served in the Labour Corps working behind the Allied lines during the war of 1914-18. The coolies were illiterate: farm boys and surplus peasant labour recruited from the North China countryside. They could not read letters if they received any, nor communicate with their relatives, nor find any recreation in their spare time. A small number of Chinese students had taken service with the Labour Corps as interpreters, and one of these, James Yen, was struck by the plight of the men. He undertook to teach them to read, was overwhelmed by the instant enormous response, and by the difficulty of teaching his pupils through the medium of the classical literary language and its large vocabulary.

The solution he devised, to limit the number of characters to those which corresponded to the actual vocabulary of the peasants themselves, and to leave aside all ideographs which were not included in this category, made possible mass education in China. The system is not unlike Basic English; Yen originally chose one thousand characters as the maximum which it was necessary to learn, this number being less than one-third of the vocabulary of the ordinary educated literate. Subsequently it has been proved that this figure can be reduced to 800. The movement which began so successfully in France was rapidly expanded in China in the years after the First World War. The educational authorities took it up, voluntary associations promoted it, and before many years had passed it was proved beyond question that with this technique and the complementary production of literature in the limited vocabulary literacy could be made universal without abandoning the Chinese script.

No opposition was made towards the programme of mass education. It was supported by all parties, and by men who disliked all the parties. It was useful to both sides, for it made possible mass propaganda. The first conspicuous example of the effect produced by the new movement was the anti-foreign agitation which followed the May 30 incident in Shanghai in 1925. The use of the new '1,000-character' press for rousing popular indignation and disseminating news, often very distorted news, had a great effect both in spreading the report of the incident and in stimulating national resentment.

The Communists certainly profited from this experience. They made the campaign against illiteracy in their areas a major part of their activity, and they used the new technique to create an army which was both literate and indoctrinated in the Communist ideology. The value of a method by which almost any man or woman as well as children can be quickly taught to read, and once literate can easily advance to a wider knowledge of ideographs, was seen to be immense. It had already, by the period of the outbreak of the war with Japan, had the effect of virtually eliminating illiteracy in the large cities. The war years probably caused a setback in these places, under Japanese occupation, but the guerrilla movement in the countryside for the first time brought large-scale educational programmes to the reach of the peasant masses.

The effect of the mass education movement would in any case have been revolutionary, even in a country where political and social conditions were more stable. The poverty of the peasant had been dumb, but now it could speak and claim a remedy. In a democratic country the result of a literacy campaign such as this would probably have been the rise of a new political party of the Left; in China it meant in practice a huge increase in strength for the Communists. The Nationalist dictatorship had little to say to the newly literate which was comforting or inspiring. The Communist message, expressed in simple language and clearly making a few easy points, struck home, and had already made a deep impression before the regime came to power. Now that only that message can be printed, and can be and is broadcast with all the resources of the State, the mass education movement becomes the chief instrument for the propagation of the new orthodox doctrine.

Under the Empire the scholars, trained in Confucian learning, and using a difficult and obscure written language, formed the élite class which governed and instructed. Their exclusive power was maintained largely through their monopoly of literacy and the arduous nature of the education needed to acquire knowledge of the written word. The State lacked both the means and the will to make education universal. Since education must be reserved for the few it was desirable that those few should all be brought up in the orthodox doctrine and taught to uphold it and the system which it expounded. The Communists have made the people the élite, and it is just as necessary for them to see that the people are indoctrinated with the new orthodoxy as it was for the Empire to maintain the exclusive Confucian training of the mandarins. Mass education makes such indoctrination possible, and the power of the new State makes it certain that all can be taught to read, and when literate will have nothing to read but literature provided by the party.

Mass education will not enable the people to read the Chinese classics, it will not enable them to read the literature of the 'capitalist imperialists' because such literature will not be translated and if it already exists will not be disseminated. They will read what the Communists decide is good for them. Since newly literate masses are always most susceptible to the truths which seem to come to them from books, and in China the ancient reverence for the written word is still widespread, it would seem certain that the next generation, literate, but only in Communist literature, will be brought up to believe that the Communist system is the only just and desirable form of society. Such echoes as reach them of the conditions of the outside world will be held to be as barbarous as the customs of the nomads seemed to the Confucian scholars. 'Creatures with the hearts of beasts', the term used in the histories for the Tartars, is not very different either in words or in meaning from the current phrases 'capitalist beast' or 'running dog of the imperialists'.

The new orthodoxy, the new religion, is thus fortified with a weapon more powerful than any in the armoury of the Empire. The Confucian doctrine succeeded for many centuries in keeping the Chinese people loyal to the system it upheld, and contemptuous of the ways of the barbarian. Then it was found that the barbarian had outstripped China in the arts of war and manufacture; the Confucian system failed to uphold the totalitarian Empire or retain the loyalty of the Chinese nation. The Communists, declaring themselves to be the true interpreters of the new foreign culture and at the same time the spiritual heirs of the old authoritarian Empire, hope to gain the support of the two main trends of Chinese thought: the desire for modernization and national strength, and the reverence for an orthodox, universal doctrine which embodies authority and co-ordinates the political, social and economic systems.

The consequences of the failure of the original republic and the Nationalist dictatorship have been to convince the mass of the Chinese people, and in particular of the educated, that modernization and national strength are impossible without authoritarian government; that imitation of the democratic West did not win the friendship of the West, but opened China to pernicious influences which sapped her power and exposed her to invasion. Mao Tse-tung, in the speech referred to above, makes a point which undoubtedly strikes home to most Chinese. Describing the movement of thought in the nineteenth century in China he says:

'Men wished to save the State, to save the State they sought to modernize, to modernize they studied foreign countries. At that time among the foreign countries only the Western capitalist States were progressive . . . in the view of the Chinese of that period Russia was a backward State, very few men thought of studying Russia. . . . Imperialist invasion destroyed the dreams of the Chinese who had studied the West. It was very odd, why should the teacher always invade the pupil? A large number of Chinese had studied the West, but it did not work, theories could never be put into practice, the condition of the country deteriorated every day, the environment restricted men until life became insupportable; doubt was born, grew greater, expanded. . . .'

Mao then goes on to claim that no solution was possible until the October Revolution in Russia came to point the way to China and the world.

In Chinese Communist writing the October Revolution in Russia becomes the equivalent of the Birth of Christ for the Christian. From that great event the world is changed, salvation becomes possible, the apostles of the Communist creed, Lenin, Stalin (and in Chinese eyes Mao Tse-tung) begin their evangel. The striking similarity between the Communist and the Christian outlook—the concepts of redemption, future bliss, struggle with evil, faith and charity are common to both —extends to the political sphere as well. Russia, the land of the Revolution, is the Holy Land of the Communist. The

Christian can now only visit the scenes of the earthly life of Christ, he cannot make close alliance with the original nation of Christians, for such a people never existed. The Kingdom of God is not of this world. But for the Chinese Communist it is very much of this world—could indeed be of no other. It is Russia; the land where Communism first triumphed.

Mao Tse-tung insists again and again in all his writings upon the sacred character of Russia and the inspired leadership of Lenin and Stalin. The necessity of close alliance with Russia is stressed. The victory of Communism in China would not have been possible without the October Revolution and the aid of Russia. The anti-Communists will find this admission damaging, but it should be noted that both in fact and in the claims of Mao Tse-tung the aid of the Russian Communist Party was not material, but ideological. 'We have fought our foreign enemies and those within and without the party. Thanks be to Marx, Engels, Lenin and Stalin. They gave us weapons, but these were not machine-guns, they were the principles of Marxism-Leninism.'

The secular religion of the Communists thus makes Russia the Holy Land; the classless society, the future paradise; the October Revolution, the starting-point of the world's redemption. International Communism is Christendom, the community of the true believers. Beyond lies the infidel world of sin. These are not all Chinese ideas; they are not really, either, perverted Christian ideas, but the product of the religious temperament geared to a secular and not to a supernatural creed. The Chinese Communists are sincere believers, almost mystics, and the party has attracted to itself the not very large proportion of Chinese who have this sort of temperament. The remainder of the nation, who do not share the faith, must be given something more in tune with their past and their traditions.

Communism bridges this gap by restoring the autocratic State, making the universal Empire of China into the universal empire of Communism, making Marxism the orthodox doctrine which governs all and instructs all. These are Chinese ideas, which can be fitted more or less into the Marxist philosophy. The combination works better now than it may do in the future. While the Communist empire is really, in the Far East, China's old zone of power, the empire of Chinese Communism, while the autocratic State governs well and satisfies the needs of the people, while the new orthodox doctrine does not require any course manifestly opposed to Chinese national character, the regime stands secure.

Yet even now it compromises; the Communism of China is not at all in practice the Communism of Eastern Europe. 'New Democracy' was evolved 'in China and in present circumstances'. Mao Tse-tung himself says as much, and Mao Tse-tung, alone of all the Communist leaders of the world who is not a Russian, stands secure among the prophets in his own right. 'Reconstruct China in accordance with the doctrines of Marx, Lenin and Mao Tse-tung.' This is the most common wall slogan in China today. Marx and Lenin are dead. Their teaching is now immutable. But Mao Tse-tung is alive, and a live prophet can still utter new truths.

CHAPTER SEVEN

'NEW DEMOCRACY'

'MAO TSE-TUNG's theory of the Chinese Revolution is a new development of Marxism-Leninism in the revolutions of the colonial and semi-colonial countries and especially in the Chinese Revolution. Mao Tse-tung's theory of the Chinese Revolution has significance not only for China and Asia, it is of universal significance for the world Communist movement. It is indeed a new contribution to the treasury of Marxism-Leninism. . . . To use the standpoint, viewpoint, and method of Marxism-Leninism to solve the problems of the Chinese Revolution scientifically, systematically and in a classic way and thereby also solve in general a series of concrete problems of the revolutions in colonial and semi-colonial countries—such a theory is Mao Tse-tung's theory of the Chinese Revolution. It is clear that this is a further development and enrichment of Marxism-Leninism and that this is a contribution of universal significance to the world Communist movement.' These words were used in a speech by Lu Ting-yi, member of the Central Committee of the Chinese Communist Party, on the occasion of the thirtieth anniversary of the founding of that party, June 25, 1951. The occasion was public, the speech given wide publicity. One must therefore assume that Mr Lu meant what he said and that this doctrine represents the views of the Chinese Communist Party and its leader himself.

Mao Tse-tung, alone of all the non-Russian Communists since the Russian Revolution, and in the select company of Marx, Engels, Lenin and Stalin only, is now to be numbered among the prophets, the rare and high beings who can enrich the 'treasury of Marxism-Leninism' and contribute further developments to that canon. Furthermore, the particular direction in which Mao's contribution is made is left in no doubt;

it is his theory—and practice—of the Chinese Revolution which contains the model for Asia and other colonial and semi-colonial areas—'the classic type of revolution in colonial and semi-colonial countries is the Chinese Revolution,' says Lu Ting-yi in the same speech. The Communists of Asia are then exhorted to study this classic model and the words of the master. It must therefore be assumed that Mao and China claim the direction of the revolution in these regions, since they are the originators of the classic model which others must follow.

Mao Tse-tung's theory of the Chinese Revolution, elaborated in several of his books and speeches, is best expressed in the term New Democracy, which must now on the strength of these claims be recognized as the special and peculiar contribution which has made him a prophet. The essence of this doctrine of New Democracy is precisely that in China and other 'semi-colonial' countries revolution in the Russian manner, in one swift all-embracing coup, is not possible, not even desirable. A semi-colonial country is one in which industry has not been developed, imperialism presses hardly upon the barely independent State, and the national capitalists themselves, oppressed and frustrated by the power of imperialist capitalism, cannot expand and have become at least in part revolutionary in the hope of shaking off foreign fetters. In fact China in the nineteenth and early twentieth century is the very type of the semi-colonial country. Not only Communist Chinese would agree.

Such being the case the working class, the paladins of Marx, are few, weak and unorganized. The peasants, whom the European Communists held in slight esteem, are numerous, poor, desperate and revolutionary. They are potentially the strongest force in the country. The small or petty capitalists, the Asiatic shopkeeper and small craftsman, are also an oppressed class, their ancient crafts and markets invaded by the ruthless power of foreign industry and mechanized factories. The national capitalists are hardly better off; a part of them, the despised compradors, may gain riches by helping the foreign capitalist to despoil the rest, but they are only running dogs, and as the ancient Chinese poet wrote, 'when the birds are slain the bow is laid aside; when the fleet deer are caught the hounds are cooked'.

New Democracy offers to all these classes the way out. Not 'workers of the world unite', but 'peasants, workers, petty and national capitalists unite'—under the leadership of the Communist Party—and carry out the first, the anti-imperialist revolution, which shall sweep away the power of the foreigner, the power of the comprador or bureaucratic capitalist, his lackey, and the power of the 'feudal' landlord, who is intimately bound up with the other two. The bureaucratic capitalist, also a Chinese phenomenon, is the official who controls the economy for his own profit, rigs the exchange, manipulates the market, establishes monopolies, seizes State property for his own use, in other words the Kuomintang. The feudal landlord is the same person, often enough, in his guise as investor, putting his gains into the land, buying out the farmer and rackrenting his tenants.

The first revolution, now 'classically' successful in China, replaces the rule of the feudal landlords, bureaucratic capitalists and their masters, the foreign capitalist-imperialists, by the Dictatorship of People's Democracy, which is the alliance of worker, peasant, petty capitalist, national capitalist under the leadership of the Communist Party. This is New Democracy. And as Mao explains in his booklet called *On the Dictatorship of the People's Democracy* it is not very democratic as the West understands the term. Towards the defeated class it is self-confessedly 'autocratic'.

It is also, of course, totalitarian. The stage of New Democracy may not yet be Socialism or Communism, but it already carries with it the essential blueprint of the future regime. Mao, in *New Democracy*, makes this quite clear:

'The problem is quite plain; we wish to eradicate the old Chinese culture; it is inseparable from the old Chinese Government and the old Chinese economic system. We intend to establish a new kind of Chinese national culture and this equally cannot be separated from the new kind of

Chinese Government and the new kind of Chinese economy.'

In this new kind of Government and economy many features of capitalism must survive for a time. The national and petty capitalists, shopkeepers and merchants, may still carry on their business, taxed but not confiscated, so long as it is in accordance with the national interest. The merchant who used in the chaotic days of the end of the Nationalist regime to import any merchandise which could be sold to someone, even if it were 'sun kist' oranges from California or scent from Paris, must now bring in goods which are of use to the 'people'—and to their Government. Merchants seeking to buy copper wire or machine tools, cotton or rubber, will be granted every facility to go abroad on their business. The shops still sell the necessities of daily life but the luxuries are frowned upon. The merchant of curios or antiques must also at least fill his shop with 'useful' goods—such as soap—behind which he may still keep a Ming vase or a Han bronze for unregenerate customers.

The period during which New Democracy must endure before ripening into Socialism or Communism—Mao uses the two terms as if there were no difference between them—is never laid down: but the conditions which are necessary before this change can come to pass, before the second stage of the Revolution is possible, are suggested. Firstly, China must become a strong industrial State from which all trace of dependence on foreign capitalism has been removed. The land reform must be complete, the workers must be educated and enlightened, the national territory fully recovered from foreign servitudes. Manifestly all this must take time. Even after the triumph of New Democracy many things remain to remind the nation of the past. China has no merchant marine and depends for her very coastal trade upon the ships of the capitalist imperialists, mostly British in this instance. Her heavy industry is almost confined to Manchuria and two or three other less developed centres. Much of this, too, was damaged in the wars.

171

Land reform, though progressing, confronts some difficulties in the newly liberated areas of the south where there was no working model to point the way as in the 'old' liberated areas of the north. The southern peasant had only vague and hearsay knowledge of what his northern cousin actually knew from close to hand experience. Land reform, under New Democracy, is not indeed a very revolutionary programme from the theoretical point of view. It is not a policy of collectivization, or even of total confiscation of landlord property. Taking a slogan of Dr Sun Yat-sen, the founder of the Kuomintang, as the text, the Communists insist that they are doing no more than was advocated by that statesman when he said 'Let the cultivator own his land.' Land is thus divided into farms regarded as adequate, depending on the region and crops grown, to support a peasant family. No one is allowed to retain more than this, but no one willing to work the land is denied title to that proportion of his former property. The landlord can 'redeem himself through work'—by becoming a peasant.

The redistributed land is granted to the new owners as freehold, a surprising concession from any Communist regime, but no doubt one which the Chinese Communists had learned was necessary to retain peasant support. In return, however, the party actively promotes the formation of co-operative movements and societies which are under party control and which, it would seem, are intended to guide and stimulate the production of the villages. The co-operative supplies better seed, better inplements, obtains a few good animals for the use of all the members, markets the village produce and advises upon which crops should best be sown. If the co-operative goes about this work intelligently it can very well so manage things that a village of private peasant proprietors is in fact producing in the same organized way as would be done by a large collective farm. In addition, the psychological satisfaction of owning land keeps up morale and prevents the indifference which would certainly be found among Chinese peasants working for a collective farm.

In nothing so much as the land policy of New Democracy is the hand of Mao Tse-tung and his followers more plainly evident and the theories of European Marxism least prominent. If this feature of New Democracy represents one of the ways in which Mao 'scientifically and systematically' applied Marxism-Leninism to the 'concrete problems of the Chinese Revo ution', it must be said that the solution is clever and sound, but is very little in accordance with previous Marxist practice or teaching, and would seem to be more a divergence than a new contribution.

It must be supposed that in that time, however distant, when New Democracy will give place to Communism, the land will be collectivized. Such at least would seem to be inevitable if Marxism is not to undergo an even greater development than Mao has already contributed. But if this is envisaged the Chinese Communist Party is very careful not to say so. No suggestion of future collectivization, no hint that the present freeholds are not perpetual, is ever allowed into print. It may safely be assumed that the present leaders, having lived with and among the peasants for twenty-five years, know what they are doing in this matter, and appreciate all the real difficulties which would meet any such policy.

The great and seemingly insoluble problem of the Chinese countryside is the pressure of population upon scanty means of subsistence. No marked decrease in China's enormous population has resulted from nearly half a century of war and turmoil. At best the population has not grown so fast as it would have done if times had been normal. Now the Communist regime has restored peace internally, has opened communications, has begun to teach elementary hygiene and to carry out the works of flood prevention and conservation which will save many thousands of lives when the next year of excessive or defective rain recurs. The party is committed to a programme of industrialization, which it is carrying forward with its great energy and organizing power, helped by the will of the educated class to whom modernization is the chief appeal of Communism.

In every other country in the world the first result of in-dustrialization is an enormous growth of population. Even in China, the great city of Shanghai, formerly a fishing port, has now six million people, all of whom live by industry. In Man-churia, too, local growth at such centres as Mukden and Anshan, the coal-mining centre, has followed the well-known pattern. Industrialization, if it can be brought about in China during the second half of this century, might bring China's population near to the level of one thousand millions. Even this would only be a doubling of the present population, and public hygiene, flood prevention and other improvements will cause an immense annual gain in numbers and thus a further natural increase. In the face of a problem in these dimensions merely dividing the already inadequate farms among those who now half live from them solves nothing.

Yet Chinese Communist literature seems determined to ignore this aspect of the internal problem. The troubles of the land are put down to feudal landlordism, its connections with foreign or native bureaucratic capitalism, and to nothing else. It is never suggested that there are too many of the people. Perhaps that would be too hard a saying in a State where the people are supposed to be the master. It is even suggested in conversation by Chinese Communist supporters that there is really no population problem at all; that it is all an exaggeration of the foreign capitalists trying to shift the blame for their op-pression of the Chinese people on to the backs of the people themselves. It is difficult to believe that the cool realists who have so successfully directed the Chinese Communist Party to victory can be thinking of their major problem in such terms of fantasy.

In other matters silence in the Communist world means always that policy is being secretly but urgently considered, and no word of the possible disputes and varying remedies put forward may be let out until the line has been established, the decision taken and orthodox doctrine is ready to be announced. It would seem very probable that this is now the situation in China. During the course of the civil war it would clearly have been false tactics to point out to some of the people on whom the party relied that they were superfluous. The help of all to fight and to die was needed. It is still needed, in Korea, perhaps in Indo-China. It would not do to start talking of over-population. But it is imperatively necessary to start thinking about it.

It may be that here lies a possible grave question between China and her fellow Communist partners. The Chinese can live with equal ease in any climate. Northern Chinese stand the rigour of a Polar climate as well as any race; Southern Chinese thrive in the tropics. Chinese of all parts seem to be very adaptable to great changes of climate. A solution which would be easy for China would be a constant flood of emigrants into Siberia in the north, into the islands and South-East Asia in the south. Such movements would be only a logical extension of those which have brought the Chinese into Manchuria, where formerly the nomads roamed, and into the south-western provinces where formerly wild tribes thinly occupied the country. China is a great colonizing power. The Communists, if they believe in the world Communist community, may see no reason why the process should be halted at the present frontiers of China, for between fellow Communist States frontiers should be unreal. Silence until this great question has been agreed upon with her neighbours would be fitting for the Chinese Communist Party.

Whether the Chinese Communists hope to solve the population problem by migration into these neighbouring regions, or by other means such as the promotion of birth control and the emancipation of the peasant women (the latter an important factor and one which the Communists do urgently further), it is certain that the pressure on the land must increase greatly for at least one more generation. The introduction of public health measures and better control of epidemics would in itself be sufficient to add millions to the population, and under any circumstances the Chinese population is certain to grow immensely during the next half century. It would seem that this fact alone will prove the greatest test and trial of Mao

Tse-tung's theory of the Chinese Revolution and of the regime constructed on that theory.

The problem is great, but it is often exaggerated by opponents of the Communist regime. Dire predictions of immediate famine when foreign food imports were cut off have not been realized even in a bad year such as 1949. The Communists have shown great skill, common sense and organizing ability in handling the distribution of the rice and grain crops. Instead of the old system of local supply and hoarding by landlords and corn factors the regime has tackled the question on a countrywide scale.

Shanghai, the great coastal centre of population, had lived since the war on imported rice. It was confidently predicted that Shanghai under the Communists would starve. The Communists, however, take the surplus rice of the great granary province of Szechuan, 1,400 miles west of Shanghai up the Yang Tze, and send this surplus straight down the river, with the current, to Shanghai. The local rice production of the Yang Tze delta goes to feed the other large cities of that district. The surpluses from Hunan in the south and Hupeh to the north of the Yang Tze, which formerly competed with the neighbouring province of Szechuan, are now sent by rail and tributary river south and north respectively to feed the huge populations of the Cantonese littoral and the deficiency areas of Shensi, Honan and Shansi. Manchurian food surplus, formerly exported, is more than sufficient to cover the extra needs of the North China region. A clever rationalization of the supplies and complete freedom to move them in accordance with actual need rather than commercial return makes it possible to feed the country on its own produce.

This system is not so modern, either, as it seems. It is in fact nothing but an up-to-date version of a very ancient Imperial Chinese economic programme, invented in the Han Dynasty by a statesman called Sang Hung-yang, and by him called the 'P'ing Chun' or 'equalizing' plan. The central idea, to institute Government control of rice and grain surpluses and transfer these from excess to deficiency provinces, so forestalling famine and preventing discontent, is entirely in line with the practice of the present regime, and is one more, and a striking instance, of the continuity between the totalitarian Empire and the New Democracy. The Communists, having the advantage of railways, and steam boats on the rivers, are able to carry out Sang's programme more efficiently than the Han statesman and his many later imitators could do. On the other hand, the Communists have to feed a population very many times greater than that of the Han Empire.

The peasant no longer pays rent to a landlord, or if his area has not yet been wholly land-reformed, he pays only a much reduced rent while waiting for the final liquidation of landlord rights. But he now pays taxes, sometimes steep taxes, instead. This fact has been eagerly seized upon by the critics and the opponents to prove to their own satisfaction that the peasant is no better off than before, perhaps worse off. The charge needs to be examined. Firstly it must be observed that in very many regions, if not in all, the peasant always did pay not only his rent but his landlord's tax as well. The tax was added to the rent. The military seized tax grain for years in advance. In some areas such as Szechuan taxes by 1942 had been collected up to the fifty-sixth year of the Republic—1967. To have half this burden, the rent, cut off, even if what is left is still large, can only be relief.

Secondly it may be observed that the issue is not between a system where no taxes are paid at all and one in which tax is collected. Alternative regimes to the New Democracy would not abolish taxation; no evidence on past showing can be produced to prove that the tax would be less under another form of government. Before it can be assumed that the Chinese peasant resents his present taxation to the point of wishing the end of the regime it must be shown that he has some reason to expect better conditions from a rival system. No such evidence exists, and the record of the Kuomintang is proof of the contrary thesis.

Thirdly the tax now collected goes to the national or local treasuries and is not embezzled in part or at all by the tax collectors. This may be only a secondary source of consolation to the taxpayer, but it is still an important psychological factor in making a high level of taxation acceptable to the public. It is not only under Communist Governments that the citizen grumbles about the weight of taxes, but in China it is only under the New Democracy that he has had reason to feel sure that his money was honestly used and reasonably well spent. It is natural that critics of the regime should fasten upon every instance of human nature's resentment against authority to proclaim it as an example of anti-Communist opposition, but if opposition to paying taxes is cited as evidence of discontent with a Communist regime, Communists can equally well point to reluctance to pay taxes by citizens of the democratic countries as proof of revolutionary fervour in those States.

The New Democracy plans, as Mao says, to build a new form of Chinese economy, a modern form, an industrialized State, with a Government which no longer limits its objectives to maintenance of the peace, collection of revenue and some major works of flood and river conservancy, but enters into the life of the citizen at every point, raises his standards and cares for his health, educates his children and shelters him against want. This ideal is shared by other modern Governments in greater or lesser degree. As is the case in other would-be welfare States, the first result of such a programme is the need for more and more money. The old Chinese economy and the old Chinese Government cared for none of these things. The citizen could look after his own health, the clan could care for their sick, the family could maintain their unemployed, the rich could educate their own children, and the poor could work or starve.

It can be argued that the numbers of the Chinese people, the poverty of the masses, the pressure on the land, the backwardness of the economy, make a programme of public welfare practically impossible of fulfilment. This argument certainly appeals to those who did not want any further development of the revolution, but it can hardly be addressed to a Communist Party, and it is not likely to make an appeal to the very large numbers of Chinese whom the revolution has made conscious of their own poverty and limited opportunities. These people will never now accept a return to the hopeless future against which they rose in arms. The New Democracy must therefore plan a programme of public welfare, and for that programme must raise large sums of money by taxation.

The peasant may not have found New Democracy to be heaven on earth, but it is very improbable that he now feels any desire to see the landlord and his 'dog leg'—his rent collector—return to the village. One may complain of the cold without wishing to be roasted alive. The merchant and the petty capitalist, also partners in New Democracy, have also experienced the weight of heavy taxation, and have not the comfort of having got rid of the landlord. These classes have therefore more to complain about. During the year 1949 and the early part of 1950 when the Government was using high taxation and forced purchase of victory bonds to deflate the economy and bring the ruinous inflation to an end these classes bore the brunt and suffered.

However, they in turn benefited more directly and more swiftly from the reforms which these stern measures inaugurated. Under the last years of the Kuomintang, and still, though more slowly, under the first year of the New Democracy, the Chinese currency suffered a fantastic, a nightmare, inflation. The 'Gold Yuan' introduced by the Kuomintang on August 19, 1948, when the old national currency had become without value, was at first exchanged in Peking against the US dollar at four to one. Five months later, when the city was surrendered to the Communists, this bogus currency, without backing or trust, had fallen to over a million to the US dollar, and no one wished to handle it. The new regime brought in its own paper money, which also swiftly, but at a less breakneck speed, declined in value. The merchant still kept his money in gold bars, US currency or silver dollars—all illegal currencies. The ending of this inflation, which had continued with mounting intensity from 1940 until the fall of the Nationalist Government, and was not finally brought under control until 1950, has been an immense benefit to merchants and business men.

The merchant class can also count among the benefits they have received in return for steep taxation the restoration of internal communications: railways, roads and river transport, which had been to a very large extent interrupted by the civil war. Foreign trade has undoubtedly declined, or been diverted to other countries, but the internal trade of China has been restored by the opening of long-closed lines of communication. Commerce may thus have found some real advantage in New Democracy, but industry, private industry, has many vulnerable aspects when in contact with Communist authority. The business man employs labour; he is therefore no longer free to hire and discharge as his circumstances suggest, for the trade union and the Government behind it has resolved that no man must be deprived of his job. The industrialist has thus had to carry a load of wages which are not justified by his sales or his income, and employ a large number of men for whom he has no work.

This situation, a form of unemployment relief directly thrust upon the employers themselves, has had its almost comical moments. A certain Chinese industrialist of Shanghai found that on the death of one of his workers, for whom he had no work, the dead man's younger brother claimed his 'job' and his wage. The employer refused to take him on. The claimant appealed to the union, who brought in the police. The employer was faced by these visitors with an accusation of sabotage, counter revolutionary thoughts and other imponderable charges.

He was, however, a member of that lively and ingenious race, the Shanghai Chinese, quickwitted, amusing and sly. He replied that while he denied any such charge, he accused, for his part, the claimant worker and the union of 'imperialism'. Shocked silence; imperialism, the worst of crimes, how could a worker, and a trade union, be guilty of that? How could he justify such an extravagant charge. 'Quite easily,' he replied. 'Tell me,' he said, 'when the Emperor died, without a son, did not his younger brother succeed to the Throne? Now this man's elder brother has died, and he claims his job by right. Is this not "The Emperor dies and the brother succeeds"? Is not that imperialism?' This ingenious argument nonplussed the authorities. An amicable discussion of the difficulty followed, and the industrialist satisfied them by giving an undertaking to employ the claimant when he had work for him to do.

The unemployment crisis in Shanghai, mainly caused by the Nationalist blockade of the port, was in time alleviated by re-organization of industry and the opening of new channels of supply. Shanghai's situation began, from the ending of the inflation in May 1950, gradually to improve. The Communist approach to the factory owner and to the large employer of labour was clearly marked by caution and distrust. It was felt that such people, being capitalists—even though national capitalists—must be watched, must be suspected of trying to play some smart trick, must be kept under very close control.

The manufacturer who was urged to open his closed factory was required to give figures showing the quantity of raw material he normally consumed in a month, the normal wage bill, the number of hands, the usual price he paid for his material and charged for his product and the normal margin of profit. The authorities then made their own calculations, and it was found that they allocated to the industrialist just enough raw material at a price just sufficiently low, and pre-scribed a selling price just sufficiently high to permit the factory to run, pay its wage bill and make a profit adequate to pay the directors a manager's salary. It was more worth while to open than to close the factory, but there was no possibility of making money or accumulating reserves. To those who inquired what would happen when large capital outlay was required for new machinery or repairs, the reply was usually made that if the owners should prove unable to run the factory, the State would have to take it over.

It might be thought that these national capitalists, under such a system, would rapidly disappear, or lose interest, and try to give up. Many perhaps have had this reaction, though few have been allowed to close their factories and withdraw their wealth. But among them, at least in some instances, another attitude has been shown. One such capitalist returning from his exile in Hong Kong, where he had fled before the Communists took Shanghai, put it this way. 'I am coming back,' he said, 'not because I expect that I shall be allowed to make a fortune out of my business, but because I am told that as I was not a hard employer the Communists have no complaint against me. I shall be able to make a living, my work interests me, and although my son will never be allowed to inherit the business, he is a good engineer and will always be acceptable as a technical expert. Under the late regime I tried to operate my business for more than twenty years. Sometimes I made big money; then all would be taken from me by some military figure, or some monopolist would be granted rights which destroyed my chance of profit. I never knew from year to year what would happen to me. Now I know; I can run the factory, more or less for the State, but making a secure livelihood, and that will go on until I die.'

It is certainly the case that the Chinese capitalist faced with the regulations and controls of New Democracy was not making as great a sacrifice of liberty and prosperity as would his foreign colleague if such a system were introduced into a country which has had the Western form of democratic government. As Mao Tse-tung has made plain, the position of the national capitalists in a semi-colonial country was in fact far less favourable than that of their rivals in developed and independent countries: when in addition they were under the corrupt rule of a Government of monopolists and military adventurers their situation was sufficiently precarious to make them largely indifferent to the terrors of Communist rule.

The Communist system of taxation which applies equally to Chinese and foreign capitalists is known as 'democratic assessment'. This system, so well suited to the present phase of Chinese economy, which lacks a large and well-trained Civil Service capable of fairly assessing taxation upon complicated industries, has to be worked by the taxpayers themselves. The authorities group together in one unit all firms engaged in similar business. These are then informed that the global figure for the tax to be levied on, say, the silk merchants, is X million. The firms themselves are then instructed to apportion the tax payable among themselves at a just proportion according to the degree of profit made by each firm, and to ensure that this is done they must at request make their books available to each other for inspection, while one firm must guarantee to the Government that his rival is paying his due tax—and reciprocally. The firm which is held in high repute is thus in honour bound to make a true return since its figures are guaranteed by a rival of equal standing. The firm of doubtful reputation will have to expose its books to the keen scrutiny of a rival before he will give any such guarantee. The Government, in either case, is sure to get its money.

This system has also been impartially applied to the foreign firms which still operate in China. Most of these are very large concerns who can survive hard times and who have something to offer China which cannot be obtained in any other way. The British shipping firms have continued to trade with the ports of Communist China, and since their services in bringing in and out goods cannot be replaced by ships controlled by the Chinese Government, they have been able to expand their business and to carry it on with at least as much return as in the days of the Nationalist Government. Better control of pilferage and more orderly conduct at the docks has greatly reduced the time and the money wasted on loading and discharging ships. The great import and export firms with their own shipping lines have adapted themselves to the new conditions of the China trade with as much skill as they formerly dealt with the Canton Hong in the time of the Manchu Empire.

The Communists, true totalitarians, prefer to deal with the big firm, rather than with a host of small men. This may seem inconsistent with the ideology and contrary to the invective so much employed against 'capitalist-imperialists', but here again, in China and under present circumstances, as Mao Tse-tung puts it, there is a need for business with these firms, and even the Communist Chinese still understand business. Towards the smaller firm, the foreigner who engaged in middleman business, the broker, the agent, the professional man, the attitude of New Democracy is more stern and less compromising. These men are not, in the eyes of the Chinese Communists, 'useful' and those foreigners who have the word 'useless' written across their residence permits will not long be allowed to remain.

The theory of New Democracy, or at least the practice, seems to imply that a stage of capitalism is a necessary evil, a kind of disease of childhood, through which every community must pass before reaching the maturity of Socialism or Communism. The capitalist is to be treated as a kind of dangerous beast, domesticated and trained under the whip of his keeper, the Communist Government. The future of such an animal when he has performed his allotted task is easily conjectured: 'when the fleet deer are caught the hounds are cooked' applies equally well to the capitalist under the new regime. But it would seem that this theory is a little too remote from actuality. The capitalist, after all, is not an unthinking animal pleased with today's fodder and careless of the future. If the Communists insist on making it all too plain that capitalists, whether national or petty, are simply being used to promote the rapid industrialization of the country and the quicker they do it the sooner will they be ready for liquidation, the capitalist, especially the Chinese merchant, who has already survived many troubles, will think again. It is not only workmen who can see the risk of working oneself out of a job.

This, indeed, would appear to be the characteristic weakness or vice of Chinese Communism: intellectual arrogance. The religious strain, the certainty of 'correctness', the undeviating belief in a dogma, the assumption that virtue is inherent in the working class and their Communist representatives, this new doctrine of the elect. All these things have appeared before in the world's history and all have carried with them the seeds of their own frustration. It would not seem probable that such weaknesses will lead to an early movement of opposition to the regime, but rather that, faced with very great problems in the future, the doctrinaire approach may hinder an objective consideration of solutions. During the period when the Communists were a minority opposition and the government of China was in other hands they showed great skill in diagnosing the evils of that society and devising ways of winning the support of the masses.

Now that they are themselves the Government, and have set up a new orthodox doctrine which must be accepted as the explanation for all problems and all policies, they can no longer so freely criticize the objective realities. Criticism must be cast into a Marxist-Leninist form; sociological studies which do not conform to that ideology must be ignored. It may be that the silence of the Communists on the most difficult of China's problems, that of population, is an example of intense study which will issue forth in a new comprehensive policy. It might also simply mean that this problem is not one which Marxist-Leninism has chosen to regard as important, because in Europe it was not important, and the original prophets of Communism had little knowledge of China.

Mao Tse-tung has indeed claimed—or others have claimed for him—the merit of contributing new truths to Marxism, and these truths are closely related to Chinese conditions and to Chinese circumstances which differ from those of Russia. Mao may, by virtue of his prestige and his real ability, be able to think original thoughts and incorporate them in the Marxist canon; but how many of his followers, or of his successors, will enjoy this privilege? It is not at all apparent that in the schools and the universities there is any trend towards academic freedom. On the whole the tendency is slowly to whittle away freedoms which were at first respected.

When the Communist regime came to power they found their warmest welcome in the universities, both from students and from faculty. The Nationalist regime had done its best to alienate the educated class. Stupid and brutal, though really ineffective, police persecution, the arrest and secret imprisonment of students on vague charges; their ill-treatment in gaol; the introduction of campus spies—bogus students who never passed an examination but were in fact police spies posing as students—all these things had completely disgusted and out-raged intellectual opinion. In the autumn of 1948 it would have been hard indeed to find one university student or one professor to defend the Nationalist regime.

The Communists at first profited by this situation and seemed anxious to prove themselves the very opposite of the late de-tested regime. The presidents of most of the universities, Government appointees, had either fled or been forced to leave the universities before the Communists arrived. The new Government waived its right to appoint new presidents and put the universities in charge of elected committees of the faculty, men who were not Communists at all, and who were freely chosen by their colleagues. The police spies were rooted out, the supervision ended, the persecutions ceased. The uni-versities breathed with relief and on all sides men and women, some of whom were not Communists, not even Chinese, but Christian Western teachers, declared that for the first time in their memory an atmosphere of freedom prevailed on the campus.

Very slowly the new order began to put out its strength. Marxism was suggested, and of course accepted, as a course in place of the political nationalism equally forced upon the uni-versities by the Nationalists. Russian was proposed as a com-pulsory subject, it was suggested that English need only be a voluntary one. The faculty of one great Chinese university accepted this suggestion, sagely reflecting that none of the students—or teachers—knew Russian, and that all of the students needed English to pass their examinations in other subjects and to study scientific textbooks. Voluntary English would not be less studied than compulsory English had been.

The professor of political science, who was a relative of one of the leading members of the Nationalist Government, found very soon that while he was in no way molested his students fell away. His courses were neglected. There was no point in studying democratic political science when in future only Marxism would count, only Communist political science would be a road to jobs and promotion. No pressure was put upon the students to change their course; they just yielded to the psychological force of the dominant ideology. Presently he felt out of it, useless and unwanted; he applied for a permit to leave the country, was easily and readily granted permission and departed with all his family.

The Communists were not going to make the mistake of persecuting university professors and proving themselves no better than the Kuomintang. But they were just as determined to oust any man whose ideas did not agree with theirs, and to see that gradually only doctrines and the interpretations they favoured were taught in the classrooms. Subsequently, professors of English have been told that many of the courses are now redundant; that there is really no job for them any longer, but that if they resign they will be offered Government employment—in intelligence work. There is really no alternative. Either you resign, and do nothing, or you resign and do what you are told to do. Academic freedom under these circumstances is clearly not at all what is meant by the term elsewhere. There is freedom for those who conform—freedom to conform. There is no other freedom.

It is certainly the academic group who most—perhaps who alone—feel the loss of these freedoms, which were at best but partially enjoyed before. The technician, the scientist, working on matters less debatable and less political are on the whole well satisfied. They find for the first time that their services are fully appreciated, ably employed and highly respected. Their word counts; their advice is accepted. No nepotism or corrupt practice hampers their work. Sticking to technical questions, shunning political overtones, they will be able to exercise influence and achieve the task of reconstruction and modernization. So long as they are allowed, as they are at present, to follow this path without interference they are quite ready to ignore any other aspect of the regime which they would not in their hearts approve.

In this field the advice of the Chinese expert has on more than one occasion been preferred against that of the Russian advisory corps. The Chinese advice, though given by men who were not Communists, was given on scientific or technical grounds, rigidly leaving all political aspects out of account. The advice of the Russians was perhaps not so objective. The Chinese Communist Party, at the highest level, preferred the strictly impartial views of its own technical men.

These are encouraging signs, not uncommon in China today. But today the great body of Chinese expert and scientific specialists is Western trained; men who for the most part went to American or to European universities after finishing their courses in the Chinese universities. They were not trained in a school of science which accepts Marxism-Leninism as the supreme directive. Their minds were formed in the free atmosphere which Western science and scholarship regards as essential to the discovery of truth. It cannot be assumed that in fifty or thirty years hence, when a large number of the Chinese scholars and specialists will either have been wholly trained under New Democracy, or else have completed their education in an Eastern European country, the same spirit of independence and scientific integrity will still prevail.

The question of how far the maintenance of this spirit of truly free inquiry is necessary to intellectual and to scientific progress is central to the conflict of Democracy and Communism. If it is true that under totalitarian direction and restraint the inventive faculty gradually withers, the inquiring mind withdraws, and the repetition of orthodox experiment and the elaboration of orthodox ideology engage the attention of men of letters and science, then it must be expected that within two to three generations the Communist countries will begin to fall back, to become out of date, to lose touch with the main stream of human thought and change. The Confucian Empire in China in the late eighteenth and early nineteenth centuries was a fine example of such a society, convinced of the perfection of its own ways, the soundness of its own interpretations, the value of its own culture, and equally convinced of the falsity, vanity and worthlessness of the 'barbarian' world outside.

The Communist Chinese will argue that this is not a true analogy; that the petrification of the Confucian Empire was the expression of its unsound class structure, its 'feudal' economy and its unenlightened masses. Once the masses have been aroused by the guiding light—the 'star of salvation' is Mao Tse-tung's own phrase—of Communism no such rigidity is possible. The Communist ideal is not one of stability but of change. New Democracy is but a stage towards Socialism—or Communism—and that in turn but a stage on the road to the classless society, beyond which it is not given to the present generation to predict what form the higher human society might take. It will be claimed that the present restrictions, the autocracy of People's Democracy, is the necessary armour against the enemy outside, the capitalist imperialist, the dislodged feudal bureaucratic capitalist, and the armed power of America and the American-protected Kuomintang remnant in Formosa.

It is indeed doubtful whether the comparison between an aged and decaying authoritarian Empire and a new, vigorous and still developing totalitarian system is valid. It may be that the Communist State will in time become what the Confucian Empire had, in a very long time, ultimately become. But it must be remembered that that Empire, which is now remembered by an elder generation in its last days of weakness, was for many centuries the most civilized, the most urbane and the most advanced of human communities. In the time of the T'ang or the Sung Dynasties, a thousand years ago, China, just as totalitarian, as orthodox and as authoritarian as she is today, led the world and achieved a civilization whose works of art and literature continue to delight and astonish.

The T'ang poets wrote under the shadow of a court as arbitrary and as self-assured as any politbureau. The Sung painters were the high officials of an authoritarian empire constantly preoccupied with the niceties of orthodox doctrine and persecuting the 'deviations' of their more original contemporaries. The personal history of the philosopher Chu Hsi, of the Sung period, is a tale of exile, police supervision and persecution, not very different from that of Trotsky. The Court of the Sung 'purged', in the most approved modern manner, those of its members whose policy was no longer in favour.

It cannot be said, on the evidence of past Chinese history, that a totalitarian regime cramps the genius of the Chinese people. They have never given greater proofs of genius than when under the most arbitrary and powerful governments. It is not the periods of weakness and division, when the Chinese Empire could not exercise its totalitarian claims, that are remembered as periods of great culture and high achievement. It is precisely under such emperors as Wu of the Han, the T'ang Empress Wu, the Sung autocrats, or Ming Hung Wu, that the Chinese achieved their greatest moments. All these were, by democratic standards, tyrants; all ruthlessly slew or liquidated anyone who opposed them, all employed the full power of the State to crush opposition, uphold orthodoxy and impose their absolute will. These were the great figures of the Chinese past; under their rule the poets sang, the painters worked and the philosophers wrote. Yet there was no trace of intellectual or any other liberty.

It would seem, perhaps, that the essential factor is not liberty or lack of liberty but the acceptability of the system to the men of intellect. If, like Western democrats, they feel that totalitarian restraint would be intolerable, would destroy their ability to produce genuine and worthy work, then they will not in fact be able to work well under such a regime. If, like the Chinese scholars of the older ages, and also of the present time, they do not question the absolute authority of the Government, nor dislike the domination of an orthodox doctrine, then they simply ignore these things and work as freely and as well as if they lived in a land of liberty.

It is plain enough that to the very large majority of the present generation of Chinese scholars, trained in the West though many of them were, the rise of totalitarian orthodoxy has not been intolerable. Most of them could have easily left the country, either before the Communists came to power, or after. They did not do so. They have in fact freely embraced the new doctrines and repudiated much of what they formerly professed. Very many have deliberately returned to China from safe and comfortable situations abroad, and have given as their reason their desire to participate in the new Chinese cultural life.

It is clear therefore that in China we are confronted with a new phenomenon, a totalitarian State of the Communist type which has come to power and retains authority with the backing and active support of very large numbers, probably the big majority, of the peasant, educated and professional classes. The small merchants do not feel any active resentment, the industrialists and large merchants accept the regime as better than they feared and hardly more inimical to their interests than the late Government. The loss of freedoms which were theoretically enjoyed by a very limited number of educated people, but which had no practical reality for the vast mass of the nation, has not greatly disturbed any section of society. The return to orthodox and authoritarian government fulfils the unexpressed desire of many, and does so, by using a modern form, in a way which is more acceptable to the educated than any outright return to some kind of monarchy could ever be.

The collapse of Western democratic influence and the rapid decrease in contacts with Western thought are regretted by a proportion of the educated, but probably almost welcomed by the mass of the people. The foreigner was never really a popular figure; the graces of Western civilization were known to few, the less attractive side was seen by many more in the port cities of China. The new hierarchy, the Communist Party, replaces the mandarin of the old Empire, and is, like his predecessor, not drawn from any stable class, but selected by an educational test. It is as possible for all, of any class, to enter the Communist Party, as it was for all, with the necessary education, to enter the imperial Civil Service. Class origin is not in China used to discriminate against persons who are sincerely desirous of joining the party. Among its members are scions of the Manchu Imperial family, and relatives of Nationalist politicians and warlord generals, in addition to real workers and peasants.

Whether this close society of the Communist Party, under a strict discipline, living a life of dedicated service to the party, cut off from normal social contacts, and deliberately dissociated from family and clan ties, will gradually become alien and out of touch with the people of China, must be a problem which the leaders have often to ponder. The need for such a body to run the revolution, to set up pure standards of administration, to remain aloof from the corruptions of Chinese society which had engulfed the Kuomintang, was so obvious and so imperative that it can be assumed that the revolution would not have succeeded without this system. Whether it must continue to be guided by so select and so abnormal an organization is not so sure. It might very well happen that the Communists would in time become as fanatical, as self-righteous and as much disliked as the extreme Puritans became in seventeenth-century England.

It might also be doubted whether, when to join the Communist Party means primarily to enter the governing élite, and no longer to endure the hardships and perils of guerrilla warfare, the quality of the membership will retain this high level. It was not only the foreign residents of Peking, but much more the Chinese themselves, who remarked upon the different appearance and manner of the Chinese and the Russian Communists of the advisory corps. A Chinese Communist, often young, gave an impression of confidence, intelligence, purpose and devotion. They had often a somewhat fanatical earnest demeanour, but they were clearly picked men and women trained and tempered by danger and discipline.

The Russians were without any expression at all. They appeared to have composed their faces into a mask of utter unresponsiveness. It was hard to tell what they were looking at, what they saw, and utterly impossible to guess what they might be thinking, if thinking at all. They seemed like stage characters acting the parts of automata. Many people asked themselves whether this difference was that between Communists of the revolution and Communists of thirty years later, or whether it was some racial characteristic. But in popular Western estimation it has been the Chinese, not the Russians, who are supposed to have an impassive appearance.

At present the Chinese Communist Party is recruited in very large measure from the educated class, the university students. Soldiers of peasant extraction educated by the army and indoctrinated during their service form the other main source of recruits. It is thus not really at all a party made up of members of the toiling masses. It could not be, because the peasants are still mainly illiterate, the workmen very little educated, and too few to supply the dominant element. The university students come from the classes which Mao Tse-tung has stigmatized as only in part reliable, and lacking in vision and courage, the former country squires or landlords, the city bourgeois and the old official families. The party has now created its own new universities and has made possible education at the older ones for many members of peasant extraction, and this leaven will in time alter the composition of the scholar class, but not for quite a long time. The present generation of recruits, taken into the party in very large numbers after 'liberation' are mainly university students, still very young. They will form the bulk of the Communist Party for another forty years.

This composition is no doubt one reason for keeping the party under such strict segregation and discipline. The membership could be easily integrated with just those elements in society which still covertly oppose the regime. The young Communist from a 'feudal' family is of course an idealist: a genuine and sincere convert. But it is just as well to keep him from mixing too much with his unregenerate relations and their friends. The new members from these mandarin families are, of course, ardent Communists, sincere believers in the New Democracy, servants of the people. They are also precisely the same group of people who have governed China for the last two thousand years. It is in their blood. They are born to rule, and whether by virtue of Confucius and the Emperor, or Marx and Mao Tse-tung, makes very little real difference. Deep rooted, not in any way destroyed by the Revolution, is the old Chinese conviction that government is an affair for the élite, for those who sit in the seats of authority, and that the qualification for such a seat is knowledge of the orthodox doctrine; not blood, nor wealth, but 'book perfume' is the real test.

The Chinese scholar class still rules, and still holds the same sort of basic philosophy of government as its grandfathers of the Empire. There is not so much a continuity of ideas as a continuity of temperament. The all-embracing doctrine, the universal society, are still dominant. The doctrine is Marxism-Leninism with the contributions of Mao Tse-tung, contributions which may well continue to 'enrich the treasury' of this canon. The universal society is now the Communist World Community, in which, little by little, the Chinese claim a larger share. The new patriotism, like the old, is not loyalty to a State, a kingdom of defined boundaries, but to a form of civilization, the only proper and sensible loyalty, which all Chinese of the past felt just as keenly as the Westerner felt patriotism for his national State.

New Democracy is not at all democratic; in some ways it is not even very new; but it is Chinese, the Chinese form of and contribution to the adaptation of Communism to Asia.

CHAPTER EIGHT

THE CHINESE REVOLUTION AND THE WESTERN POWERS

IT USED TO be said of the Chinese, by their Western critics, that 'this people yields nothing to reason and everything to force'. Two observations can be made on this saying; firstly, in the amoral field of international relations between sovereign States it would be difficult to find an example of one nation yielding any substantial portion of its power or sovereignty to reason. The European States have only to look at their own records and history to see that the aphorism applies equally to themselves. Secondly it is necessary to inquire what it was that the Chinese were expected to yield to reason. For unless it appears that these things were such as the Chinese might reasonably concede, the criticism is pointless.

The first Western nations to come into contact with the Chinese were the Portuguese, the Dutch and the English. The Portuguese came to the Eastern seas with ideas derived from their Iberian background, ideas formed by the intolerance of the long struggle with the Moors. To them the nations of the earth were divided between Catholics and infidels. Between Catholic States relations were based, in theory at least, on Christian morality and the feudal chivalric code. Between Catholic and infidel kingdoms they were based on force. No faith could be expected of the faithless and no oath towards them need be binding. Therefore the pagans of the Far East, though apparently less ferocious than the Moslems of the Near East, were no more entitled to fair dealing and Christian charity.

With these ideas in mind the early contacts of the Portuguese with China were unfortunate. The Chinese were not, as is often alleged, unaware of foreign nations and unfamiliar with overseas trade. They had received the visits of the Arab traders along their southern coast for over a thousand years. They themselves traded to the East Indies and Ceylon. There is nothing in Chinese history to suggest or confirm the view that these Arab traders were a source of disturbance or friction. The Arab trading communities in Canton, Ch'üan Chou and other southern ports were large, yet there is no record of any attempt to seize these cities or establish fortresses on the coast of China.

The Portuguese, from the very first, tried to do these things. They had successfully done so elsewhere, on the African coast, in India, the islands and in Brazil. They did not see any reason to change their policy in China. There were therefore armed affrays; the Portuguese were driven from one port after another, and finally only allowed to trade from the safe distance of the anchorage at Macao. The Chinese formed the opinion that these seafarers were of a different and more piratical type than the Arabs, and must be treated with care and severity. When the Dutch and English arrived things went no better. The Dutch were Protestant and considered themselves entitled to despoil the Portuguese and seize their bases. They did not behave along the Chinese coast with any marked improvement over their rivals, and Chinese history records tales of their plundering forays upon the coastal towns and island monasteries.

These early contacts left a deep and bad impression. The Chinese decided that the sea foreigners—Ocean Devils—as they were called, were a dangerous and unwelcome breed. They must be contained and confined to minimum contacts. Thus when the foreigner asked to be allowed to trade at all ports he was refused and kept to Canton; when he wished to send missionaries to teach the people Christianity, he was suspected of stirring up trouble and denied. These things were not yielded to reason because to the Chinese they were not reasonable. The proposal to station a diplomatic representative at the Chinese court, as was done in Europe, was to the Westerner very reasonable, but firmly rejected by the Chinese. They did not see this request as reasonable, but as impudent.

There was only one sovereign in the world: barbarian kings could and did send tribute- or gift-bearing missions, which were properly entertained and sent away with appropriate rewards and presents. No foreign king had ever sought to keep a mission permanently in Peking; thus the sea foreigners' request was not normal or reasonable, and probably concealed some further noxious design. The Arabs had traded with China for centuries without diplomatic missions, and if all the Western foreigners really wanted was trade, they too had no need of diplomatic representation.

It must, moreover, be doubted whether the European nations really were only interested in trade. The record of their dealings in Asia elsewhere gives rise to the belief that they traded where they were too weak to conquer, and conquered when trade had opened to them a sufficient opportunity. Such had been the story in India, in the islands, and was nearly the case in Japan, until the Japanese, becoming suspicious of the Spanish and Portuguese missionaries and their long-term designs, turned all foreigners out of the country and closed their ports to trade. The Chinese can be blamed for taking inadequate, and the wrong, precautions against the power and aggressions of the West, but not for seeing the danger of those intentions and suspecting the ultimate aim.

As the precautions were wrong, they failed to prevent the danger. The Chinese were successively forced to open their ports, admit the missionary, accept the diplomat, and then lose first their protected dependent kingdoms, next the control of their own ports, and finally to face the prospect of large-scale invasions and annexations. Indo-China, Burma, Hong Kong, Formosa and Korea were all either dependent kingdoms or integral portions of China one hundred and ten years ago. The Concessions in the treaty ports, the leased territories and the tariff privileges, extra-territorial rights and legation guards were all successively yielded by China to force. They were withheld from China by force, and by force they have for the most part been won back. In the history of Chinese relations with the West the consequences of weakness and strength, first on one side, then on the other, are conspicuous; the operations of reason and the validity of claims to rights and wrongs are not apparent.

The Western powers approached China at the end of the seventeenth century with considerable caution; the Empire was vast, it appeared to be also strong, well governed and rich. The early missionaries, themselves the subjects of Catholic Spain or Bourbon France, had no fault to find with its absolutism and its ignorance of democracy. Their only complaint was that it was not Christian. The traders thought they saw an opportunity of a vast expansion of their business; the lure of the Chinese market, that will-o'-the-wisp, had begun. The Chinese were not at all impressed by the foreigner, in so far as they took note of him. They did not cross the seas to see him at home, and thus formed no just idea of his real strength or civilization. They did not particularly require, or admire, the products of his industry, and they had no desire to embrace his strange religion. They could see little to be gained from contact with these remote peoples.

When the Emperor Ch'ien Lung rejected the British request for a permanent diplomatic mission in Peking he did so with the patient kindness of a superior being explaining something rather simple to a dull-witted yokel. It was useless, and would be embarrassing for the British king to send one of his officers to live in Peking. He would not understand the language, he would know nothing of Chinese etiquette and ceremony, he would be quite unfit for polite society. Ch'ien Lung tries to explain this in words which will not cut too deep; he clearly feels that an improper and foolish request has been made by one who does not appreciate the indelicacy of his conduct. As for trade and intercourse, the British king, 'living in the depths of the sea' at the ends of the earth, must see that such trade as went on was not important and not worth the notice of the Emperor. The Celestial Empire, moreover, produced all things necessary in the utmost abundance and had no need for the strange and curious products of faraway people.

The passage has often been quoted as a proof of the blindness and ignorance of the Chinese Government and the impossibility of dealing with them in normal ways. Since the Chinese would not understand reason, force must be used. Ch'ien Lung was certainly ignorant of the real power of Europe. His language sounded strangely in the ears of the polite aristocrats of the eighteenth century, yet it would be wrong to dismiss the Emperor as wholly ridiculous. Ch'ien Lung was a deeply learned man, a very good Confucian scholar, a student of history who made pointed and illuminating comments on his predecessors of the past. He was a good emperor, efficient, hard-working and courageous. He was in fact a good totalitarian. He understood that the Chinese Empire and its claims and doctrine were all of one piece. Invade those rights, relax those claims, and the whole fabric was endangered. He may have known enough of the king who lived in the depths of the sea and his admirals to realize that India had experienced more than mere trade ventures from England.

Moreover, the points he made were, in spite of the un-flattering language, valid. The foreign diplomat could not accommodate himself to Chinese court etiquette, which required, for example, that the envoy prostrate himself nine times—the kowtow—which no Western representative was prepared to do. The language difficulty was real, and continued to trouble the relations between China and the powers. The trade situation was, at his time, also as he described it. The British had in vain attempted to find a market for their manufactures in China. They had to pay silver for the Chinese products they sought to export; not until they discovered that opium, grown in India, could be sold to the Chinese and the habit encouraged did their trade balance improve.

Ch'ien Lung was really right, and the Chinese have always secretly thought so. The consequences of his successors yielding to force, where he would not yield to reason, proved him right. The result of unlimited foreign trade was the lop-sided development of such cities as Shanghai, the ruin of Chinese handicraft industry, the impoverishment of the peasant and consequent unrest, the invasion of new and subversive ideas, the situation which in the end brought the Chinese Empire to revolution. Ch'ien Lung may not have foreseen all this, but he can claim the credit of distrusting the consequences of foreign contacts.

The later Manchu Emperors gave way step by step, yielding to force, but never believed that they were doing the right thing, never trusted the foreigner and never believed in the ideals he was forcing upon them. During the Empire the Chinese foreign policy was called 'playing off one barbarian against another'. That is, using the jealousies of the various powers as a brake upon their aggressions. This policy was in the circumstances wise and clever; it does not deserve the censure which European writers have bestowed upon it, for unless it were founded on real dissensions it would not have been of any avail. There is no doubt that by the eighties of the last century the Chinese Empire was only saved from partition by this policy, which the foreigners were able to detect and describe, but too mutually hostile to counter.

Indo-China had been taken by France; Hong Kong by Britain. Russia had encroached in the far north of Manchuria—a territory which no Chinese then regarded as a real part of the Empire, but merely as a Manchu possession. Spheres of influence were marked out in which each power had the right to build railways to promote its occupation when the time for partition came. Britain claimed the vast Yang Tze Valley. The French pegged out their share in Yunnan and Kuangsi, provinces neighbouring their present possession of Indo-China. The Germans, late in the field, claimed Shantung. The Russians were to have Manchuria. The rest of North China might perhaps, with Peking, be left to the Chinese—unless Japan had to be bought off. The Italians, very late comers, tried to put in a claim for the maritime province of Fukien and demanded a lease of the harbour of San Tu Ao. The Chinese had the judgment and the courage to refuse.

This situation was not improved by the movement of furious xenophobia which swept North China under the name of the Boxer Rebellion. The Boxers were crushed; the court, which had turned their fury from itself against the foreigner, was punished by further servitudes. Troops were now stationed in Peking itself, where the Legation Quarter was fortified. These troops had also the right of garrison at all points between Peking and the sea at Shan Hai Kuan. Further Leased Territories were exacted in other parts of China, extensions of the Concessions, new Treaty Ports. Yet the Boxers did do something. They frightened the home Governments. Troops had had to be sent to China in 1900. The war had been not entirely a walkover. The prospect of widespread Boxer rebellions if spheres of influence were converted into colonies alarmed the home Governments. It was decided that a weak Chinese Government dominated by the powers was preferable to the risks of partition, especially as the allotment of territories seemed more likely to lead to quarrels among the powers themselves than to peaceful possession.

The Republic did not succeed, as was hoped by many Chinese, in recovering the lost rights by the voluntary surrender of the powers. The enthusiasm of the republicans for Western forms of government was partly due to the belief that by establishing these institutions China would automatically become a real member of the club, and would be treated as an equal. The special rights might be justified by the archaic character of the Manchu Government; but a republic was surely a modern State by definition; to retain extra-territorial rights and Concessions, Leased Territories and legation guards in the territory of a sovereign republic was unseemly.

The foreign powers did not agree. They saw that China was less orderly than under the Empire; that all reforms were on paper and none in practice. They talked of renouncing their rights when the Chinese Government had 'put its house in order', had 'modernized its administration', had in fact done those things which many another foreign State, suffering no such disadvantages, had never done or tried to do. Gradually the Chinese came to feel that these excuses were unreal; that power could only be regained by force.

The Nationalist movement of the late 'twenties was motivated mainly by the resentment all educated Chinese felt against the Western nations and Japan. Russia was now *persona grata* since the Revolution. The foreign policy of China became aggressive, directed to recovery of the lost rights and territories. Maps published by the Nationalist Government marked all the lost territories with notes showing how and when they were taken. No claim was abandoned, no cession really accepted as final. Here once again the differing conceptions of law which prevail in the West and in China made real under-standing with the West very difficult. To the Chinese all terri-tory which had once acknowledged the Empire as lord, all territory which had been part of China, was for ever Chinese. Its cession was a concession to force, without validity. The old idea of the universal Empire still influenced Chinese thinking; it was inadmissible that a territory once reclaimed for civiliza-tion should be abandoned to barbarians; such had been the viewpoint of the rulers of the Empire throughout the ages, and in the modern form of a national right to all territory once Chinese it still holds.

It was this strong inheritance from the past which prevented the Kuomintang from pursuing a realist foreign policy. The facts were plain enough. Japan was powerful and aggressive, aiming at the extension of her footholds in China, ultimately planning to conquer the whole country. The Japanese had con-vinced themselves that this was their 'manifest destiny', to succeed to the vacant throne of the Manchus. Against this real menace China should have used every artifice of diplomacy to supplement her military weakness. The policy of playing off one barbarian against another was more than ever necessary, and would have repaid far more than in the nineteenth century. For now all the Chinese had to do was to play off the West against Japan. The West was already beginning to fear that Japan had proved too apt a pupil. The Japanese conquest of China, or even of a large part of China, would have meant the end of the Western colonial position in the Far East; the West was equally menaced, but at one remove. Japan intended to conquer China first.

On the other hand the Chinese had now nothing serious to fear from the Western powers. The age of confident imperialism was over, killed by the First German War and the rise of Asiatic nationalism. It was plain to every thinking European that the West could not hope to retain its old domination in Asia for more than a few years; it was really only a question of whether these colonies and concessions would be conceded to Asians who had accepted Western standards of administration and law, or yielded to force wielded by peoples who had made no such reforms. The Boxers had halted the movement towards the partition of China; henceforward the West was prepared to defend what it had, but not willing to undertake new commitments. The Nationalist movement in 1925-27 threw the West on to the defensive; it became a question now of how much longer the privileges could be retained, and under what circumstances they should be given up.

This being so it was China's interest to sacrifice the lesser in order to defend the greater; to leave the Concessions alone and enlist the aid of the West to save Manchuria. The Concessions would have come back to China sooner or later, Manchuria once lost would be hard to recover. Yet the Kuomintang, sensing the weakness of the West, put constant pressure upon those nations to renounce their Concessions and rights, while towards Japan they followed a policy of appeasement. This policy was a double failure: Japan was not appeased, but her appetite whetted and her programme accelerated: the Western powers talked but would not act, they negotiated but never agreed. After the first wave of Nationalist advance in 1927 had obtained for China the British Concessions at Hankow and Kiukiang, and the abolition of the restriction upon her tariffs, no real gains were made by the Nationalist policy of recovery of sovereign rights. From 1927 until Japan struck in 1937 these questions, extra-territorial rights, Concessions, Leased Territories, the International Settlement in Shanghai, were constantly and fruitlessly debated.

The Western powers took their stand on law. If the Chinese legal system were modern and effective they would renounce extra-territoriality. If China could guarantee order and normal legal practices in Shanghai the Settlement could be given up. But they contended that these things were not yet true. A commission of inquiry into the situation in Shanghai was appointed as an outcome of the Washington Conference of 1921. The commission reported in 1926 that while in some minor matters, such as extra-Settlement Roads (roads built by the International Settlement in the suburbs of Shanghai, and in Chinese territory), the Chinese had some legal grievance, the main case for the maintenance of Settlement and extra-territorial rights could not be challenged. The report henceforward became for the foreigner in China a kind of charter of rights. It was quoted back to the Chinese whenever the issue was in dispute, and it satisfied the Westerners; for it was a legal production, the work of judges. The Chinese saw no such sanctity in legalism; to them the report was just a dodge adopted by the foreigner to baulk China of her just rights.

Seen in perspective the whole argument about law and rights, the foreigners' claims and the Chinese demands, seems unreal and beside the point. The Western nations were in any case only established in China because they had profited by the passing weakness of the old Empire to impose themselves and their trade outposts. They had no real strength, no abiding power in the Far East. Their homelands were immensely remote from China, the home populations very little interested in what happened in China. The moment some great strategic issue arose, some real national crisis, the West would leave its holdings in the Far East to their fate, to concentrate on the defence of vital regions. The moment that these nations were faced in the Far East by real power and open force, they would yield without argument their rights and their claims. Law would be forgotten. Had China concentrated not on diplomatic arguments but on the building of a strong army, she would have recovered her lost rights very quickly and without trouble. As it was the use of force was left to Japan, who soon drove a cart and horse through all the legalisms.

In 1931 the Japanese annexed Manchuria; the Kuomintang

protested, but made no armed resistance. They thought that armed resistance would be in vain, and Chiang did not wish to give up his war upon the Communists. Had China shown fight at this critical moment the West would have been placed in a most uncomfortable position. Open war would have meant a Japanese blockade of the coast and an end to Western trade with China. War might have meant the defeat of China, but it might also mean the ruin of the European trade and the fall of the Western bastions in the Far East. Victorious Japan would have made short work of the Concessions and other rights. The West, including America, would have made great efforts to avert such a war, or to end it if it began. America was by now willing to check Japan, and would have co-operated with the League of Nations to that end. But when China yielded to force, the West lost interest; if China would not fight, the European nations were certainly not going to interfere. Japan was strong, a useful ally who must be conciliated lest she become a dangerous enemy.

It was not only China who suffered the consequences. The Japanese had shown that force could win all, and law was of no avail to stop it. The next year, in 1932, they made the whole argument for the retention of the International Settlement at Shanghai ridiculous by using that Settlement, or rather the eastern half of it, as a base for a further attack upon China. This time the local Chinese forces did resist, they fought back, and fought well. They did not respect the border of the International Settlement any more than the Japanese had. The whole dispute about the Settlement was rendered meaningless. So were the claims of the foreigner to the protection of law, and his fear of coming under the arbitrary authority of Chinese military men. The Westerner soon found himself under the still more harsh authority of Japanese military commanders.

In 1938 the Japanese, then in control of Tientsin, imposed a blockade of the British Concession. All who entered were stripped and searched. Particular attention was paid to the foreigners, who were thus humiliated in the eyes of the Chinese people. Or so the Japanese hoped; actually, such conduct, by making the foreigner suffer in the same way as the Chinese, won them, for the first time for many years, some sympathy from the Chinese people.

The Japanese invasion of China in 1937 thus made a swift end to the whole Western structure of rights and privileges. Shanghai's Settlement was once again used as the Japanese base, and once again the Chinese fought well in its defence. In this struggle the foreigner, who had taken such pains to defend the Settlement against the prospect of Chinese attack in 1927, was now a powerless spectator, who saw his factories and his property in the eastern part of the Settlement bombarded by both sides. The Japanese as they conquered and advanced paid no attention to the extra-territorial rights of British and other Westerners. Business men were imprisoned, Concessions ignored, the legation guards, still in Peking, withdrawn lest they should clash with the occupying Japanese troops.

The main reasons for the supine attitude of the West in the face of these molestations were firstly the obvious fact that if Japan were to be restrained or challenged it could only be done at the risk of war. Secondly the prospect of war in Europe with resurgent Nazi Germany was now so imminent and so menacing that the Far East occupied but a very inferior place in the anxieties of the Western Governments. In the face of force in the Far East and danger in Europe the whole century-old fabric of Western imperialism in China went down like a house of cards. The Chinese, who had fought so well against the Japanese at Shanghai and in Shantung, could now see, too late, that if they had been the first to use this show of force they would have gained all as easily as had the Japanese. This lesson, though not of any use at that time, was not forgotten.

What the Japanese had done by force was later ratified by the Western powers, who gave up, by treaty in 1942, all that they no longer possessed in China: the International Settlement, the Concessions, the extra-territorial rights and the legation guards; Wei Hai Wei and Kuang Chou Wan, the British and French Leased Ports. Hong Kong alone was excluded from this general retreat. At that time none of these rights were operative and all of these territories were in Japanese hands.

The surrender of Japan thus opened a new, third phase in China's relations with the West. Almost all the old postulates were changed, almost all the old landmarks swept away. The post-war world in the Far East resembled the era of the Concessions and Treaty Ports no more than it resembled that of the Canton factories of the eighteenth century. Of the main participant powers, Italy and Germany were wholly eliminated. France was reduced to a tertiary role, Britain had receded to second place and America was dominant and supreme. The Chinese had recovered all the special privileges and Concessions. They had not recovered Hong Kong, but the British had given up Burma, also contiguous to China, and the French were fighting a losing battle to retain some hold over Indo-China. Formosa was occupied by China in expectation of its outright legal restoration when peace was imposed on Japan. All Japanese rights, outposts, conquests and concessions were abrogated.

Had China been united and ready for post-war reconstruction this would have been a fair prospect. Her enemies were either converted into friends or reduced to nullity. Even Russia, the enigma, was behaving in Manchuria with more restraint than could have been expected. The factories were indeed looted, but the Russians evacuated the country. Had the Chinese been of one mind as to who was to take it over, no hindrance to their doing so existed; the fatal division between the Nationalist and Communist parties ruined this opportunity, and at the very moment when the Nationalist aims were about to be achieved, they were overthrown from within by the social revolution.

The post-war scene in China was wholly dominated by the struggle between the Communists and the Kuomintang; consequently such foreign policy as the Government pursued was also conditioned by this conflict. The Western European nations played no part in the contest, and were in effect spectators only. America alone counted in China. The policy of the Nationalist Government was therefore to enlist American aid in the war against the Communists. In this, as is known, they were to a point successful, but only to a point. The American people refused to get too deeply involved; the American experts on the spot were very dubious about the wisdom or propriety of engaging in the Chinese civil war. Yet the fear of Communism, as an extension of Russian influence, and the strategic commitments in the Far East which America had acquired by conquering Japan, led the United States on into the Chinese swamp.

The Americans never really reconciled two divergent trends in their outlook, and thus in their policy. On the one hand tradition, anti-colonial sentiment and democratic feeling prompted them to rejoice at the fall of the European imperialism in the Far East. The Americans had no desire to restore Concessions, insist on special rights, or even to see their European allies become once more possessed of their former colonies. America was listless towards French aims in Indo-China, indifferent to the British intention to recover Hong Kong, which indeed was only accomplished by British initiative acting independently of the Allied Supreme Command in the Pacific. America would gladly have seen Asia independent, democratic—and capitalist.

On the other hand, almost without realizing what had happened, America had become an imperial power, and thus found herself accused of 'imperialism'. She had conquered Japan, and now ruled that country. She also occupied, on an even more indefinite tenure, the Liu Chiu isles which include the great air base of Okinawa. South Korea had come under her guidance; she controlled the former Japanese South Sea Islands. In actual terms of commitments America thus now became the heir of all the imperialists in the Far East; she took over Britain's sea power, Japan's empire and the leadership of the Western nations in China.

It is true that many of these commitments were supposed to be temporary, were mere wartime accidents; but such accidents are the real foundation of empires. It is not by cold and calculated aggression that the enduring empires have been built. They grew through a series of accidental acquisitions, through occupying places which could not well be left alone. So it had been with Britain in Asia, haphazard improvisations for the protection of this or that interest, the defence of some ally, or the suppression of some lawless regime.

The conquest of Japan imposed empire on America whether that suited American tradition or not. The occupation might be ended in the main islands of Japan, but the Japanese cannot then be left either unprotected or without guidance. They must receive American protection to preserve them from Russia; they must be under American guidance to keep them from making terms with Communist China. The bases which America retains in Japan after peace has been signed are in fact just as much the lynch-pins of empire as Hong Kong or Singapore. Whether the Japanese have nominal sovereignty or not is without significance. The Sultan of Bahrein is also the sovereign of that British base in the Persian Gulf. Moreover in the Liu Chiu Islands and the Pacific possessions or mandated islands of Japan, America is not ending her occupation. These territories must not be called colonies, but their real situation is in no way different from that of the old European colonies.

The logic of power also forced America into the Chinese Revolution. The defence of Japan against potential Russian attack, a danger which grew in the post-war years with the increasing tension between Russia and the West, has step by step compelled America to adopt the policies of defeated Japan. To secure her flank Japan has sought to dominate, and then to annex Korea. America occupied South Korea, tried to leave it, and has been brought back there to fight a long and hard war. Manchuria in Russian hands threatens Japan as much as China. To keep Russia out of Manchuria was long Japan's aim. It became America's purpose also. The Communists might hand over Manchuria to Russian control, so the Kuomintang must be assisted to recover that country. So, too, in North China, the Communists had to be opposed if possible, and the friendly Kuomintang assisted. This, too, the creation of a friendly regime in North China, had been the aim of the Japanese when they were responsible for ruling Japan.

The Japanese had no democratic traditions; they were un-inhibited in the game of power politics, and had no psycholo-gical obstacles to overcome upon the road to empire. America has not been able to face the fact of her empire, because empires were hateful to her in the past; she cannot admit the necessity for holding territories against the will of the inhabitants, because the idea of strategic bases was part of the imperialist complex which America was taught to abhor. She cannot accept that revolution can be Communist, and Communists sincere, because the revolution is a sacred word in American tradition and means the overthrow of imperialism, not social conflict. Consequently the real facts were not faced, the real causes not explained, and the real dangers not recognized.

Once America had become Japan she must follow Japanese policy, or devise another. She did not see the necessity. To follow the Japanese line it would have been necessary for America to undertake to conquer the Chinese Communists. If they won the civil war there would be a regime in control of China hostile to the power controlling Japan, and friendly to Russia. So such a regime must be prevented. This meant giving all aid to the Kuomintang. But the Kuomintang were a corrupt dictatorship, a thing hateful to Americans, and contrary to all their ideals. They could not bring themselves either to assist Chiang in an all-out war or to leave him to his fate unaided. Therefore he was beaten and America incurred the hostility of the Communists and the Chinese people.

There may have been no alternative, but it is at least worth while to consider what might have happened if the Americans had not fallen between the two stools of their democratic tradi-tions and the fact of their unadmitted empire. It was not pos-sible for Americans, on the morrow of victory, to adopt whole-heartedly the cold and ruthless imperialism which they had just overthrown; it might have been possible to follow a real anti-imperialist policy in the Far East, which would have accorded with American ideals, but not with the Japanese inheritance.

To do this it would have been necessary to leave the Chinese civil war to its own logical conclusion and in no way intervene or give aid to either side. The Communists would then have rapidly compelled Chiang Kai-shek to make a compromise coalition. That regime, although undoubtedly gradually moving to the Left, would have made no sudden break with the democratic world, would have been under the restraint of Chinese non-Communist opinion, and would have slowed up the tempo of revolution.

It would also have been necessary to bring the occupation of Japan to an early end, to make peace with the Japanese on terms similar to those imposed on Italy, and to have withdrawn from all bases acquired during the war on the western side of the Pacific. This would have confirmed the fall of the European domination in the Far East, and left those countries to face the possibility of Russian advance or internal Communist revolution without any prospect of aid from the West. For these reasons such a policy was rejected, if ever put forward, and finds few advocates.

On the other hand, by adopting neither the complete Japanese imperialist programme in the Far East, nor the democratic policy of non-intervention, America and the West have become involved in the evils which both policies imply. The peoples of Asia are in revolution, and revolution with a Communist direction. The colonies of the Western powers are under attack, and seething with internal disorder; the Western powers have been led into war on the mainland of Asia; war which can have no final end, unless, like the Japanese, they are led on to attempt the conquest of China.

The advance of Communism can be arrested only by open armed intervention, and then only if the intervention is on a massive scale. The European domination in the East has all but collapsed, and is now sustained only by clinging to America for support. Thus America has incurred all the odium attaching to these regimes, and lost all the good will which her former anti-colonial policy gained for her in Asia. America can thus neither advance nor retreat; to advance means open war with

China, and therefore before long with Russia too. To retreat would mean to abandon Japan, South Korea and Indo-China to speedy Communist control or guidance.

The fall of the Nationalist Government in 1949 once more entirely changed the relationship between China and the Western powers. In place of a weak and divided China, distracted by a long civil war, there has emerged within the last two years a strong unitary State, in complete military and civil control of every part of the mainland territory, with a powerful central Government, an honest administration, and a well-disciplined effective army. In fact the powers who used to claim that what they hoped to see was a 'strong, united and independent China' have been granted their wish—with a twist. For this strong and independent China which has suppressed disorder, abolished corruption, given peace to the country and stabilized the currency is a Communist China, which was not what any of the Western powers wished to see.

In place of the Nationalist regime, which bad though it was, and authoritarian in practice, still professed friendship for the West and claimed to be striving towards democracy—a fiction which all found it convenient to accept—there is now a totalitarian regime which does not profess any friendship for the 'capitalist imperialist' powers, has no hesitation in proclaiming its friendship for Russia, and despises the democratic practices of the West. China has chosen the Communist side in the world struggle, and therefore Russia's enemies are her opponents, America's foes are her friends. This development, although it logically followed from the victory of the Communist Party in the civil war, has yet taken the Western world by surprise.

The reaction of the West is not, however, uniform. To the majority opinion in America, and to many in other countries, the Chinese must now be treated as enemies, the allies, probably the satellite, of Russia. Aid and assistance should be given to the remnant of the Nationalists who still survive in Formosa. The faults of that regime, both past in China and present in Formosa, must be ignored, because it is at least anti-Communist. Chiang must be rearmed, his forces landed on the south coast and backed in a renewal of the civil war.

This programme is to adopt the policy of imperial Japan when all the cards the Japanese held are already lost. To suppose that a Chinese party which could not retain power when all was in its hand could now regain it with limited foreign support is to fly in the face of all history and indeed of common sense. It is certain that nothing could so well please the Chinese Communist leaders as to see Chiang's forces landed on the coast of China. In Formosa they can neither surrender nor be destroyed; on the mainland both surrender and rapid destruction would end the Nationalist Party for ever.

The British Government, the large majority of the British people, the European nations of the non-Communist West, and the newly independent Asiatic peoples such as India and Pakistan, do not accept the premises which dominate American thinking. It is felt in the European West and in non-Communist Asia that the identity of interest between Communist China and Russia is not necessarily everlasting, that in any case the mere fact of becoming Communist does not make a nation an enemy, and that whether the new regime is good or bad, friendly or hostile, it has come to stay.

The Kuomintang does not find any advocates in Europe where it was never very well liked; no European or Asiatic statesman would consider extending aid to Chiang Kai-shek, no European believes that his party will ever regain power. The peoples of the European nations who once had Concessions and rights in China are now very hesitant to interfere in that country again. They regard the phase of Western domination as past, and have no desire to embark on further adventures. All these nations would like to treat China as a neutral in the cold war, and induce America to leave the Chinese question alone, so that her aid to Europe shall not be diverted to Far Eastern activities.

In so far as they were still struggling to maintain position and prestige in China, the Western Europeans are now ready to acknowledge defeat and to resign all further pretensions to influence in that country. In so far as they hoped to see China remain among the non-Communist powers, they have abandoned all faith in the Kuomintang and rather look to some future disagreement between China and Russia. In fact the Europeans accept the Chinese revolution as final, the Americans do not.

The Asiatic countries go farther; to India, Pakistan, Burma and other nations recently become independent, and formerly under European government, the Chinese revolution is seen primarily as a great defeat for colonialism and a great liberation for Asia. They do not feel strongly on the issue between Communism and democracy, because to them the issue of independence against subjection is still vivid and dominant. They tend to divide the nations of Asia into the free and the subject, and to count Communist China as one of the leaders of the free. The antithesis between the free world of democracy and the totalitarian world of Communism, so stressed in American policy and thought, is largely unreal to Asiatics. These people not only accept the Chinese revolution, they secretly, almost openly, admire it.

In this situation it might be thought that the new Government of China could with ease and success adopt the Manchu foreign policy of playing off one barbarian against the other. The British recognized Peking, the Americans did not; what could be more simple than to welcome the British, who are now weak, and treat them with friendship and consideration. Such conduct would certainly antagonize large sections of American opinion, inflame disagreements on policy, drive a wedge of disunion between the partners of the democratic front. The Asiatic peoples could easily be brought into such a policy, their fear of American economic power played upon, their recognition of British wisdom in granting independence applauded and encouraged. If China were the satellite of Russia, only serving the interests of the Kremlin, this would be the policy which Russia should advocate, for by it the unity of the democracies would be impaired, and the case of the Left Wing European critics of America greatly strengthened.

China has now little to demand from Britain, who has recognized Peking, would have supported Peking's claim to the
UN seat of China, and would no doubt be prepared in time
to negotiate upon the future of Hong Kong. That colony's
future is in any case not in doubt in the long run. The territory
is composed of the main island and some smaller ones which
were ceded outright, and the new territory and leased territory
on the mainland, which are held by Britain on a lease expiring
in 1998. Without the mainland territory and the port installa-
tion of Kowloon, many of which are leased territory, Hong
Kong could not exist. Long before 1998 an agreement must
be negotiated, for no Chinese Government, Communist or
Nationalist, will ever renew the lease.

If it was apparently to China's interest to drive this wedge
of division between Britain and America, and certainly to
Russia's interest, why in fact did the Chinese Government
pursue a very different course, rebuffing British overtures,
repelling advances, treating the British as satellites of America,
and thus weakening the force of elements in Britain who were
ready to disagree with America on this issue. Peking's conduct has been puzzling to friends, gratifying to opponents,
and mystifying to many of the Chinese people themselves.

The Chinese Government, when refusing to implement the
British recognition by exchanging ambassadors and appointing
a Chinese diplomatic mission to proceed to London, alleged as
its reasons three grievances. Firstly that the British had failed
to support Communist China's candidature for the seat on UN
and had continued to accept the Nationalist representative as
the legal delegate of China. The issue had arisen a few days
after British recognition was announced, and it had been plain
that at that time no other member State except the Soviet
block would vote for Peking. Secondly the Peking Government complained that the British still had consular officers in
Formosa and thus had dealings with the Nationalist regime
there. Thirdly they alleged that Chinese aircraft in Hong Kong
had not been handed over to the Communist authorities, but

were retained in the British colony under pretext of legal decisions as to their ownership being still pending.

Not one of these reasons for so grave a step as the rebuff to friendly intercourse was adequate. The British in any case soon changed their line at Lake Success and repeatedly voted in favour of Peking's representation. The consuls in Formosa were occupying long-established posts, which had been open in the nineteenth century when the island was Chinese, had continued during the period of Japanese rule, and would no doubt be still maintained if the island passed under Chinese Communist control. Their presence no more gave support to the claims of the Kuomintang than the presence of the British consuls in Mukden and Peking had given support to the Communists when they took those cities from the Nationalists in 1948 and 1949. The aircraft in Hong Kong were claimed by an American concern which started legal proceedings to justify their ownership. The courts rejected their case, but it was then taken on appeal to a higher court. The law has its delays.

It must therefore be due to some other reason that the Chinese Communists adopted a policy which denied them considerable benefits. It must be remembered that if they had agreed to exchange diplomatic missions, not only would their ambassador have occupied the embassy in London, which is not to be despised as a listening post and centre for collecting information, but Chinese Communist consuls would have had to be admitted to Singapore, Penang, Kuala Lumpur and other Malayan towns, where the Malayan Communist rebellion was raging. That these officers would have given moral support at least, and material aid if possible, to the rebels cannot be doubted.

What is still more curious is that while denying themselves these advantages the Peking Government has conferred them upon the British. There is a British Embassy in Peking, complete with all its staff except the ambassador. The embassy has the usual cipher and bag privileges. There are consuls in all the main ports, Shanghai, Canton, Hankow and Tientsin. What profit China can reap from this one-sided intercourse to offset that which the British obtain is wholly obscure.

It has been suggested that in fact the Chinese Communists have gone back in this, as in other things, to the attitude of the Empire, the period of Ch'ien Lung. Once again a British envoy is denied the status which normal diplomatic intercourse requires. Once more exclusion and indifference to foreign contacts rule the minds of the masters of Peking. The British king 'dwelling in the depths of the sea' need not be treated with courtesy or permitted direct contact with the Government. This is an amusing idea, but hardly fits the facts. The Peking Government has exchanged ambassadors with India and Burma, and also with all the Communist countries. There is no suggestion of Manchu exclusion in their treatment of Russians, Czechs or Poles, nor of indifference to foreign affairs in their Press or their propaganda. On the contrary the international character of Communism, the brotherhood of Communist peoples is always stressed, even exaggerated.

The British, not being Communists, are of course excluded from the inner circle; but the Indian Government is more sharply opposed to Communism at home than is the British Government; the Government of Burma is actually at war with its own Communist insurgents. The fact that the British are capitalists, and were imperialists, should make their presence in China obnoxious, rather than exclude the Chinese diplomats from London and Malaya. No direct and wholly convincing answer to this riddle can be given, but one may try to consider the problem from the peculiar angle of Chinese Communist thought.

In the eyes of the Chinese Communists, America is their sworn and implacable enemy; the capitalist imperialists can never approach a Communist State with truth or good will; they must always be enemies, because they represent the class conflict, and that is based on unchanging material factors, wealth and poverty, exploitation and slavery. Britain is the ally, in their eyes the client, of America. Britain will always in the end respond to American pressure, yield to American insistence, and forget her own objections, because being also a capitalist society her real interests, or the interests of her governing class, are in the end identical with those of their American colleagues. British recognition was thus either a trick, by which America hoped to use the British for their business in China, or else a British independent initiative which America permitted, but which she might at any time repress.

There was another reason: the recognition by Britain was welcome to many Chinese of all classes, who were glad to see that one of the foreign powers had accepted the revolution, and were also glad to see that China was not by reason of having a Communist regime to be cut off from all intercourse with the West. These sentiments were not in accordance with the ideas of the Chinese Communists. They considered that the desire to have the favour of the powers was a bad mental habit dating from the weakness of the Republic; that the hope of continued normal intercourse with the West was evidence of reactionary ideas, and lukewarm acceptance of the revolution. No; the Chinese people must be taught that the West was no longer to be regarded with affection or respect. Britain only recognized China because she hoped to save her trade; capitalists are only swayed by monetary considerations, indeed all mankind are only moved by economic motives, and those of capitalists are necessarily inimical to proletarians.

By permitting the British to appear in Peking, but disdaining to send Chinese to London, the Communists hoped to prove to their people how strong they were; how little they cared for the favour of those powers whom the Republic and the late Empire had courted. In time, when the lesson was well learned, and the regime and its ideas more firmly established, then it would be useful to have a mission in London; but the sacrifice of this convenience was well worth the moral reward in prestige at home.

It may well be that they no longer think so; there is no reason to believe the Chinese Communist leadership, able though it is, infallible. But it is hard to see how the interests of Russia could be served by the rudeness and exclusive policy of the Peking Government. It has been suggested that this refusal to complete the exchange of missions with Britain was made

on Russian insistence; that Russia does not want the Chinese
Communists to have too many contacts abroad, to meet foreign
statesmen in friendly ways, and get to know the real sentiments of the West. If that is so it would have been best to
forbid the Chinese to accept any recognition, to prevent the
exchange of ambassadors with India, and to close Hong Kong
to all contact with China. It is certainly hard to believe that
these alleged Russian fears outweighed the advantage to the
Communist cause of having Chinese Communist consuls in
Malaya.

The truth would seem rather to be that the Chinese Communists have fully realized the fact that it is not the Western
European nations who now matter to them in the Far East.
The contest is between America and Communist China and
Soviet Russia. Those moves which serve to check America
are worth while, those which would merely serve to soothe
the feelings of the West or satisfy some section of Chinese
opinion are not worth consideration. The Chinese Communists
are insistent that every act of the State shall redound to its
credit and enhance its prestige; they have the totalitarian outlook of the Empire and of Communism combined. No move
which suggests compromise, no softening towards the enemy
until he has first acknowledged weakness, must be allowed.
When the British had been kept waiting long enough, and
had voted often enough for Peking's admission to UN, China
would have sent her ambassador. Then came the Korean War.

The invasion of South Korea by the North Korean Communist army was not an event which served any Chinese interest, and it has therefore been generally accepted in the West
as a Russian inspired move. The Chinese Communists had had
little to do with North Korea. That satellite State had been
created by the Russians when Japan surrendered; it came into
existence *de facto* long before the Chinese Communists came
to power in China, and some time before they were in control
of all the neighbouring part of Manchuria. Korean exiles who
had fought with the Communists against Japan returned to
North Korea, just as Korean exiles who had fought with the

Nationalists or Americans returned to South Korea. The existence of a Communist regime in North Korea, the region which adjoins the most important industrial area in Manchuria, and therefore in China as a whole, was very satisfactory to the Chinese Communist Government. That friendly regime in North Korea ensured the necessary co-operation in maintaining the electric power stations and their dams, which, built by the Japanese, serve both North Korea and the adjacent region of Manchuria.

The Chinese were thus interested in the protection and existence of the North Korean State: the fate of South Korea was unimportant as a strategic question to China, but engaged their sympathy with North Korean aspirations on the ideological plane. When North Korea invaded the south, alleging a previous South Korean infringement of the 38th Parallel, Peking supported this claim, which the West had rejected as a fiction, and gave verbal encouragement to North Korea. No Chinese armed support was given, and the Peking Propaganda Department was not prepared for the invasion, and did not get its directives for nearly twenty-four hours. This fact does not exclude the possibility that the leaders of Communist China were privy to the intended invasion; but it suggests that if this was so they were only informed at a very late hour, and that the information was not passed to the second rank of the hierarchy, who prepare the news for the Press. The disarray of the Chinese Communist Press during the first twenty-four hours of the Korean War is an interesting and suggestive fact.

President Truman, meanwhile, had issued his declaration urging the United Nations to rally to the support of the victim of aggression; he also coupled this appeal with a unilateral declaration, for which United Nations support was neither asked, nor given, neutralizing the island of Formosa and the Pescadores group from any Communist Chinese attack, 'for the duration of hostilities in Korea'. The President thus assumed Chinese Communist complicity in the North Korean invasion, and took the first step which actually involved China in that quarrel.

Coming as the culmination of steadily deteriorating relations between the Peking Government and the United States this declaration on Formosa cannot be regarded as surprising. It nevertheless marks a very important stage in the development of Communist China's relations with America, and the other Western powers. America had aided Chiang during the civil war, by supplying arms, aircraft and petroleum, and by sending missions to train the Kuomintang forces. American troops had not, then or later, intervened in the actual fighting between the rival Chinese armies. The American Navy had evacuated its base at Tsing Tao when the Communist forces advanced on that port. Between material aid and armed intervention there is a very wide gap, a gap as wide as that which separated American aid to the Allied powers prior to Pearl Harbour, and American participation in the war after that event.

The neutralization of Formosa, followed by military consultations in that island between General MacArthur, then the United Nations Commander-in-Chief, and Chiang Kai-shek, the subsequent considerable military aid supplied to the Nationalists in Formosa prior to Chinese participation in the Korean War, all these things unquestionably constitute overt intervention in the Chinese civil war. Formosa was the last stronghold of the Nationalist Party; in the opinion of military observers it would not have resisted a well-prepared Chinese Communist attack. All Chinese regard the island as a part of China's national territory, and therefore as a legitimate prize for whichever side in the civil war can hold or take it.

The Chinese Communists and the Russian bloc subsequently accused the United States of aggression on China for this act of intervention. As the United Nations and the United States still recognized the Nationalist regime in Formosa as the Government of the Republic of China it was held that no charge of aggression upon a sovereign State could be sustained. This is another example of the legalism which Chinese do not understand or admire.

The Formosa question has thus become, far more than the

Korean War, the real bone of contention. The Korean War can be—has been—brought to an end by the mutual renunciation of hopes of conquering the part of the country held by the other side. North and South Korea after a year of war continued to exist, ruined, but within much the same boundaries. Aggression has been repelled, the Chinese security zone in North Korea preserved. While unsatisfactory to both sides, this compromise at least affords a way for both to withdraw from a contest which had ceased to be profitable to either. But the question of Formosa remains, and will remain, to poison relations between China and the West, and to disturb those between America and her Western allies.

So long as Chiang Kai-shek, with American recognition and massive financial and material support, remains in possession of the island and rules over its eight million inhabitants, there can be no final peace for China. The possibility, the oft suggested threat, of landing the Kuomintang army re-equipped with American arms, on the coast of China cannot be discounted. If it were to happen, it is very probable that the Nationalist army would be swiftly routed and compelled to surrender. No evidence has been produced to show any sign of real support for a restoration of the Kuomintang, or the possibility of defection by any army of the Peking People's Republic. Chiang has five hundred thousand men, and at least one-third would have to remain in Formosa to guard against a rising by his dissatisfied Formosan subjects.

If he could, with US aid, transport two hundred thousand men to the Chinese coast—and without US participation and shipping he could never do any such thing—he would be faced by armed forces at least ten times the size of his own. He would have no base, no supplies other than those brought from Formosa; he would be invading a hostile land. Where the Japanese failed after eight years, although they already had bases in China, it is hardly likely that the discredited Chiang would succeed.

But it is always possible to make raids on a coast line, to land small forces, and attack coastal shipping. If American protection of Chiang were to mean the continuation of such futilities, without prospect of an end, it is obvious that the Peking Government would be provoked to make an attack upon Formosa in one way or another. American protection has, however, been of a negative type; no Communist assault on Formosa will be allowed, but no Nationalist attack on China will be permitted. Neutralization means what it says. This implies, if the policy is maintained in the future, the separation of Formosa from China, and its *de facto* creation as an independent republic, a client State under American protection. The consequences of taking over an empire are still inexorably pushing the Americans into the role of imperialists.

The American policy is thus, if peace continues, bound to lead to the creation of an American protectorate in the island; if war comes, it will become an American base for air attack on China. In either event it constitutes the grounds for the abiding hostility of the Chinese People's Republic, and for the resentment of the Chinese people, who by virtue of this policy see the threat of civil war or alien attack kept hanging over their heads.

The foreign policy of the new Chinese regime towards the Western powers is thus defined in shades of hostility. Towards America, the supporter of Chiang, the declared enemy of Communism anywhere and at all times, the protector and neutralizer of Formosa, there can clearly be no hope of friendship or of normal relations for a long, perhaps an indefinite, time. Towards Britain, who has dissociated herself from the more extreme policies of America, but yet follows American leadership in all major questions, there may be a reserved and chilly intercourse, largely due to the mutual benefits of trade and the common value of Hong Kong to both countries. Towards France, who still seeks to turn back the clock and re-establish a colonial regime in Indo-China, no closer relations are likely, until, at least, this Indo-China policy is reversed. Towards the rest of the Western world, Australia, Canada, Holland and the European democracies of Scandinavia and Belgium, the attitude of the new Chinese Government resembles that adopted towards Britain, with slight modifications of favour or disdain, dependent on the policy of recognition or non-recognition. The Chinese consider these countries as more or less satellite to America; those who show more independence are given slightly better and more cordial treatment; those who follow the American line closely are ignored.

The policy of China today is thus in some ways a reversion to that of the Empire in its days of power. The Western powers are treated with indifference and only admitted, under close supervision, to trade. The Americans, by virtue of their empire in Japan and her former colonies, are treated as enemies. The Russians, and all Communist States, are treated as friends. There is here a modernization of the old ideas. The Communist world is now the equivalent of the Chinese Confucian world Empire. Those peoples who have received the one orthodox culture, this time Communism, are 'civilized' and admitted to the family of nations, those who have not accepted Communism are treated as dangerous and barbarous, each according to the measure of his power and proximity.

Conflict between Communist powers is not admitted—officially—as a possible risk; there can be no divisions between the faithful; those who accept the orthodox doctrine must thereby accept the Communist world community. There could be no two suns in the sky, no two Emperors of China; now there can be no two Communist parties, no two sources of orthodoxy in the Communist world.

This ideal may not be easy to achieve; the basic differences between Russian and Chinese are profound, and cannot be always ignored. The question of how far China and Russia can proceed in company, whether the identity of doctrine must mean unity in policy, and whether Marxism in China can wholly replace the Confucian ideal, and substitute the theory of a world party for that of a Chinese Empire, must next be examined.

CHAPTER NINE

THE CHINESE REVOLUTION AND THE FAR EAST

'CH'IEN MEN CH'U HU, Hou Men Ch'in Lang—Drive out the tiger by the front gate, and let in the wolf at the back gate'—the old Chinese proverb aptly expresses the criticism to which the Communist foreign policy is most exposed. The tiger, be it the Japanese or the Western 'imperialists', has certainly been driven out by the front gate of China. Shanghai and the Concessions are now wholly under the control of the Chinese; the Treaty Ports are gone, the gunboats no longer sail upon the Yang Tze. But what has been happening at the back gate? Is it not the case that there the wolf—the Russian wolf—has certainly made an entry, and will he not take possession of the whole house?

The defeated Nationalists in Formosa and the American official propaganda make great play with this argument, varying the line between outright statements that the Chinese Communists are nothing but the tools of Moscow, to the 'more in sorrow than in anger' attitude which deplores that the Chinese Communists have had to buy Russian support so dear, and that it is still to be hoped that they will see the unwisdom of their action and expel the Russian invader while there is yet time.

The charge is backed up with specific accusations; that Outer Mongolia has been taken from China by Russia; that Manchuria, if still nominally Chinese, is in fact under Russian domination, and that Sinkiang is in the same situation. It is often implied that these countries have been alienated by the Chinese Communists and were before their advent to power wholly under Chinese authority. Since such a policy of concessions and retreats would make the Communist record in face of Russia worse even than that of the Kuomintang in the face of Japan it is necessary to examine the charges very care-fully; if true they certainly portend the impending fall of the Communist regime, for the Chinese people would not con-tinue to support a Government devoted to a policy of national surrender. But to see the foreign policy of Communist China clearly one must also look not only at relations with Russia, but at relations with the West and with China's neighbours in the Far East.

The clue to China's new policy towards the Western powers is that, with the exception of America, they do not any longer count in the Far East, and that America is seen as the successor to Japan and to Japanese imperialism. Whatever changes war and revolution may bring, two abiding facts remain in China's foreign relations: Japan is the only Asiatic power near enough to be a menace to China; Russia the only European power with a common frontier with China and an Asiatic extension of its homeland. The intrusion of the Western powers into the Far East was a distraction, a major irritant, but never really contained the potentiality of disaster. Japanese invasion could perhaps, one day, as it very nearly did, effect the conquest of China. Japan backed by America would be the most formidable danger the Chinese have ever faced. Russia also could add large Chinese provinces to her empire. These two powers alone can really bring their force to bear upon China. It is therefore with these two in view that a wise Chinese Govern-ment must align its foreign policy.

The Nationalist Government, threatened by Japan in the years before the war, could not bring in the only sure counter-poise, Russia, because the Nationalists were attempting to crush the Chinese Communist Party and therefore could not expect the friendship of Russia. The People's Republic today is not at this disadvantage. Faced with the Japanese danger in new guise, the American control of Japan and her former sea empire and the American hostility to Communism, and there-fore to China, the Peking regime can invoke the alliance with Russia, an alliance which comes naturally, is indeed almost a sacred obligation upon any Communist regime. Thus so long as America, controlling Japan, neutralizing Formosa, defending South Korea, supplying the French in Indo-China, stands as the heir to the Japanese Empire, a more potent danger still than Japan before the war, China must necessarily, being Communist, accept the Russian alliance, however unwelcome.

It will be said, or hoped, that China has another alternative. Even without renouncing Communism, Mao Tse-tung could follow Marshal Tito and stand out as a leader of an independent Communist China, hostile to Russia. It is quite true that this course would be possible. If Russia has found it wiser to confine her attacks upon Yugoslavia to words, she would not be likely to follow the Japanese into an endless war upon China. But it must also be asked just what China would gain by such a course. To begin with the Chinese Communist Party sincerely believe that their programme is in the best interest of the Chinese people; the Chinese people has shown itself at least very willing to give the Communists their chance. There is thus no incentive for a renunciation of Communism in China either by the party or the people. Yugoslavia was driven into heresy or schism by Russian arbitrary demands and overbearing treatment. Mao Tse-tung, so far as is known, has suffered no such oppression. He has been able to accept or decline Russian advice, as in July 1948, at will.

Moreover, Mao and the Chinese Communists have little reason to suppose that if they broke with Russia they would receive from the Americans and the West satisfactions which Russia denies to them. It is unfortunately a fact that in the Far East the Americans, as successors to Japan, occupy the regions and the bases which China traditionally controlled or possessed; Russia does not infringe upon China's sphere to the same degree, nor in the same way. Russia has a lease and an agreement for joint control of Port Arthur and Dairen for a limited period. She also still has rights, on a partnership basis, in the Manchurian railway. These Russian positions are described by Western statesmen and propagandists as though they constituted the outposts of aggression, and were the pegs marking out the Russian claim to seize Manchuria. It is necessary to see this problem from the Chinese point of view, historical and contemporary, in order to test the validity of this assumption.

Western and anti-Communist policy is based on the hope that the Chinese people will before long resent and resist Russian encroachment in Manchuria; if the Chinese Communist Government does not itself oppose Russia, then the people will transfer their support to some party that will. This thesis is so clearly based on European experience, so manifestly postulates a situation in China resembling that of Poland or Yugoslavia that it must be treated with caution and subjected to minute scrutiny before applying it to China.

The similarity between the situation in China and that in the Eastern European countries which are either Russian satellites, or once were so regarded, is slight. It consists in the single fact that both China and these European countries have Communist Governments. Neither in background nor in the social system is there any resemblance. China was not, before the Communists came to power, a small succession State only recently liberated from a long period of foreign rule; her social system included, besides a large impoverished peasantry, an extensive class of literates who were not aristocratic landowners or city bourgeois, but members of a widespread small landowning class, a class which had for many generations provided the officials of the Civil Service by which the Empire was governed. Few of these were rich, few had hereditary wealth, almost all depended on their career for a living. There was thus no striking change of personnel when the Communist Government took over. Members of the educated class who had become Communists replaced members of the same class who had not.

The governing class in China today, as before, is the literate section of the population. Communist plans to enlarge that section by bringing into it large numbers of workers and peasants are in action, but cannot affect the composition of the governing literate group for a generation. The policy and outlook of the new selection of the scholars, the Communist group, differs only in some respects from those they have displaced. Both groups had already broken with their common past, the Empire. Their dispute was how to carry forward the Chinese Revolution, not whether there should be a Revolution at all. There is thus no large class of dispossessed persons who look back longingly to a fallen regime. There are no Chinese 'Whites'.

It will be argued that the Kuomintang remnants in Formosa are 'White Chinese', and much Right Wing American misconception of the Chinese Revolution is due to this belief. But it is false. The Nationalists are failed revolutionaries; men who had the revolution at their feet and did not give it the right direction, modernizers who went stale and failed to find a cure for the evils of society. They have no following among the Chinese people, and no longer offer anything to the Chinese educated class.

There is thus no close analogy between the internal Chinese situation and that of, say, Czechoslovakia. Nor does the Chinese historical relationship with Russia in any way resemble that of the Eastern European nations. Russia was, to the Chinese, for a long time the most remote and least known of the European nations. Although the two empires had a common frontier on the Manchurian and Mongolian borders, this fact had very little significance for either. Manchuria, especially North Manchuria, which bordered on Russia, was a country which had only been part of the Empire since the Manchus had conquered China. Mongolia was the traditional home of the enemy of the Chinese cultivator, and the conquest of this country by the Manchus, while the Russians were conquering the Tartars of Siberia, was rather an example of co-operation between the two civilized empires in putting an end to the nomad scourge, than an example of rivalry between them. The Chinese did not want Outer Mongolia for themselves, they only wanted it neutralized so that no further nomad power should arise in that region.

The advance of Russia in Siberia was thus not seen in China as the approach of a danger, nor feared as the incursion of an alien people into regions where China had once been dominant. China had never succeeded in conquering the Siberian Tartars, and had only very rarely sent expeditions so far to the north. But it was well appreciated in China that these distant countries were the reservoir from which the nomad races poured forth to war, and the end of this menace was a subject for congratulation. The conquest of Indo-China by the French, an encroachment into a region close to China and of Chinese culture, was much more serious. Meanwhile Siberia remained far from Russia also. The communications were bad and the population scanty. No land hunger could impel the Russians to invade overcrowded China.

This picture began to change with the building of the Trans-Siberian railway. That great work brought the distant Russian possessions on the Pacific coast into close contact with St Petersburg, and then the Russians found that the best way to connect their Pacific base at Vladivostok with the main region of Siberia was to build the railway through North Manchuria, thus shortening the line and opening up a much richer countryside. Later, following the defeat of the Manchu Empire in the Boxer War, Russia obtained the right to extend her railway southward to the sea on the coast of South Manchuria, the Liao Tung Peninsula, where she built a modern naval base at Lu Shun (called by foreigners Port Arthur), and a civil port and trade mart at Ta Lien Wan, which was named Dalny by the Russians, and came to be called Dairen, from the Japanese pronunciation of the first two words of the Chinese name.

The Russian penetration of South Manchuria was a very different matter in Chinese eyes to their advance to the Pacific in Eastern Siberia. The Liao Tung Peninsula was an old Chinese territory. It had been part of the Empire, its north-east frontier zone, since the Han Dynasty in the beginning of the Christian era. It had been made a part of Shantung province, across the narrow thirty-mile Chih Li Strait. It was lost by the Ming to the rising Manchu kingdom, but it was in Chinese eyes and in history an integral part of China. The effect of Russian railway building in Manchuria was to merge this ancient

Chinese region around the sea coast with the wild and hitherto nomadic interior of Central and Northern Manchuria, which had never been Chinese.

The land was accordingly rapidly developed. Russian labour was far too distant; the nomads do not work the land, nor dig in mines. The Chinese from Shantung and Hopei, the nearby provinces of the north, were innumerable and poor; they gladly poured into Manchuria to work and settle, when the Manchus were forced to abolish their ancient prohibition on Chinese settlement there. Even before the Russo-Japanese war had rolled back the Tsarist Empire to North Manchuria the Chinese had already occupied the land in very large numbers. The Japanese, although they urged the need for new lands for their own over-crowded population, in practice preferred and encouraged the influx of the hardy Chinese who could work in the harsh climate better than Japanese, and asked less wages. In less than thirty years, from 1905 to 1931, the population of Manchuria increased by thirty million, and almost all were immigrant Chinese from Shantung and Hopei.

Manchuria, at China's doorstep just beyond the Wall, comprising an old Chinese territory in Liao Tung and new lands recently colonized to the north, is thus for ever a part of China. Ethnically, economically, culturally and also in its political allegiance the region is nothing but an eastward extension of North China. The Chinese call it Tung Pei, the north-east; the term 'Manchuria' is foreign, coined to denote the original kingdom of the Manchus before they conquered China.

The north-east is very close to China, and very far from the centres of Russian population and power. The region can be detached from China, as it was by the Japanese when they set up their puppet State of Manchoukuo, but it cannot be made non-Chinese. Moreover, as the Japanese found out, to separate Manchuria from China means sooner or later to advance into North China also. The two regions are too intimately linked; once North China is entered, there is no boundary to be found, no limit to be set, and so the invader is forced into the attempt to conquer China.

This strategic truth first appeared in the tenth century when the Kin Tartars set up their kingdom in Liao Tung at the end of the T'ang Dynasty. They next were led into North China, to protect their frontier, and from there they were compelled to engage in constant war with the Sung—the Chinese—till they had advanced to the Yang Tze. The Mongols did the same; the Manchus followed suit. Finally came the Japanese. It is often supposed that Russia must be dragged along the same road. This ignores one important difference; Russia is really a European power. Siberia is the most distant part of her domains, Manchuria still farther. She has no need to dominate Manchuria in order to defend Siberia; at best all she needs is the railway across to Vladivostok. And as a fact Russia has never annexed Manchuria, but has, both under the Tsars and the Soviets, contented herself with economic privileges and strategic railways.

It is thus possible for Russia to accept a limited aim in the Far East, to refrain from any attempt to annex Chinese territory, the more so as she can be sure of the economic co-operation of Manchuria under the Chinese Communist Government. That the Soviet takes this view can be assumed from the fact that Russia evacuated Manchuria when she had conquered that country from Japan in 1945. She did not need to do so. Treaty provisions made it her duty, but she has not heeded similar restrictions elsewhere. She could have alleged the Chinese civil war, the certainty that if evacuated Manchuria would become a scene of operations, and Russia's railway suffer—as indeed it did. She could have offered to hold Manchuria intact and safe until the civil war was over, and then hand it back to a recognized and stable Chinese Government. It would have been difficult to deny the propriety of such action, and impossible to dislodge the Russians if they had refused to go.

In any assessment of the Chinese attitude to Russia these facts have to be weighed. Nor are they alone in speaking to the Chinese in favour of Russia. After the Revolution in Russia the new regime, when it had taken over Siberia, renounced its special rights and privileges in China, agreed to a modification of Russian rights in Manchuria, and handed back its Concessions. This was twenty years and more before any other power abandoned any rights. The Chinese were deeply impressed, and the impression has remained. It is not easy to make any Chinese feel that the Soviet is a threat in the way that Japan was a threat. Even comparisons with the Western powers were often in favour of Russia. The Communists, of course, stress these facts, and ignore all that detracts from their merit.

To the non-Communist Chinese the actions of Russia which seem improper and insincere are the retention, even on a basis of partnership, of the naval base at Port Arthur, and the city of Dairen. When other powers have renounced such strongholds, the Russians insisted on regaining these places from Japan, as a price for their intervention in the war. It is true that the Russians have now signed a treaty with Communist China which promises restoration upon the signing of peace with Japan, or not later than 1952. Yet this is an old story and does not wholly convince. It must certainly be true that the Chinese Communists are aware of these doubts and misgivings; what cannot be known is whether they share them.

Most Chinese, contrary to what is often supposed, would probably agree that Russian pressure in Manchuria has been less, and less sinister in intention, than the encroachments which China has experienced from other powers in other parts of the country. The Communists profess to see no risk at all, to have no fears, and to think that such suggestions are only the reflection of the guilty consciences of the capitalist imperialists. What these wish to do, or have done, they attribute to the blameless Russians. Yet even if the Chinese Communists have some doubts about Russia, some fears that the Russian privileges in Port Arthur and Dairen may prove long enduring, they would still say, sincerely, that such sacrifices are necessary and worth while. The Russian alliance may have to be bought at this price; but the return is high and the price light.

From the Russian alliance they have gained complete security on the most exposed frontier of China, the north-east.

They have gained Russian co-operation in restoring the Manchurian industries to full production. It is true that these only ceased to produce in full because the Russians stripped the plant during their occupation after the war; but that was, perhaps the Communists would admit it, a mistake, due to a failure to foresee the rapid success of the Chinese Communists. If the Russians have now to atone for this mistake by greater efforts to repair it the Chinese Communists may not regret a situation which gives them some moral right to claim such assistance, instead of having to beg for it. The Chinese have also gained the support of an ally who will certainly not oppose their claims in other regions, and will be glad to see China grow strong at the expense of the Western colonial powers or America. In the regions of old Chinese imperial ambition the Russians will not oppose Chinese aspirations, will further them willingly.

China can for her part acclaim the Communist policy in Europe; Europe does not matter to China; she can follow Russia in denouncing capitalist imperialists everywhere. She is already at odds with the chief of these, America, and can lose nothing by giving Russia verbal support. But China can now attempt to push her influence in South-East Asia, to recover her lost territories and her former suzerainties, and do all these things in the name of Communism and in full agreement with Russia. If China's relations with her Asiatic neighbours and powers having a land frontier with China are in turn examined it is plain that she has much to gain from the Russian alliance, and that there is little which America could offer to outbid the Russians.

Mongolia, in the far north, was lost to China in 1917 when the last Chinese army and governor, the warlord called 'Little Hsu', were expelled by the Mongols in alliance with Russian Whites. Soon after that the Red Russians expelled the Whites, and helped the Mongols to form an independent State, which was, of course, framed on Communist lines. For thirty years Outer Mongolia was ignored by China. It could not be recovered; it still appeared on the maps of China; it had virtually no Chinese inhabitants, and no Chinese cared whether it was supposed to be independent or not. It was in any case a territory which had only been incorporated in the Empire by the Manchu Dynasty. Now that the nomad menace was for ever dispelled by modern weapons and numbers, the question of Mongolia no longer mattered.

By virtue of the Yalta agreements Russia and the Allied powers agreed to persuade the Chinese Nationalist Government to consent to a plebiscite in Outer Mongolia which would ratify the fact of its thirty-year-old independence. The plebiscite was held, and the result, a foregone conclusion, made Outer Mongolia a legal sovereign independent State. The Mongolian question was closed. No Chinese, Communist or Nationalist, wishes to reverse this verdict. The Chinese could not be tempted to break with Russia to get back Mongolia.

Korea, excepting Russia herself, the next foreign State to have a land frontier with China, has had a long historic connection with China. Geography has made Korea the natural bridge between China and Japan. Korea is also the assembly ground for a seafaring nation's invasion directed at Manchuria. The Chinese first occupied North Korea, and made it a territory of their empire in the Han period, two hundred years before Christ. Later they lost the country, when the barbarian invasions swept over North China under the weak dynasties which followed the Han. The T'ang Dynasty, when the central Empire was restored, once more undertook the conquest of Korea, north and south alike this time, and beat off the first Japanese intervention in that country.

The T'ang held Korea for two hundred years, and under later dynasties the Korean kingdom accepted the position of a tributary and protected State without demur. The Ming fought a long war against Japan in Korea, to protect the Korean kingdom and drive out the Japanese. The Manchus imposed their suzerainty on Korea, and held it until the end of the nineteenth century. Not until 1895 was China deprived of her authority over Korea, which was then to fall under Japanese domination. Korea has never stood alone in the Far East, she has always been either a Chinese protected State or a Japanese colony. The Chinese protection is by very many centuries the more enduring of these alternatives. It thus can hardly be surprising to find a strong China once more asserting her interest in Korea, and opposing the influence in that peninsula of the rulers of Japan.

The North Korean State was brought into existence by Russian occupation at the end of the war with Japan. At that time the Chinese Communists had not gained control of Manchuria and were in no position to make claims upon Korea. The consequences of the North Korean attack upon the south, and its failure to achieve the conquest of that area, gave China a chance to intervene and restore her ancient suzerainty in Korea. The advance of the United Nations army towards the Yalu gave China also the kind of pretext which would insure popular support for such intervention. China, though successful in repelling the United Nations forces out of North Korea, was not able to conquer South Korea, and consequently has proved willing to negotiate a cease fire, the purpose of which is clearly to safeguard her position in North Korea, the more important part of the country. China will no doubt bide her time and wait for an opportunity to promote the reunion of the whole peninsula under a Communist Government. This, if achieved, would give China a modern version of her ancient relationship with the old Korean kingdom, and satisfy her security requirements.

But beyond Korea lies Japan; the real reason for American resistance to the Communist domination of all Korea is not so much belief in the democratic character of the regime of Syngman Rhee as the fear that if Korea is lost Japan will be exposed to the danger of Communist attack. This fear is based on the view that all Communist countries pursue alike the aims of Russian policy; and that China if dominant in Korea would be willing to embark on an attack on Japan at Russia's behest. If it were Russia herself who constituted the only danger, her possession of Vladivostok and Sakhalin is in itself as much a menace to Japan as Chinese control of Korea could ever be. If the fear is confined to what might happen in the event of general war, it can hardly be supposed that South Korea could be defended in such circumstances against both Russia and China.

It is reasonable to suppose that the objective of China's policy towards Japan is to promote in that country a revolution which will bring Japan into the Communist world. Only if Japan were under a friendly regime could China feel perfectly at ease with this dangerous neighbour whose past record is so black. Certainly a Japan allied to America and rearmed by the United States can only be regarded in China with deep suspicion. Yet it must be thought very doubtful whether the Chinese Communist Government believe that an armed invasion of Japan is the best way to bring that country to Communism. Such an invasion, by a country lacking all naval power, would be at best impossible for many years to come. The Chinese must have a more immediate and more practical programme.

Japan before the war depended to a very large extent on the raw materials of China and Manchuria; her finished products also found their widest market in China. Both source and outlet are now closed, and Japan suffers bitterly from the lack. China can now feel assured that, failing a general war, she has nothing to fear from Japan in the way of military attack. Japan lacks both the naval power and the military strength to renew an enterprise which failed even against Nationalist China. China today is far more powerful and prepared than twelve years ago. It is also probable that the majority opinion in Japan no longer favours such adventures. Japan, like England after the Hundred Years War, has learned that the hope of conquest upon the Continent is vain. The future of the island power lies upon the sea, and that future is not at present open to her ambition.

China can therefore exert pressure upon Japan, or relieve her wants, by opening or closing her market and supplying or retaining her raw materials. At the very time that American opinion became incensed at the trade between Hong Kong and

China, Japan, under American occupation, was permitted to continue her trade with China in order to obtain Chinese coal. Japan, once more her own mistress, if still subservient to America in her broad international policy, will surely seek to enter into commercial relations with China. Such relations will involve a measure of political neutrality, which will find strong advocates in Japan. As Japanese trade with China expands, to the mutual benefit of both nations, the urge to remain on friendly terms will increase. As Japanese rearmament grows the possibility of an independent policy will also increase. The essence of pre-war Japanese imperialism in China was the use of force to secure the Chinese market and the raw materials of Manchuria. Force is no longer available and these necessities will have to be secured through friendship. The long-term policy of China will be to warp Japan by commercial pressures towards the Communist camp, by way of neutrality.

In China's policy towards Japan as towards Korea there is nothing which conflicts with Russian aims, but much which marches in common. The attainment of China's desires would be pleasant to Russia, and no Russian aim in those countries need be harmful to China. If this is the case in the crucial area of Korea and Japan where both parties have their interests and their close contiguous territories, it is still more the case farther south.

Formosa is an island inhabited by people of Chinese descent; the few aborigines have no political significance. It is at present retained by Chiang Kai-shek and his Nationalist remnants through American protection and armed power. Here is a striking instance of American opposition to the objectives of Chinese policy, objectives which Russia would further if she could do so without war. Whether, in certain circumstances, Russsia would be ready to afford China the assistance necessary to invade Formosa must remain unknown. The main obstacle to such an incursion is the lack of naval power, or compensating air power. It would be difficult for Russia to lend ships of war to the Chinese Communists, but the supply of aircraft is far easier and less liable to identification.

It is probable that if American protection for the regime of Chiang Kai-shek were withdrawn, or merely allowed to lapse, such an invasion assisted by aircraft supplied by Russia would follow. The American declaration neutralizing Formosa was made by President Truman, without the concurrence of other member States of the United Nations, at the outbreak of the Korean War, but several months before Chinese intervention in that conflict. It was stated that the neutralization of Formosa was a measure of security for the American forces engaged in Korea, and would endure only as long as the war in Korea continued. If peace is made, or the war brought to an end by a permanent cease fire, it is not easy to see what justification can then be produced for continued American intervention in what remains in law a Chinese civil war. It can be taken as certain that no Government ruling in China, whether the present Communist regime or any other, will abandon the claim to Formosa.

The colony and leased territory of Hong Kong comprises the island of that name and the city of Kowloon, with some lesser islands, ceded outright to Great Britain, and a larger area on the mainland behind Kowloon, with certain other islands, which is leased territory, the lease being due to expire in 1998. The whole colony and territory support a population of nearly two millions, the overwhelming majority of whom are Chinese. Very large numbers of the inhabitants are not natives, but migrants who come in to work from the neighbouring province of Kuangtung. Under the Nationalist regime an incessant campaign of pin pricks was maintained against the British in Hong Kong. Incidents, in themselves trifling, were made the occasion of protests, retaliation and Press campaigns. It might have been thought that the alienation of the Hong Kong region inflicted on China an evil far greater than the loss of Manchuria.

Since the Communist regime came to power this attitude has changed. Relations with Hong Kong have been normal, even peaceful, though not exactly friendly, since the Communist authorities have not made any visit to Hong Kong nor invited any British officials to Canton. But there have been no Press campaigns against the British in Hong Kong, no overt incitement to disorder, no active demand for the retrocession of the colony. This restraint caused considerable amazement in Hong Kong, and has been felt by many to be the calm before the storm. Even when the forces garrisoning Hong Kong were sent to Korea to fight against the Chinese army there no change in the normal relations on the Hong Kong border was experienced.

It can hardly be doubted that the policy of the new, as of any conceivable Chinese Government, is to recover Hong Kong. The reason for the restraint now shown is thus not indifference to the question, but policy. It has been argued that the Communist regime, sure of its power and certain of its stability, is prepared to wait until the end of the century approaches; when the last years of Britain's lease are at hand it will be necessary to negotiate a settlement of the Hong Kong question, and since the colony could not now exist without the territory, and the lease will never be renewed, that settlement must be in some form a surrender of the colony. The longer the Chinese wait, the more certain are they of getting Hong Kong on their terms. The British hold a wasting bargaining counter, therefore the Chinese are ready to wait.

Another view, complementary to the last, is that the Chinese Communists realize very well that the present standard of living of the Chinese industrial workers and commercial classes in Hong Kong is very much higher than that of the corresponding classes in China. To incorporate Hong Kong now would mean a great loss of trade and prosperity to a city which, now a free port, would then be brought within the Chinese tariff. The workers would suffer, and the comparison they would make between capitalism and Communism would be unflattering to the latter. If China waits it is to be hoped, at least by the Communists, that the standard of living in China will rise until not much difference remains between Hong Kong and China; then incorporation of the colony could be effected without dislocation or unfavourable comparison.

Both of these views presuppose that the Chinese Communists are so strong and secure that they can afford to ignore and frustrate national feeling for a period of up to forty years. This seems too complacent an assumption. It would be surprising if the Hong Kong question is allowed to sleep so long. It would seem more probable that the Peking Government has left Hong Kong alone because in the present circumstances Hong Kong in British hands was more useful to them than an agitation to recover it would be. Hong Kong became with the Communist victory the chief port for China. From Hong Kong the coasting vessels of various nationalities sail safely to Chinese ports, immune from Nationalist attack. As long as Formosa remains a potential base for Nationalist blockade or naval patrol, Hong Kong serves China very well. It also acts as a centre for intelligence, for communication with other countries, and for financial operations. It is dependent on China for its daily food, and cannot therefore adopt stringent measures of trade boycott or control such as could be enforced in other parts of the Far East.

It is thus certainly at present in the Chinese interest to leave Hong Kong alone. It is not necessarily a Russian interest that China and Britain in Hong Kong should live on easy terms, but it does not do Russia any harm. The good will between Hong Kong and China serves, also, as an irritant in Anglo-American relations, and from the Chinese and Russian point of view this alone makes it almost worth while. The time will come when China can exert pressure on Britain to re-cede Hong Kong. The place being half on lease makes its defence as an ultimate aim impossible, and Britain can be counted upon to give it up on some terms, rather than make its fate an issue for war.

The frontier between China and Indo-China is, after the Korean and Siberian frontiers, the most important and vulnerable of China's borders. The mountains which divide the Chinese province of Kuangsi from Tonking, though rugged, are by no means impassable. The flat lands of the Red River delta are ideal for the construction of air bases which can dominate all South China. Northern and Eastern Indo-China are also within the Chinese cultural sphere; the languages of the peoples of this region are closely related to Chinese, their literature based on Chinese models, and their art inspired by Chinese ideas. The connection between Tonking and China is both intimate and old. From the beginning of the Christian era Tonking has alternated between being a province of China or an independent but tributary kingdom. Chinese authority was never directly imposed on the southern and western parts of what is now Indo-China, but the Red River Valley and the rich plain of Tonking were for many centuries Chinese territories.

The Chinese Empire in the middle of the nineteenth century fought a war with France to retain this suzerainty, a war in which the Chinese were not altogether unsuccessful, but which was none the less concluded by the renunciation of Chinese authority in Indo-China and the establishment of the French protectorate. This result was extorted from the weakness of the Manchu Empire; it was not, in Chinese eyes, in accordance with natural justice or based on any enduring verity of geography or history. It was a situation which had to be accepted until China was strong enough to reverse it, and no longer.

After the fall of France in 1940 the isolated colony and protectorate of Indo-China was left, under a Vichy governor-general, at the mercy of Japanese power. Japan accordingly imposed herself upon the country, virtually deprived the French authorities of any control, and used Indo-China as the staging point for her advance into Malaya and Siam. The fall of Singapore was in no small measure due to the surrender of Indo-China to the Japanese. These events not only destroyed the authority of the French colonial government, but also its prestige and its moral claim to rule. At the Japanese surrender the Indo-Chinese, particularly the Annamites, formed their own Government, adopted the old Chinese name of Viet Nam (in Chinese Yueh Nan, 'the Further South') for the country, and under a leader who had for many years opposed the French, Ho Chi-minh, proclaimed their independence.

This situation, so similar to events in Indonesia, and not unlike those in Burma, was not met with the wisdom which the British showed in Burma, or the Dutch, more tardily, displayed in Indonesia. The French attempted from the first to regain control, and after a series of abortive negotiations, in which no real point of agreement was present, passed into open warfare with the Viet Minh Party, as the Indo-Chinese nationalists were called. At this time although Ho Chi-minh was himself a Communist most of his followers were not, and the Viet Minh Party was much more nationalist than Communist. The Chinese Communists were then still in the north of China, more than a thousand miles from Indo-China, and in no way responsible for events in that country.

Four years later, when the advance of the Chinese Communists brought them to the frontiers of Indo-China, Ho Chi-minh was still in the field waging a guerrilla war against the French, who, although they had occupied the main cities, had very little control over the open country and were unable to penetrate the mountain zones. The situation of the French in fact closely resembled that of the Kuomintang in China in the years following the war. In both cases the authority of the legal Government was rejected by the mass of the nation, and its power confined to cities where garrisons were stationed.

The Viet Minh movement being led by a Communist, and having, as is the way with resistance movements elsewhere, gradually become more and more under Communist direction and control, it was inevitable that the Chinese Communists should regard it with favour. The triumph of the Viet Minh would assure to the new regime in China a friendly and sympathetic Government in Indo-China, and thus secure China's southern exposed frontier. Moreover the French Government was already applying to America for assistance in the Indo-Chinese war, and striving to convince the West that this conflict formed an essential part of the general resistance to Communism.

This view was only with some difficulty accepted by the American and British public. In the Far East the conduct of the

French in Indo-China and their reliance on the discredited ex-Emperor of Annam, Bao Dai, had not inspired very much confidence or enthusiasm. Among the Asiatic nations, such as India, the cause of the Viet Minh was popular and that of the French detested as an attempt to revive a fallen colonialism. The slow and hesitating steps taken by the French to transfer some authority to regimes of their own creation in Indo-China, which were claimed to be based on popular support and deserving of international recognition, were much criticized in Asia; India has refused any recognition of these Governments.

No doubt aware of the weak case that the French made in Asia, and determined to assert their support of the Viet Minh, Russia and China recognized the Government of Ho Chi-minh as the legitimate regime in Indo-China, and have exchanged diplomatic representation with that Government. There is thus an open breach between the West and the Chinese Government on the question of Indo-China. Both sides have given support to their protégés, and although no American or Chinese troops have yet been engaged, it is certain that China has helped Ho Chi-minh with arms and advice, just as the French have received American munitions. The Chinese have the assurance of the support of Asiatic opinion in what is viewed in that continent as a war of liberation against colonial reconquest. But it may be doubted whether, if the Viet Minh ultimately win, the independence of Indo-China would be very substantial.

It is an obvious Chinese interest to see a Communist regime, dependent on Peking for moral and material support, established in Indo-China. Such an outcome would restore in that country the old relationship between China and Tonking in new guise. It would also guarantee that no foreign or hostile Government could use Indo-China as a base for attack upon China. That this fear is real can be seen from the fact that as the war progresses the French depend more and more upon American aid, and such assistance could well lead to American occupation of part of the country. This would in the Chinese view be a direct menace to her security. China will therefore give Ho Chi-minh all the aid he needs to resist the French and if possible expel them from the country. If American intervention becomes overt Chinese counter-intervention will be certain. Indo-China could easily become a new Korea, but one in which the sympathy of the Asiatic peoples would be overwhelmingly on the Communist side.

In this question also the interests of America and China conflict, and those of Russia and China coincide. America is determined to resist the advance of Communism, even if this means upholding a French colonial regime which is widely discredited. The Chinese are equally determined to expel what they regard as a hostile regime from a territory of vital strategic importance to China. Russia can give China support in this without sacrifice to herself. There is no settlement of the Indo-Chinese question which the West can offer more favourable to China than that which she seeks with Russian support. Every issue in which Chinese interests are opposed by the West and supported by Russia makes the Chinese alliance with Russia more solid. It is thus to Russia's interest to give China that support, which costs Russia very little.

The only other country with a frontier directly contiguous with China is Burma. This frontier running through a region of very high and precipitous mountains, intersected with deep and swift rivers, covered with jungle, and almost roadless, is not an area where military operations can easily be undertaken. It is not a sensitive and dangerous frontier for China. Consequently, although in Burma also a Communist revolt disturbs the country, and the regime is very unstable, there has so far been no evidence of Chinese assistance to the Communist rebels, nor of open antagonism to the Government in power. Burma and Peking have exchanged recognition and diplomatic missions. But China has clearly indicated that if Burma accepts American aid and becomes identified with the Western democratic bloc, her attitude would change. Burma seems to understand just what this means.

Chinese indifference to Burma's troubles, her non-intervention, and her attitude of friendship is clearly a Chinese policy, dictated by the facts of her frontier with Burma and Burma's independence. It is not the policy of crusading Communism, such as Russia might inspire in the hope of raising further trouble in South-East Asia. Although Burma was in former centuries a tributary kingdom, the relationship with China was very loose and implied no Chinese control of Burmese affairs. It would seem that to the Chinese Communists the fact of Burma's entire independence and detachment from the American bloc is sufficient.

Beyond Indo-China, and southward of Burma, are Siam and Malaya, two countries in which a very large proportion of the population are Chinese, and which form for China the natural outlet for her southern population. In Siam the existing Government, the regime of the near-dictator, Pibul, is openly anti-Chinese, not merely anti-Chinese Communist. The power of the Chinese merchants in Siam, their monopoly of commerce and industry, their energy and their skill, have made the Chinese of Siam the economic masters of the country. Long before the Communists came to power in China bad relations between China and Siam were normal. The Nationalist Government repeatedly protested against the anti-Chinese legislation of the Pibul regime. Believing that however much China might protest, nothing could be done by her to defend her subjects in Siam, the Siamese Government continued on its course.

Now a different situation confronts the Government of Bangkok. China is Communist. She is also strong, and although no common frontier exists, the strip of Burmese and Indo-Chinese territory which separates China from Northern Siam is narrow and easily overrun. The Chinese of Siam are largely merchants and shopkeepers, classes in themselves not prone to favour Communism. But the Chinese regime does not at present persecute small capitalists, nor suppress commerce. The Chinese of Siam have perhaps more to fear from Siamese chauvinism than from the Communism of their own country. The greater the restraints laid upon them by the Siamese, the more inclined they become to support the home Government and to look to it for protection. The Communists will have little difficulty in building a formidable fifth column in Siam. Here, too, the ultimate establishment of a Communist regime, under the control of local Chinese or half-Chinese (a very numerous element in the Siamese population) would be a Chinese interest, and one for which there would be strong local support from the Chinese community.

While Indo-China, Burma and Siam are all either contiguous with China proper, or separated by short land distances, Malaya, lying beyond these countries, is relatively remote from China, with which its communications are by sea and not by land. Until the development of railways or roads between China, Burma, Siam and Indo-China has progressed very much further than is at present the case, Malaya is still in relation to China to all intents an island. It is, however, a land with a large Chinese population, forming nearly half the total, and a considerable section of this Chinese population is either actively or passively supporting the Communist rebellion which for three years has maintained guerrilla warfare against the British authorities.

The Chinese Communists in China proper were not yet in the ascendant and were still confined to North China when the Communists of Malaya, very largely Chinese, rose in open rebellion. The Malayan Communist Party had risen to strength during the war against Japan, when it provided the only guerrilla resistance movement to maintain effective and sustained opposition to the occupying Japanese forces. After the war there was a brief period of legal political activity, but when the policy of labour agitation and infiltration of trade unions failed to give spectacular results, the party once more went into open insurrection and took to the jungle.

It would seem natural to suppose that an intimate connection exists between the Chinese Communist Party of China and the Malayan Communist movement. There can be no doubt that some at least of the insurgents in Malaya once served in the Chinese Communist army. But there has never been any definite evidence published which confirms the view that the insurrection in Malaya was either projected by the Chinese Communist Party or is now directed by their agents. There has, in fact, if the confessions of captured and surrendered Malayan Chinese Communists are to be credited, been some evidence pointing to a separate control and a chain of command which reaches back to Moscow rather than to Yenan or Peking.

The Chinese Communist Press has also pursued a relatively cautious and moderate line in dealing with the Malayan movement. While the 'People's Liberation Army of Malaya' receives the praise and support of the Press, its actions in murdering European planters and Chinese merchants are not reported. The fact that it is almost 90 per cent a Chinese force and a Chinese Party is never brought out, and it is only when the British authorities deport Chinese squatters to resettlement areas that the fact that these 'persecuted peasants' are Chinese is mentioned. Then the reports carefully refrain from connecting the episode with the Communist insurrection.

From these indications it may be possible to draw certain conclusions respecting the Chinese Government's policy in Malaya. Firstly, had the Peking Government wished to give active and open support to the Malayan Chinese Communists the easiest method would have been to implement the exchange of diplomatic missions with Britain, and thus gain the right to station consuls in the principal towns of the Malayan Union and in Singapore. These consulates, however carefully watched, could certainly have rendered valuable services to the Communist rebels. The fact that the British authorities in Malaya were greatly perturbed at the prospect should have encouraged the Chinese to claim this right. The Chinese Government has, however, by its own choice and action renounced this opportunity, which must have been sad news for the Communist rebels in Malaya.

The tepid character of the Press support, the concealment of facts which do not accord with Communist policy in China (such as the slaying of Europeans) and the failure, so far as is known, to assert active control over the Malayan movement suggest that Peking has its reservations about the insurrection in Malaya. These reservations are probably not concerned with the desirability of Communist victory, but with the probability of that victory. Malaya cannot be reached from China except by sea, which the Chinese do not control and have no hope of controlling for more than a generation. China cannot in fact give the Malayan Communists that decisive support which she afforded to the North Koreans and could at any time give to Viet Minh.

Communism, like other religions, must always be right and always triumph. There can by definition be no possibility of the people freely rejecting Communism; they may be crushed, or they may be deceived. In Malaya they (the Communists) are likely to be crushed, not quickly, nor perhaps finally, but still effectively for many years. If the triumphant Communism of China were to be publicly associated with a failure, and a failure which concerned other Chinese Communists, it would be harmful to the totalitarian ideal and inspiring to enemies or opponents nearer home.

But if the 'Malayan' (not specifically 'Chinese') Communist Party is crushed by the 'capitalist imperialist' British it is no doubt sad, but does not involve China. China remains the great potential liberator of the future, to whom all good Malayan Communists will be wise to look, and upon whom they will in future have to rely. Malaya is a natural objective for future Chinese policy; its large Chinese population is in itself a reason and provides a claim. But the time is not yet; Malaya is too far and too well defended. It is in the second category of Chinese objectives, and the prestige of the regime must not be damaged by premature and unsuccessful intervention.

It is sometimes suggested that Russian interests require the progress of the Communist rebellion in Malaya, and that therefore China will be goaded by Russia into further activity and support. It is obvious that a rebellion which hinders the production of rubber and tin, destined to support the programme of Western rearmament, is useful to Russia. It is, however, not certain that the movement could have more than a nuisance

value for Russia. Were the Malayan Communists to triumph
it would devolve upon China, not Russia, to protect and
sustain the new and distant Communist republic of Malaya.
It would be a remote commitment hard to hold. As a potential
fifth column in being, in case of world war, the Malayan
Communists are valuable. It is unlikely that the direction of
their movement is really a bone of contention between China
and Russia.

The Chinese assertion of the former Manchu suzerainty over
Tibet has made China a neighbour of India. The advance of
the Chinese into Tibet was put forward by Western propagandists as a bogy to frighten India out of her attitude of
neutrality towards China and the Korean War. It failed to have
this effect, largely because it was an ill-chosen weapon apt to
wound the hand that wielded it more than the enemy. The
Chinese claim to suzerainty over Tibet is, in international law,
quite unchallengeable. No Chinese Government, least of all
that of the Kuomintang, has ever renounced China's rights over
Tibet, or ever signed any agreement acknowledging the *de facto*
independence of that country. The Tibetans maintained that
independence, which no foreign power ever recognized *de jure*,
simply because the Chinese Governments of the Republic were
too weak or too occupied with civil war to organize an expedition capable of retaking the country. When the Communists came to power and united China they were able to do
what every previous Chinese Government hoped and intended
to do.

Another weakness in the accusations of aggression against
China for reoccupying Tibet is that if this charge is sustained,
it will cut out the ground from under the feet of those who
support the French reconquest of Indo-China, for in law the
two cases are identical. In Tibet, as in Indo-China, the legal,
alien, sovereign power is attempting to reassert its right to rule
the country. In Indo-China, as in Tibet, a native Government,
formed during the period when the alien rule was in abeyance,
resists this reconquest. The only differences are those of power
and time. The Chinese can certainly retake Tibet; it is not at all

certain that the French can reimpose their authority on Indo-China. Tibet was free from Chinese control for forty years; Indo-China has been free from French authority for only four or five. But international law takes no cognizance of such factors.

India, perhaps reflecting on these aspects of the problem, and finding more substantial comfort in the height of the Himalayan mountains which divide her from Tibet, has made plain her acquiescence in the restoration of Chinese suzerainty. No serious fear of an invasion across these bleak and lofty regions—a feat never yet performed in history—disturbs the tranquillity of India. It is not Chinese armies from over the Himalayas that India fears, but Chinese ideas and examples, which come to her people from the spectacle of China restored to strength and unity by a Communist movement. India lies beyond the realm of Chinese military power, but her social system and her economic problems expose her wide open to the influence of Chinese Communist ideology.

This examination of China's relations with her neighbours has not touched upon those island States such as the Philippine Republic, Indonesia and more distantly Australia and New Zealand, which being situated in the Pacific, at greater or lesser distance from China, fall within the theoretical scope of Chinese policy. The theoretical aspect is, however, here all important. China has no naval power; many years must pass before she could build up and train a navy strong enough to challenge the present sea kings of the Pacific. The most that China, however Communist and fanatical she may become, can do is to give moral support to those elements in the island lands who oppose America and incline towards Communism. In Indonesia, where a large Chinese community exists, this community can be used to some extent as a fifth column, valuable perhaps in war, but in no sense comparable to the huge Chinese minorities which almost overtop the native population of Malaya and Siam.

It would seem more probable that China will hope for the trend towards Communism in these island lands to continue and triumph through local causes, which in the Philippine Republic at least, would seem to be more than likely. These countries, like Malaya, are really in the second category of Chinese objectives. They may, by becoming Communist States, move into the first category, but China is not in a position to exert direct influence on their destiny. It can be safely assumed that China would prefer to see the island lands close to Asia under Communist rule. That development would deny them to the West and remove the threat of Western air power to a safer distance. This objective can more easily be attained by encouraging the native Communist movements than by direct intervention.

It is therefore clear that although the Communist revolution has restored to China the might or the potential authority of the old Empire, the scope of her effective power has not been enlarged beyond that pale. All the countries either threatened by or experiencing Chinese intervention were territories or tributaries of the Empire. Those Far Eastern countries which lay beyond the zone of the Empire's domination lie now equally beyond the power of Communist China. To secure this ancient protective zone around the frontiers of the Empire China has the support of Russia, whose interests in no way conflict, and meets the opposition of the West. America and her allies can offer China nothing except at the expense of those allies themselves. Russia can offer to support China in regaining all, for none is or ever was Russian.

No occult sympathy between Communist States, though such does indeed exist, no Russian domination, no blind sub-servience to international Communism is needed to explain why Communist China prefers the Russian alliance to whatever form of toleration America would be prepared to offer. The old and hard facts of international relations, the fear of war, the jealousy of foreign powers, the demands of the military, and the supposed necessities of security, are the motives which have impelled resurgent China on this course and will maintain her in it until her claims are satisfied and her fears allayed. Since this requires surrenders by the West which there is no inclination to make, it is improbable that any early solution to the tension in the Far East will emerge from either war or peace in Korea.

For a long period, since the beginning of the nineteenth century, the West has had no need to take into account the interests and aims of a strong China. Weak and divided China had all her energies expended on merely avoiding conquest and partition. Now that strong China has once more appeared it will be found that her minimum demands are incompatible with the survival of any European colonies in the Far East or with the presence of Western armed force in that region. This would have been the consequence of the reappearance of China as a power under any regime. Under the Communist regime it is likely to be more swiftly apparent than would have been the case in other circumstances. But that is the only difference.

CHAPTER TEN

POSSIBLE DEVELOPMENT OF THE CHINESE REVOLUTION

'WE ARE NOT vain idealists, we cannot separate ourselves from the reality of the conditions we see before us.' Mao Tse-tung makes this sound observation in the eighth chapter of *New Democracy*, a chapter devoted to the criticism of those Left extremists who could not see why the two-stage revolution was necessary in China, and denied the need for the intermediate period of New Democracy. In considering how the Chinese Revolution may develop in this and later ages it would be as well to follow Mao and take account of the reality of the conditions we see before us, rather than indulge in wishful thinking. Among a very large number of Western students of China and the Far East the hope, or the wish, that the Communist regime will prove transitory still dominates. The permanence of a distasteful situation is too unwelcome to be admitted.

Since few who have studied the actual working of the new Government can find grounds for the belief that it is losing internal support, the hope of its overthrow tends to centre in the expectation of a world war and the victory of the Western powers. The possibility of such a war, and of such a result, is certainly one of those realities which Mao urges his followers to recognize. No one can feel sure that the cold war can be maintained for many years without leading to an all-out contest between the rival worlds, and no one can be sure that the outcome of that struggle would be the certain victory of either side. Consequently the first decisive factor in the future of the Chinese Revolution is whether it is to develop under conditions of world war or of uneasy peace.

If war is to come it may be expected before many years have passed, and therefore before any extensive change has occurred in the internal social and economic condition of China. War will find China, as at present, only very lightly industrialized, with forces only partially armed with modern weapons, and with a communication system which is inadequate for the size of the country; without a navy, and with an air force dependent on Russian supply. These are unfavourable conditions for waging victorious war against the highly industrialized and rapidly rearming West. Russia, of course, would be China's ally, and the main enemy of the Western powers. But Russia would find her own strength fully engaged in such a struggle, and would not be able to spare much of her war production for China. China would be the weaker partner, but would she be, in fact, 'the soft underbelly' of the new totalitarian coalition? If that were so it might be supposed that Western military thinking would have chosen China as the objective for the decisive stroke.

It does not appear, however, that this is the case. In the Senate Hearings on the dismissal of General MacArthur the question of what would have happened if the General's policy of making war on China had been adopted was very fully examined. Both General MacArthur himself and Secretary Marshall gave ample testimony to elucidate this point. The General had advocated the use of Chiang Kai-shek's army to make a diversion upon the coast of China, but when asked whether he thought that action would result in the overthrow of the Communist regime, or whether Chiang's forces unsupported by American troops would be able to maintain themselves on the mainland, he took refuge in evasions. His only purpose, he repeated, was to relieve pressure on the hard-pressed United Nations forces in Korea. He did not appear to have considered—or to care—whether the Nationalist army would or would not establish itself in China proper.

The Senators who found this attitude inadequate pressed hard to know whether American troops would then be called upon to support, or to evacuate, Chiang's army. General MacArthur, concurring in this with the Administration and General Marshall, was vehement in denying any such intention. No

American troops were to be committed to the Chinese mainland; no idea of following up a Nationalist invasion was entertained. Military thinking absolutely rejected the notion of any
American attempt to reinstate the Nationalist regime by force
of arms. The policy he advocated was to bomb the Chinese
bases and industrial establishments in Manchuria and, if necessary, to bomb and disrupt the communication system in China
itself. Chiang Kai-shek's forces were clearly considered to be
'expendable', to be used to make nuisance raids and limited
landings. It must be assumed that if world war were to follow
the adoption of MacArthur's policies this would be the pattern
of American action against China.

It can be regarded as certain that the industrial plants of
Manchuria would then be largely destroyed; the railways would
be frequently and seriously disrupted. Certain cities would be
bombed out. The coast would be effectively blockaded. In fact
the situation of the Chinese Communist regime would be
similar to that which it experienced before it came to power,
though it would not be so bad. Then their armies, equally or
even more unprotected by any air force, were exposed for
years to the attacks of the Nationalist, then Japanese and lastly
American-supplied Nationalist Air Force. Then they could
make no use of the railways, which they indeed disrupted.
Then they could not shelter their troops in the cities, which
their enemies held. Then they were cut off from the sea and
from all sources of foreign supply. And under those conditions,
after effectively depriving the Japanese of control over vast
rural areas, they won the civil war against forces three times
as numerous and equipped with modern American arms.
Communist China may be the geographical underbelly of the
Communist world, but it is not soft.

If the West would not make the conquest of China the
primary objective of a world war, but would rather pursue a
defensive policy in the Pacific, while concentrating on the
overthrow of Russia, the Chinese Communist regime will
certainly not be destroyed by aerial bombardment, blockade
and raids by Nationalist forces from Formosa. On the contrary,

the Chinese would no doubt react by attempting to use their main resource, manpower, and their principal military skill, guerrilla war and mobility, to invade the remaining strongholds of the West on the mainland of Eastern Asia. South Korea, Indo-China and Hong Kong could hardly be held if the West were concentrating on Russia. Malaya and Siam would be endangered, and might have to be abandoned.

If the West were to use Japanese forces to contain China and menace Eastern Siberia such a campaign might prove very wasteful of resources. The Japanese navy no longer exists; the army has to be retrained and re-equipped, the air force rebuilt from nothing. It may also be doubted whether the Japanese people would be altogether ready to undertake, with less preparation, and on behalf of Western interests, the task which cost them so dear and failed so utterly when embarked upon by a Japan well armed, long prepared and fighting for her own profit.

Certainly if a new invasion by Japanese forces were to be the strategy of the West in a future war with China and Russia, such a plan would rally the entire Chinese people behind the Government. It is very doubtful whether the Nationalists in Formosa could countenance such a project, or participate in it if launched by others. Unless the Japanese were promised the restoration of their former position of dominance in the Far East, and provided with the means to achieve it, they would not be a party to a policy which would treat their forces as MacArthur wishes to treat the Nationalist Chinese: 'expendable' troops designed to create diversions but not to make permanent conquests. Rearmed Japan could be relied upon to defend herself against attack and would be valuable to the West as the principal force necessary for containing the Communist powers in Asia, but such an employment of Japanese strength would in no way shake the Communist regime in China.

It will be argued that as in the last world conflict, the fall of the lesser partner will follow upon the destruction of the greater. Once Germany had been conquered Japan was certain to surrender. Once Russia has been overthrown, China must yield. The argument ignores two differences in the situation of the present and the late totalitarian alliance. Russia is a country many times larger than Germany, and China is not only many times larger than Japan, but is a continental power contiguous to Russia. From the Elbe to the Pacific coast of China the Communist powers stretch across the world.

All this territory, on the German analogy, must be over-run, must be occupied, and must be administered after defeat. The Germans did not surrender until the Allied armies from east and west were about to meet. Although the Nazi regime was disliked by large classes the German people fought invasion to the last mile. The Russia after 1941 had also resisted German invasion with unity, courage and endurance. There is every reason to believe that had Hitler won the battles of Stalingrad and Moscow the Russians would have continued the fight beyond the Urals, and the Communist regime would have remained in power.

No evidence of discontent produced from Russia, and certainly none from China, can sustain the belief that the Russian and Chinese peoples would not resist invasion as long and as fiercely as they did ten years ago. The idea that after some atom bombs had destroyed the main cities of Russia and the communications of China these countries would submit to peaceful occupation has no basis in any known evidence. It would seem very much more probable that a nationwide resistance, based if need be on guerrilla warfare, would continue inspired by horror and hatred of the destructive invader. The area which would have to be occupied and pacified is so immense, the prospects of such an operation succeeding so slight, that the Western powers would almost certainly refrain from committing the Japanese error on a scale ten times as great. They would hope that the demonstration of their power would suffice to prove to the Communist leaders the impossibility of conquering the world, or destroying the democracies. They would in fact seek on a world-wide scale the solution which is looked for in Korea: partition and cease fire, defence and not conquest.

In attempting to achieve this end to the conflict the Western powers will concentrate on Russia. It will be on Russia that the atomic bombs will fall. The vast, unorganized and dispersed economy of China offers no satisfactory target. Peace or cease fire achieved, the West would demand that China withdrew from any local conquests in Korea or Indo-China which she had made while the democracies were engaged with Russia. The experience of the Japanese occupations of these countries in Asia has already shown that while the invader may be ultimately forced to leave, the former overlord does not recover his prestige or his authority. The eggs will be much more thoroughly scrambled by a Chinese Communist conquest than by a Japanese military occupation. The Japanese wished only to eliminate the European Governments: the Chinese Communists will destroy the whole of the former social system and set up New Democracies. It is by no means certain that the inhabitants as a whole will wish to be liberated from this system for the benefit of their exiled landlords or former colonial governors.

It would seem probable therefore that whether the world war was lost by the Communist side, or a stalemate achieved, the Chinese Communist regime would certainly survive. As the probability of a military deadlock (with outright victory for neither side) is very much greater than the total victory of one or the other, the probability that New Democracy will continue in China and cannot be overthrown by outside force is still stronger. The circumstances in which such a war ended and the effects of the war upon the economy of China would, on the other hand, have profound consequences upon the future of the regime. China might gain in international stature by the weakening of Russia, or she might, as a consequence of her sufferings, be forced more firmly into dependence on a Russia less able to give her the help she would need. The West, unable to achieve total victory, would have no incentive to help to restore the economy of a Communist and hostile power. The Chinese Communists would still certainly reject any such offers if they were made.

It is therefore improbable that the outbreak of a world war will result in an abrupt reversal of the course of history in China. If the present situation of half-peace, disturbed periodically by local wars, continues for several years, there is no reason to expect that the present Government of China will be dislodged. The fact that the Nationalist regime in Formosa pins its last hopes to a world war is sufficient proof of the impregnable position of the Peking regime in time of peace. Limited attacks, or restraints, the denial of recognition, the refusal to admit Peking to the United Nations, the protection of Formosa, the aid to Bao Dai and the French in Indo-China, these activities which are described as 'containing Communism' probably strengthen the regime in China itself. They tend to underline Communist propaganda, to prove it to be true to people who doubted, and to rally non-Communist support to the regime, all of which happened in Russia at the time of the White resistance to the Bolshevik regime of Lenin.

It is also very doubtful whether such limited hostility, 'willing to wound and yet afraid to strike', is not rapidly winning support for the Chinese Communist regime in countries beyond her borders. Neither the Formosan Chinese, nor the Indo-Chinese can be expected to accept the role of 'expendables' on behalf of the West with enthusiasm. In India and other mid-Asiatic countries sympathy for the Chinese Government—or people—and hostility to the policy of America is much stronger than the fear of Communism. Affronts to China are felt as snubs to Asia. China is likely to find diplomatic allies among many non-Communist Governments in Asia. So long as the arbitrament of war is not involved the present American policy towards China is certainly strengthening the regime internally and improving its standing among the peoples of Asia.

General Marshall has stated that the United States will oppose any attempt by the Peking regime to 'shoot its way into UN', and will therefore continue to refuse the admission of the Peking delegate as the representative of China. The United States, according to the testimony of General Marshall, will also continue to prevent Formosa from passing under the control of the Peking Government. At the same time the American administration has made it clear that a cease fire in Korea, near to the 38th Parallel, will be welcomed. Further, a settlement of the Korean issue and of other problems connected with the Far East is expected to follow from the cease fire. If the Chinese Government which implements the Korean armistice is not to be recognized as a Government, its acts have no validity. If the settlement of Far Eastern problems is to rule out most of the acute questions as prejudged, no such negotiation can have any reality.

The peculiar balancing of incompatible procedures which American internal politics make necessary for the Truman administration will not appeal to Asiatic opinion, and disturbs the solidarity of the democratic Western alliance. Both the European and the non-Communist Asiatic States want a real settlement to result from the Korean armistice, and know that such a settlement must recognize what Mao Tse-tung has called the 'reality of the conditions we see before us'. Among those realities is the fact that it is the Government in Peking, not that in Taipeh, which controls China. Clearly there will be increasing pressure to conclude a true settlement with China, unless the turn of international events tends towards world war. If peace prevails it will be necessary, in order to tranquillize the Far East, to concede much to the new China. General recognition, the seat of China on the UN and the cessation of American intervention in the civil war, by which Formosa is protected under Chiang Kai-shek, will be the minimum demands upon which any settlement can be constructed.

The Formosan question, which is the most difficult to solve, is often presented to the Western public as if it were a question of either protecting that island or handing it over to the Peking Government. But these are not the alternatives. It can never be reasonably suggested that America or any other power should expel Chiang Kai-shek and the Nationalist regime by force. All that can be suggested is that America returns to the policy in force before the Korean War, and leaves Chiang to defend, or to lose, the island as best he may. In the view of all Chinese and in equity, Formosa, whether allotted to one Government or the other in a peace treaty, is certainly Chinese territory, taken from the Empire by Japan in 1895. The question of which Government should hold the island is therefore a question to be settled by the course of the civil war, just as the fate of the other large Chinese island, Hainan, was so decided.

The most equitable suggestion for a solution of the Formosan problem, and one which it is probable would be endorsed by the free vote of the Formosan people themselves, is that the island should be freed from the Nationalist regime, which is locally detested, and left under a Government of its own inhabitants, guaranteed by the United Nations. After a space of ten or more years the Formosan people would then choose whether they wished to be associated with China, and to what degree. Just because this proposal is so sensible it is not very likely to be implemented. Chiang and his mainland army would have first to be removed—an act politically difficult for America or the UN to carry out. The Communist regime would also have to consent to the arrangement, which is most improbable. In the eyes of the Chinese Communists the UN is at present nothing but an organ of 'American imperialism' and any system connected with UN would be regarded as a sham or as cover for American designs. Finally some power would have to uphold the United Nations guarantee of Formosan independence. This could not be the United States, too suspect in Chinese and Russian eyes, but unless naval power was available on the spot no such guarantee would be effective.

The Formosan question is therefore likely to disturb the Far East for several years to come; China will never drop her demand, the United States will not at present consent to abandon the protection of the island; the Asiatic nations, anxious to prevent wars, will give moral support to China, and the European democracies will give tacit assent to the policies of these Asiatic democracies. The existence of an open question of dispute with the West, the threat of nuisance raids from Nationalist forces, the potential use of Formosa in a war as a base for attacks upon China, all these factors will strengthen the Chinese Communist regime at home and reinforce its alliance with Russia abroad.

Under conditions of war or what is now called peace it is thus probable that the Chinese Revolution will continue to be guided by the Chinese Communist Party and that New Democracy will persist. It is, however, not at all so certain that the character of the regime will remain as unchanging as its name. One of the realities which must be taken into account is the fact of the different history of the Communist Party in China and elsewhere, and the difference in administrative techniques and of political procedures which have resulted from this background. Mao Tse-tung has now been recognized as a contributor to the Marxist truths, and the originator and leader of the particular kind of revolution suitable to Asiatic countries. However the faithful may interpret this claim, it affords proof to non-Communists that there are now in fact two kinds of Communism officially admitted as co-existing without either being condemned as heresy.

Asiatic Communism is instructed to look to China and follow Mao Tse-tung; European and American Communism must be assumed to be still taking the October Revolution as the model and Stalin as its prophet. Mao Tse-tung it is true only claims that New Democracy is a stage on the road to the Communist State and the classless society; but he also says that it will be a lengthy stage, and the commentators have suggested that it might in fact extend over two generations. If it is assumed that there can be no Communist State without industrialization, it is not unreasonable to expect that half a century and more must pass before the vast extent of the People's Republic has been converted into a modern industrial State. In fifty years Mao Tse-tung himself, and Stalin also, will be long dead.

Communism denies the view that great personalities sway the course of history, but the actual story of all the Communist States since 1917 tends to confirm this theory. In no modern

263

country other than Germany and Italy, self-confessed believers in the 'leadership principle', has personal power been more conspicuous than in Russia under Lenin and Stalin, and China under Mao Tse-tung. It is only these heads of the Communist States who have been accepted as having the power to propound new doctrine. No academic Marxist, no scholar and no lesser statesman has added a comma to the orthodox dogma. There is no higher criticism of Communist doctrine; there is revelation and obedience.

The co-existence of two prophets at the same time, certainly an uneasy situation, may be tided over by the agreement that one utters truths for Asia and the other for the rest of the world. Moreover, Stalin is a much older man. The course of nature will before many years pass lead to a vacancy in the Russian politbureau. It is not at all clear to non-Russians, Communist or not, who will succeed to Stalin, and it is quite clear that no present personality in Russia commands the prestige, the respect or even the recognition of the outside world. Few Chinese other than the adepts of the party know the names of any other prominent living Russian, Molotov perhaps excepted. If such a figure succeeds to Stalin he could not expect that in China he would outrank or even equal Mao Tse-tung in the eyes of Communists or others. When Mao becomes not only a prophet for Asia, but the senior and sole surviving 'contributor to the treasury of Marxist thought', the relationship between Asiatic and European Communism will be very greatly changed.

An eighteenth-century French diplomat, watching the sanguinary palace revolutions of St Petersburg, remarked that 'Le trône de Russie n'est ni héréditaire ni électif, c'est occupatif'. The history of events since the death of Lenin would suggest that this is still true. The principle on which the Communist succession is established has never been made clear. It is certainly not hereditary, and though it would be claimed to be elective, it may well prove, as under Paul and Catherine, to be 'occupative'. The possibilities for the choice of occupant are many. Whoever gains the prize will be a figure of far less stature than Stalin; the support of Mao Tse-tung and China, the ratification of the Russian succession by the other chief Communist power, will be useful for internal acceptance and essential for foreign prestige. The Russian aspirant will be anxious to have that support. Mao Tse-tung, being Chinese, will know what is meant by a bargain.

In China itself the same prospect, perhaps more distant, but still inevitable, awaits the regime. Mao Tse-tung must one day die. His successor will either be a personality agreeable to his Russian colleague, or one whom the future ruler of Russia would rather see excluded from the highest post. In either case there is room for disagreement, for resentments, for divergences and for recriminations. The present excellent relations, as far as is known, which prevail between Stalin and Mao are no safe guide to the future. Stalin is too big a figure, too settled and assured, to fear a rival. He can afford to acknowledge the genius of his Chinese colleague, and accept him as a friend. Mao Tse-tung is too able to be treated as a subordinate, has too great a following to be given orders, and has too great a respect for Stalin and the Russian Communist Party to seek a quarrel. But this harmony does not rest on defined principles and constitutional rights, but on personalities. In this respect the new regime resembles the old Empire very closely.

Under the Chinese Empire in all dynastic periods there was in theory a settled rule of succession. Primogeniture by the chief wife or sole empress was the law; younger sons and brothers only had the right to succeed to the throne if the main line failed. Yet in practice it is recorded in history that this rule was as often broken as observed. Some of the very greatest of Chinese emperors did not inherit the throne in a legitimate manner, but by violence or force. In one of the greatest periods of Chinese history, the first one hundred and fifty years of the T'ang Dynasty, not one Crown Prince succeeded to the throne without question. Every emperor in that period was a younger son, some even the sons of concubines. In other periods a similar story can be told and it would be truer to say that the appointment of an eldest son as Crown Prince was more a guarantee that he would not in time become emperor than that he would. If this was the course of events under a system of hereditary monarchy, when at least the choice was confined to members of the Imperial family, it would seem probable that under a system of autocratic government which has renounced the hereditary principle, the possibilities of an 'occupative' succession are infinite.

There are thus in the prospects of the Chinese Revolution two factors making for uncertainty: the extent and future scope of the tolerated divergence called New Democracy, now proclaimed as the model for Asia, and the future occupancy of the supreme power in Russia and in China. The view that Communism is by nature more intolerant of variations than any other totalitarian system or authoritarian religion is not certainly true. Until the rise of the Chinese Communist Party there was no scope for such divergences. Tito, the first to assert independence of Moscow, was too small to be tolerated, though too close to the West to be suppressed by force. China is so large that Mao Tse-tung must be accepted, and so influential in the Asiatic movement that his views must be followed. There exists the possibility that in China there will arise a 'Gallican Church' of Communism, orthodox—the 'Most Marxist Movement'—but also independent of the immediate jurisdiction of Moscow.

A powerful trend towards this development exists in the difference of national tradition and spirit. To the Chinese Communist his non-Communist fellow countryman is not so much a class enemy as a misguided neglected creature who must be taught the truth. 'Re-education', the great slogan of the party at the present time for internal affairs, means the conversion of doubters and opponents into believers and supporters. Re-education is an essentially non-violent process, depending upon the awakening of the social conscience, the inculcation of faith in the 'people' and the belief in collective action. Re-education consists often of courses in which professors or other urban intellectuals go to a village to share the life and toil of the peasants. Re-education for the mass of the community consists in the demonstration of better social behaviour.

Reckless motor drivers are stopped by the police, lectured in the public street, told the error of their behaviour and then allowed to go on. Train conductors give, between stops, lectures on how to behave at the station. 'Do not get on till others have alighted; do not push, the train will wait, let the elderly and the weak go first; move up to let another passenger sit down . . .' all familiar enough to the European traveller, but new in China. There is little of the atmosphere of regimentation about these instructions. The party men in charge more often adopt the tone of kindergarten mistresses gently teaching young people how to behave. The assumption is always that the public are the 'people' who may be ignorant, but are always sublime.

Underlying the theory and practice of re-education there would seem to be a constant tradition from the past. The bourgeois is a selfish creature who needs to be made to realize his duty to his fellows, but he is redeemable, he can 'change his body over', the untranslatable term *fan shen*, which means to undergo the process of conversion. Confucius and his followers, above all the great thinkers of the Sung period, also said, 'Man is born good, but his nature is corrupted by the evil of the world', and, 'Like dust upon a mirror, the nature of man only needs to be purified to become radiant and clear'. What is not found in modern China or in ancient thought is the concept that some special class of citizens has the monopoly of virtue and that all others are for ever damned.

The Chinese, Communist though he may be, thus still believes that ideas are more potent than laws, that content matters more than form, that man is by nature good and can be redeemed by following right doctrine. The nation as a whole can be made 'good'; the workers may be the spearhead and vanguard, but they are not the only ones for whom salvation is reserved. The Buddhist butcher could, in aeons of time, rise from the lowest hell to Nirvana; the capitalist, much more swiftly, can be re-educated. This is a most powerful influence in the Chinese attitude and one which draws away from Russian practice and Russian tradition.

If in the imponderable spiritual forces which still act upon Chinese thought there is much which is strange to the Eastern European whose experience of any form of civilization is by many hundreds of years shorter than that of the Chinese, there is also a very material difference in the situation of China and the Slav nations. The Eastern European States live in and by Europe; they were till 1945 intimately linked with the democratic western part of the continent, their culture is largely West European, their economy close-linked to Central and Western Europe. Communists in these countries may well feel that the only real solution, on Marxist lines, lies in world revolution. The Balkans and countries of the former Austro-Hungarian Empire have had sufficient experience to realize that independence is for them a lure and a sham. No safety lies in small national armies, no economic future in narrow autarchies.

The Chinese have no real reason to share this view, except in wide theoretical terms. The affairs of Europe are remote; those of the Americas and of other continents such as Africa hardly impinge. Asia is now more closely in touch than ever before, and in Asia the Chinese Communists are clearly very interested. But the rest of the world gets scant attention in their Press. A few Tass messages, set on the back page, are all that the party thinks necessary for foreign information. Nor do the majority of readers pine for more. The Chinese Communist would seem to be quite prepared to let the farther parts of the world progress, or regress, as they may, provided they no longer have any influence in China.

It may be doubted whether 'World Revolution' does not mean Asian revolution in practice; whether the claims of Mao Tse-tung to set up the Chinese Revolution as the model for Asia does not reflect a real agreement to limit Chinese aims and activity to those parts of Asia which are of interest to China. Such a settlement might be convenient to Russia at the present, even if it contains within it the seeds of dissension and heresy for the future. If that were so, and even if no such precise definition exists, it is important to consider just what the claim for the second classic revolution, the model for Asia, implies. How far west in Asia does this model apply? The term 'semi-colonial country', if apt for China under the Kuomintang, will fit Iran, Irak and Egypt also. Yet these countries have hitherto been far beyond the scope of Chinese imperial ambition.

There is implied in this problem another important difference between the Asiatic and the European Communists. In Asia the Communist leadership has been and still is wholly national. Mao Tse-tung and all his colleagues are pure-bred Chinese, without any trace of foreign ancestry, not men from border areas of mixed blood, but from the very heart of China, the south central provinces, the least touched by foreign contacts. The Korean Communists are also Koreans, Ho Chi-minh a pure Annamite. The situation in Russia and Eastern Europe is very different. Stalin is a Georgian. Many of the leading Russian Communists are of similar border peoples, or partly Jewish. The heads of the new Eastern European Communist States are all persons of mixed origin, of doubtful nationality, and certainly not drawn from the most national elements of the population.

Communism in Asia is in fact much more national, much less interested in world revolution, more concerned with the expulsion of the foreign imperialist, and prepared, as New Democracy proves, to make a reasonable accommodation with native capitalism. It is very doubtful whether a Mongol or a half-Tibetan could occupy the position of Mao Tse-tung in China. Such persons, if Communists, are sent to preside over the 'autonomous' areas in which their own people dwell. New Democracy as preached and practised by Mao Tse-tung is a recognition of these facts, though not always an open recognition of all the facts. It is declared that the two-stage revolution is necessary because China was backward industrially; it is not openly said that it was necessary because the mass of the people still felt more resentment against the foreigner than against the landlord and the native capitalist.

Mao has clearly realized that the strength of his movement in part derives from frustrated nationalism; that the great surge of opinion which has swept him into power is not altogether a class war, but a war to free China from her weakness and her bondage to the West. As his panegyrist points out, 'The characteristic feature of the Chinese Revolution . . . headed by Mao Tse-tung lies in it being a revolution in the biggest colonial and semi-colonial country. In addition the Chinese Revolution took place in the East where a population of more than one billion has been living under the long-term oppression of imperialism.'*

If the characteristic feature of the Chinese Revolution lies in this appeal to nationalist sentiment, to the desire to be free from foreign rule, and to become strong and 'modern', it is clear that the second classic example of revolution has only a limited scope, and is by no means a world-wide formula. In Asia today, in Africa tomorrow, the model will be studied, the lesson learned and the teaching accepted. But elsewhere Mao Tse-tung's contribution will hardly apply. The system of New Democracy is not even so advanced in social progress as the capitalism of the welfare State in Britain or in the Dominions. North-Western Europe would have little to learn from Mao, and much that could be taught to him. The Communist parties of Europe and America, of Australia and New Zealand, will not find much in the works of Mao Tse-tung which they can apply to the situation of their own countries. Just as the Western doctrines of Christianity and democracy could find no secure lodgment in the alien structure of Chinese society and thought, so Asiatic Communism, which may well have 'solved the problems of the Chinese Revolution' has nothing to offer to societies whose past history and present character are so utterly unlike those of China.

The two worlds, which seemed in the nineteenth century to be drawing together, have in the twentieth century collided, and with all the force of their momentum violently rebounded

* Lu Ting-yi. Speech. 'The World Significance of the Chinese Revolution.' NCNA. Peking, June 25th, 1951.

from each other. The Westerner in China today often feels as if he were living a hundred and fifty years back in the era of the Canton factories. In a few years time such Western visitors as can enter China may well be reminded rather of the days of Mathew Ricci in the late Ming period, when the rare stranger was an object of mingled suspicion and curiosity, a passing entertainment for the court, but not a person who should be allowed any contact with the people.

This, at least, might be the consequence of the domination of the more national elements in the Chinese Communist Party. But there is also the other strain, the pure Marxist, and therefore European tradition, which continues to emphasize the unity of the working class throughout the world, the debt to Russia and the West (though not the debt the West still claims), the ultimate goal of the world classless society. This influence is certainly strong and implicit in all Marxist writing. If the world does in fact develop as the Communists believe it will, the capitalist empires fall and the Communist republics triumph everywhere, then it might be supposed that China in common with the rest of humanity will enter into the Communist World State, and gradually sink her identity in some new all-embracing culture.

These possibilities are hardly among the realities which we see before us. The present trend, the avowed aim of the non-Communist world, is to resist any such development, to fortify its limits, to provide the basis of power for the two-world era. In most of the strongest countries of the West, Communism is a weak force, unable to win wide support, under the stigma of alien control, maintained by a fanatical minority. In the marginal countries of Europe—perhaps of South America also—Communism could only triumph with outside aid at the cost of a bitter civil struggle which would divide society for generations. In the greater part of Asia, Communism has a very fair prospect of victory. Here no real ideological opposition exists; the conflicts of society are violent, the needs of the poor extreme.

The real prospect before the world is therefore rather a

struggle to control the marginal lands, those in which there is a stronger or weaker inclination towards the Communist solution; the great base lands of the rival systems will never be conquered by the enemy; they will perhaps be devastated in inconclusive wars, but they will survive. If in future Communism is to be tailored to suit the character of the region in which it aspires to success, the Chinese Revolution is the classic example for Asia, and it is Asia that is really in question today. In Europe, Communism is not making progress beyond the region under Russian control; in the Americas the overwhelming strength of the United States makes the prospect of a Communist revolution in any South American country almost hopeless. Such a movement would be crushed. In Africa, perhaps one day to be the scene of the 'third classic example' of Communist revolution, the time is not yet ripe.

The importance of the Chinese Revolution and Mao Tsetung's claim to be the leader and teacher of Asia thus lies in the fact that it is in Asia that the ideological struggle is most in doubt, it is in Asia that Communism has won its most striking triumphs since the October Revolution, and here alone that whole populations are either ready to accept or actively to support Communist Governments. Russia would seem to have accepted the more difficult and less promising task of converting Europe: China by her circumstances and geographical position is inevitably taking over the leadership in Asia.

The degree to which China will use her position of teacher and leader to promote what are really Chinese imperial ambitions as in Korea and Indo-China, or to further what are primarily ideological aspirations, such as the rise of Communism in India, Indonesia and farther afield, will determine the role of the Chinese Revolution in international politics. In the party and in the nation there will be a conflict between two strong trends: the age-old Chinese conception of the exclusive Chinese State exercising authority over the nearer neighbours of China, and entertaining only distant and formal relations with more remote peoples; and the new ideas which the revolution, both pre- and post-Communist, has so deeply instilled: the desire to be modern, to make China strong and to raise the standard of living, the worship of natural science, and the belief in the world-wide unity of the working class.

It does not follow that this conflict will divide the party or the people into hostile factions, for the struggle is one which goes on in each individual soul. It may be that Mao Tse-tung has solved the problems of the Chinese Revolution in so far as such problems were political and social; it is not so clear that New Democracy has solved the problem of the Chinese intellectual. The generation which cast aside Confucius as inadequate has been offered Marx and Mao and promised a translation of its old ideals to a world-wide scale. But while advocating world unity, the advance of science and the modernization of the economy, the Chinese intellectual is in fact being cut off from his former Western contacts and colleagues; he is no longer able to study the scientific progress of the West, and must rely on what Russia and Eastern Europe can offer. The resources which could have rapidly transformed the Chinese economy will not be available, because they are 'capitalist imperialist'.

The Chinese Communist Party, like every previous regime which has governed in China, must, to survive, conciliate the interests of the peasants and those of the scholars. Hitherto, aided by the inept tyranny of the Kuomintang, they have realized the coalition of the two essential classes, fitted Marxism to reality and called the scholars 'workers'. But the Chinese scholars are not really workers in the Marxist sense. They are in fact the same class which produced the Civil Servants of the old Empire, and government is their inherited trade. They will serve the regime which gives them their career and their reward, but they continue to form a close corporation with their orthodox doctrine, be it Marx or Confucius, Mencius or Mao Tse-tung. They have always based their membership on the tests of education and orthodoxy rather than on birth and wealth. They can accept the peasant boy or the factory worker, but when he has studied among them he will issue forth

T

neither a peasant nor a worker, but a scholar and a bureau-
crat.

As the messianic qualities of the early revolution fade with
time, the hardships of the guerrillas become a legend and no
longer a personal memory, the abiding character of the ruling
class will reassert itself, though not necessarily in the same way
or with the same defects as in the past. Corruption, a function
of the economy rather than of the morality of the old China,
may disappear for ever, as it has in other bureaucracies. The
ruler, whatever his early origin, must be trained to govern;
he cannot in a modern State remain either a peasant or a
worker; the innumerable mass of the population cannot in
fact ever have more than limited and strictly local political
power. The established bureaucracy of Communist China—
unlike the position in some 'satellite' countries—will be essentially and wholly Chinese. As its prestige rises and the influence of
China in Asia increases the bureaucracy will become more intolerant of innovations not of its own choosing; it will become
less susceptible to foreign doctrine and more self-sufficient.
The increase of Chinese scientific workers and experts, the very
great ability of the Chinese intellectual and the barriers of language will tend to decrease the number of and the need for
Russian advisers or experts.

It is rather in this inevitable trend towards independence and
equality than in the expectation of sudden and violent disagreement that the future of Chinese relations with Russia holds hope
for the West. The gradual emergence of divergent policies in
Asia, while probably in the first instance highly disagreeable to
the Western colonial powers, against whom such policies will
be directed, nevertheless foreshadows the eventual disruption
of the Communist World Movement into regional variations.
When to later generations the expectation of world-wide Communism is no more real than the millennium has become to
the Christian, the sharp hostility towards the unregenerate part
of the world will also fade. The modern European can with
difficulty enter into his medieval ancestors' feelings towards the
Islamic world. The future Chinese Communist, assured of the

stability of his own system and no longer deluded into the belief that it is about to be accepted by others, will be ready to understand and practise toleration.

The prospect of future stability does not remove the fact of present tension. The Chinese Communist Party today, fully in control of the country, buoyed up by a great wave of national resurgence, is bitterly hostile to the Western world, pathologically suspicious of American policy, largely uncritical of Russian ambition. Nothing in the present policy of the Western powers holds any promise of changing this attitude or softening the animosity which wide classes of Chinese, and of other Asian peoples, feel towards the West. Every move made since the triumph of the Communist Party has tended to convince that party, and many of the Chinese people, that the alliance with Russia is the only defence which saves China from immediate invasion either by Nationalist forces armed and equipped by America, by Japanese similarly supplied or even by American forces.

The more moderate policies of Britain have been disregarded partly because the British Commonwealth as a whole did not follow the lead of the United Kingdom, partly because British statesmen have lost no opportunity for proclaiming that any difference in policy with America was purely superficial, had no real significance, was nothing but a matter of local expediency, and would be abandoned at once if any issue of substance arose. If a nation openly declares that its policy is not an expression of conviction but of expediency, and frankly admits that such convictions as exist will be given up on demand, it can hardly be surprising if such a policy is without effect.

In Asia today the West acts without conviction and plans without consistent principle. Democracy and independence are the ideals revered by all Americans. But neither democracy nor independence are found in Indo-China; democracy is a sham in the Philippines, denied in Formosa. Britain renounced her empire in India, but supports the attempts of the French to retain theirs in Indo-China. No one pretends that these policies represent a reversal of belief, a change of ideal. No one believes that colonial empires in Asia can endure, or that 'democracies' of the landlord oligarchy type are sound and viable States. But as the alternative to the colonial empires and the bogus democracies is some form of Communist regime, the West blindly opposes all such movements. The fact of widespread support is not equated with 'democracy'. The craving for independence is not admissible under a Communist inspiration.

The result is that while Communist policy in Asia appears to the peoples of these nations as consistent, idealistic and sincere, the actions of the Western powers appear opportunist, hypocritical and selfish. The arms may exist by which Communism can be contained in Asia, but the unity of purpose, the conviction of principle and the expectation of victory are all on the other side. History has often recorded the consequences of this disparity.

To the West it appears obvious that the smaller and weaker nations of South-East Asia cannot stand alone as viable independent States in the modern world; it seems reasonable that they should accept either the assistance and guidance of the great democracies, or some form of association with the erstwhile dominant power. These ideas are fully in accordance with the known limitations of the economic development of the former colonial territories. But all these considerations in fact apply equally well to most of the former colonial powers themselves and to their European neighbours. Neither Holland nor Portugal can hope to survive as independent States unless guaranteed by the might of America. France can only feel safe from invasion if the Atlantic Pact becomes a reality. Yet the European powers are still strongly swayed by purely nationalist considerations which no longer suit their real situation. It is hardly surprising that these outmoded ideas are still in fashion among the newly free peoples of Asia.

Consequently the appeal of the West falls on deaf ears; it appears to be nothing more than a plea for continued colonialism, an attempt to frighten the resurgent nationalists with a

Communist bogy. To many who understand the validity of the argument based on the inadequate economic development of these countries, the rival claim of Communism or New Democracy is at least as attractive as the aid of the West. Mao Tse-tung has claimed to solve the problems of Asia as well as those of China by his theory of the Chinese Revolution. The Chinese prescription, which amounts to a promise to aid the other South-East Asian countries to set up their own New Democracies, backed by China and Russia, but free to rule themselves on these lines, has great appeal. The West is under suspicion as 'imperialist': the argument that Communism is also imperialist is simply not accepted by Asiatic opinion, and is not supported by what Asian peoples know of events in China.

It is therefore almost certain that in the coming years the Chinese Revolution will be taken as a model, and many attempts to put Mao's theory into practice will be made. China will certainly do all within her power to forward these move-ments, nor is it yet possible to say when or where her power will be proved too weak. Until the West can find some way of satisfying Asiatic peoples that the aid of the democracies is not in fact concealed imperialism and economic bondage, tending to maintain in power the least desirable of privileged groups, the influence of the Chinese Revolution will continue to work like yeast in the politics of Asia.

There remains one supreme question concerning the future of the new China and the outcome of the Revolution. It has been shown that in many respects the Chinese people have turned back to older ideas, and when they have given these ideas new form they have repudiated the theories of the demo-cratic West and taken their new knowledge and new political doctrines from Russia. Freedom as the West has known it has been subordinated to orthodoxy, and individualism to mass action. The history of the West has taught its peoples to believe that all such repudiations are retrogressive, ephemeral and disastrous. The idea is still strongly held that progress or civili-zation is synonymous with the liberties which the West has

established, but which it has rarely exported to others. Whatever claims can be made for the great authoritarian systems of
the past, whether Imperial Rome or T'ang China, these
systems did not live in daily competition with democracy and
free thought. The question must therefore be asked, even if the
totalitarian system suits Chinese mental habits and past traditions, can it in fact satisfy the modern Chinese when it is not all
embracing and world-wide, but must stand the constant criticism
of another, opposed ethic?

It will not in fact be possible for the rulers of modern China
to behave or to think in the way which the T'ang or Han
Emperors found natural and normal. It is not possible to pretend that beyond the confines of China and her Communist
allies all is barbarism. It can be argued that the West is hostile,
the capitalist system harsh to the poor, but not that in those
countries no good life exists, no opportunity for men of
culture and intellect to make their mark. In the old Empire
the few Chinese who fled, for political or personal reasons, to
the nomads, there to act as secretaries or advisers to some
Tartar khan, were known as *Han Ch'ien*, 'renegade Chinese';
men who had renounced civilization to live with and serve the
barbarian. As such they were both pitied and despised.

Now, there is little real likelihood that the democratic or
capitalist West will rapidly succumb to Communist conquest
or revolution. The Chinese who go abroad, or who have
failed to return, cannot really be equated with the *Han Ch'ien*
of the past. They do not live in misery among barbarians, they
are not conscious of their fallen status, but in many cases enjoy
opportunities for creative work which they could not find in
China. Whether they are political opponents of Communism
or merely scholars who prefer the free academic atmosphere of
the West, they constitute a kind of intellectual opposition very
different from the outcasts of the old Empire. There can be no
doubt that this competition of the attractions of the West is
the main opponent of the system which Mao Tse-tung has
built.

It is not an opponent which shakes his hold on the mass of

the peasants and people. To them the old made new, still having the ethos of the old, but infused with the energy and enthusiasm of the new, is indeed the solution of China's problems. But the scholars, who are still the essential second wheel to the Chinese cart, will perhaps not be wholly satisfied if present national hostility to America and her allies becomes a mould in which the whole future of Chinese thought and culture is to be formed.

The coalition of peasant and scholar has been the key to the triumph of Chinese Communism, just as it was the secret of Ming Hung Wu's victory over the Mongols and his rivals. The future depends on the success with which the Communist rulers can continue to satisfy both these classes. The fact that Mao has not publicly recognized that this is his problem need not matter. The equation of scholars to workers and the recognition of the alliance of 'peasants and workers' amounts in practice to an acknowledgment of the old basic truth. The next step must be to put into practice measures which not only assure the peasants of their livelihood and better conditions, all they have ever asked, but also provide full scope for the ambitions and abilities of the scholars. In the period of reconstruction this can be done by giving all men of skill and good will ample opportunities, and in this way the vast majority have been reconciled.

Yet there will remain the men of speculative temperament, of ideas rather than of techniques, who will ask for more than this. They will not be satisfied with the hard-and-fast dogmas of Marxism and Maoism. They will wish to interpret, to compare, to analyse and to criticize. In the past under the Confucian orthodoxy there were always such thinkers, and even though they were seldom honoured and often persecuted, their teaching was not utterly suppressed, their criticism remained to be read; in the end it often became in turn a part of the orthodox doctrine. If New Democracy is to remain new and not to fossilize, and if it is to become more democratic rather than stiffly hierarchic, these men will be needed.

INDEX

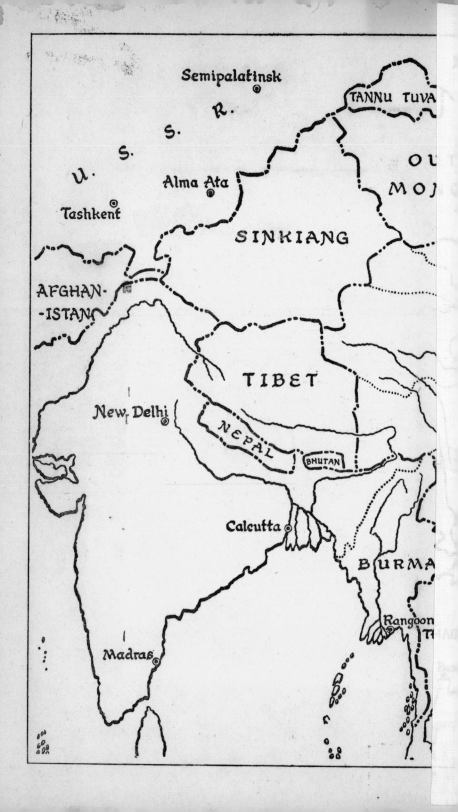